Anarchist Women
1870-1920

American Civilization

A Series Edited by Allen F. Davis

Gospel Hymns and Social Religion: The Rhetoric of Nineteenth-Century Revivalism, by Sandra S. Sizer (1978)
Social Darwinism: Science and Myth in Anglo-American Social Thought, by Robert C. Bannister (1979)
Twentieth Century Limited: Industrial Design in America, 1925–1939, by Jeffrey L. Meikle (1979)
Charlotte Perkins Gilman: The Making of a Radical Feminist, 1860–1896, by Mary A. Hill (1980)
Inventing the American Way of Death, 1830–1920, by James J. Farrell (1980)
Anarchist Women, 1870–1920, by Margaret S. Marsh (1981)
Woman and Temperance: The Quest for Power and Liberty, 1837–1900, by Ruth Bordin (1981)

Anarchist Women
1870-1920

MARGARET S. MARSH

Temple University Press
Philadelphia

Temple University Press
© 1981 by Temple University. All rights reserved
Published 1981
Printed in the United States of America

Library of Congress Cataloging in Publication Data
Marsh, Margaret S   1945–
    Anarchist women, 1870–1920.

    (American civilization)
    Includes bibliographical references and index.
    1. Anarchism and anarchists—United States—
History. 2. Feminism—United States—History.
3. Women revolutionists—United States—History.
4. Women's rights—United States—History. I. Title.
II. Series.
HX843.M29   335'.83'0973   80-18109
ISBN 0-87722-202-9

Two lines from "The Couriers" in *Ariel* by Sylvia Plath
Copyright © 1963 by Ted Hughes
Reprinted by permission of Harper & Row, Publishers, Inc.

Acknowledgments

I would like to express my gratitude to all of those who have helped me, in various ways, during the past five years while this book was being written. I am grateful for the assistance of the late Mollie Steimer, an anarchist woman who shared her reminiscences, photographs, newspaper clippings, and documents. Renée de Cleyre Buckwalter, granddaughter of Voltairine de Cleyre, answered numerous questions and granted me permission to quote from her grandmother's unpublished papers. Paul Avrich, the noted anarchist scholar, not only shared his own work with me, but also read and commented on an earlier draft of several chapters.

My colleagues and friends at Stockton State College have been especially generous with their help, particularly the current and former members of the college's History Colloquium: John Alviti, Demetrios Constantelos, William Lubenow, and James Miller, all of whom are still at Stockton; Edward Muir, now of Syracuse University; and Bruce Jennings, now of the Hastings Institute. This group has heard most of the material in the book over the past few years, and its members have offered numerous suggestions and comments. In addition, Professors Lubenow and Muir read and commented on the manuscript as a whole. Annette Muir, of Syracuse University, helped me to edit, clarify, and reorganize several of the chapters. The assistance of Allen Davis, the series editor, has been invaluable. And Barbara Evans Clements, of the University of Akron, kindly shared with me material from her then-unpublished biography of Aleksandra Kollontai.

The staffs of the following libraries offered considerable assistance: International Institute of Social History, Amsterdam, Holland; Labadie Collection, University of Michigan; Houghton Library, Harvard University; Tamiment Collection, Bobst Library, New York University; New York Public Library; Library of Congress; Alexander Library, Rutgers University. I would like to extend special thanks to Carmen Williams of the Rare Books Department, University of Florida Libraries.

Financial support, and perhaps more important, research time, came from Stockton State College through its Grant Program for Research and Professional Development. The institution has been generous in its support. Finally, I want to thank my typist, Jacki Smith, for an excellent job.

This book is dedicated to three members of my family for their loving encouragement: my husband, Robert H. Marsh; my sister, Wanda S. White; and my cousin and dear friend, Kathleen A. Sammartino.

Contents

	Illustrations	ix
	Introduction	3
1	Commencing a Revolution: Anarchism and American Society	6
2	True Freedom: Anarchist Womanhood	19
3	No Purely Feminine Women: Anarchist Feminism	45
4	A Ring of Gold: Love, Sex, and Marriage	65
5	Successful Propagandists: Anarchist Activism	100
6	No Illusions: The Anarchist Life of Voltairine de Cleyre	123
7	Neither Heroines nor Heroes: Radicals and Feminist Politics	151
	Conclusion	171
	Appendix: Women as Activists	175
	Notes	183
	A Note on Sources	205
	Index	209

Illustrations

1	Helena Born	33
2	Mollie Steimer	34
3	Marie Ganz	34
4	Emma Goldman in 1911	35
5	Emma Goldman in 1919	35
6	Lillian Rubell, Becky Edelsohn, Louise Berger, and Alexander Berkman	36
7	Voltairine de Cleyre in 1897	37
8	Voltairine de Cleyre at home in Philadelphia	37

Anarchist Women
1870-1920

For Bob, Wanda, and Kathy

Introduction

> You never know what is enough until you know what is more than enough.
>
> *William Blake*

Most people, however reluctantly, accept the limits placed on their behavior by the institutions within which they live. The anarchists of late-nineteenth- and early-twentieth-century America did not, and their continued fascination lies in the extravagance of their refusal to submit to external constraints. These anarchists repudiated all authority, extending the idea of individual liberty beyond the reaches of any sort of legal system. Many of them also denied the need for informal social controls exercised by the community. Anarchism is an ideology of "logical extremity," as George Woodcock has noted,[1] and its followers, of all of the radicals and reformers during the latter half of the nineteenth century, came closest to a total renunciation of not only law and government but also traditional cultural values and social norms. Although it is obviously impossible to grow up within a particular culture and remain completely unaffected by it, the vehemence of the anarchist denial emphasized the intensity of their rejection.

For women there was special significance in this phenomenon. Nineteenth-century America was acutely conscious of gender, a consciousness embodied in the feminist movement as well as in the popular sanctification of domesticity as a female trait. Anarchism, at least as it came to be interpreted by many women within the movement, offered them a way out of the gender trap. The women who embraced anarchism worked to restructure the society as a whole, but they also wanted to transcend conventional social and moral precepts as individuals in order to create for themselves independent, productive, and meaningful lives. The chief difference between them and their counterparts in the socialist movement and in mainstream feminist organizations was the extreme lengths to which they carried their repudiation of traditional views about the nature of womanhood. Although they often found themselves more bound to their culture than they had thought, although their dreams exceeded their abilities in many cases, and although their struggles sometimes overwhelmed them, they emerge from the past as women of strength and power, their defeats somehow enhancing rather than diminishing them.

The anarchist-feminists and their ideology possess a significance that extends beyond anarchism. The purpose of this study is not so much to examine anarchism through the lives of the women who espoused it as it is to understand the ways in which a group of women responded to the social, sexual, and economic upheavals of the late nineteenth and early twentieth centuries. The anarchist women are important in this sense because we have come to realize that the antistatist, antiauthoritarian, decentralist visions of the anarchists, as well as their emphasis on discovering the "natural" constraints on human behavior, are an integral part of our intellectual heritage. While I do not go so far as David de Leon, who asserts that anarchism *is* the American radical tradition, I believe that its impact on American thought has been misunderstood and underrated.[2] Anarchist excesses in thought and action signify more than eccentricity; the anarchists carried to their logical and extreme ends tendencies that already existed in American society. Anarchism provides us with a useful yardstick for measuring the boundaries of acceptable deviation from conventional patterns of behavior.

Although the anarchist women considered themselves exempt from the notions of womanhood that restricted their less liberated sisters, we realize that their connections to the larger society were closer and more complex than they themselves recognized. It is in this context that the role of these women as feminists becomes important not only in terms of our understanding of their relationship to the women's rights movement of a century ago but also in terms of contemporary feminism. Although late-twentieth-century feminists may recognize that political and legal rights wrested from the state have not resulted in fundamental equality, they still emphasize the passage of the Equal Rights Amendment or other antidiscriminatory statutes, partly because legal equality with men is a gain that the existing institutional structure can accommodate without fundamental changes in the structure of society. It would be much harder for feminists to retain the support of political moderates if they asserted that political, legal, and economic parity, while essential for an egalitarian society, does not assure true equality. For the most part, contemporary feminists have not confronted the question of whether inequality may be inherent in our more intimate institutional arrangements, such as the family. Some radical feminists, perhaps most notably Shulamith Firestone, have argued that we must eradicate existing notions of family life and alter our patterns of sexual behavior if we expect to eliminate inequality of the sexes.[3] But, on the whole, feminists have confined their scrutiny of familial and sexual relationships to such issues as an enhanced role for fathers in childrearing, the necessity for readily available and affordable child care, housework-sharing, and the right to abortion. All of these are important concerns, yet they do not come to grips with the question of the extent to which the family relationship itself may be inegalitarian. Among the anarchist women of a century ago we find the kind of serious probing of sexual and familial relationships that could serve as a preface to a new feminist analysis.

The anarchist-feminists insisted that female subordination was rooted in an obsolete system of sexual and familial relationships. Attacking marriage, often urging sexual varietism, insisting on both economic and psychological independence, and sometimes denying maternal responsibility, they argued that personal autonomy was an essential component of sexual equality, and that political and legal rights could not of themselves engender such equality. Although in seeking liberation they often went to extremes—even from a twentieth-century point of view—their recognition of the significance of sexual and domestic relationships in developing a feminist theory commends them to our attention.

1
Commencing a Revolution: Anarchism and American Society

> That generation which commences a revolution rarely completes it.
>
> *Thomas Jefferson*

In late-nineteenth-century America the mention of the word "anarchist" brought to the minds of most people a particular image: an unkempt, bushy-bearded man, swarthy and dirty, lurking in a dark alley with a bomb hidden under his coat. Couple the word "woman" with that of anarchist, and the picture became even more appalling: a monster who had repudiated her femininity to become a "shrieker and a termagent," distinguished only by her "wild recklessness."[1] Normally reasonable men and women were terrified of the anarchists, and if we can understand the nature of that fear, we can begin to understand the complicated relationship between the anarchists and the larger society.

One source of the American response to the anarchists is relatively easy to identify: the Haymarket bombing. On May 4, 1886, an unknown terrorist threw a bomb into a group of policemen during a labor demonstration at Chicago's Haymarket Square. One of the policemen was killed outright, and six others died shortly afterward as a result of the attack. The authorities never discovered who threw the bomb; novelists and historians continue to speculate about the terrorist's identity. The anarchists claimed publicly and disingenuously that it was the work of an agent provocateur, but Dyer D. Lum, a prominent anarchist in Chicago, later hinted that he knew the assailant, suggesting that the bomb-thrower was one of their number.[2]

The lack of an actual assassin did not deter the police from indicting eight men for murder—on the charge that they were anarchists and were therefore morally responsible for inciting terrorism even if they did not perform the deed themselves. Seven of the eight were sentenced to death. One of the seven, Louis Lingg, chose not to wait for his execution and committed suicide by blowing his face off with a dynamite capsule that Lum had smuggled to him in prison. Four of the others were hanged: Albert Parsons, August Spies, Adolph Fischer, and George Engel. Samuel Fielden and Michael Schwab had their sentences commuted to life imprisonment. They and Oscar Neebe, who had been sentenced to fifteen years imprisonment, were later pardoned by Governor Altgeld. These men were convicted not on the basis of actual involvement in the bomb-throwing act, but on the grounds that as anarchists they urged people to destroy the social system. As the prosecutor himself argued, "Law is on trial. Anarchy is on trial. These men have been selected . . . because they are leaders. They are no more guilty than the thousands who follow them. Gentlemen of the jury, convict these men, . . . and . . . save our institutions, our society."[3]

Although the Haymarket bombing was a specific event to which Americans could attribute their fear of anarchism, it precipitated rather than caused the hysteria that followed it. Even before Haymarket, ordinarily sober observers of the political scene, such as the economist Richard Ely, responded to the anarchists with alarm. In an article written just before the bombing but not published until shortly after it, Ely characterized the philosophy of the anarchists as one of "gunpowder, petroleum, and dynamite, and their cry is away with religion, away with the family, away with the state." Warning his readers that "doubtless two or three hundred thousand" men and women in the United States were either committed anarchists or sympathizers (an estimate surely inflated by fear), Ely concluded anxiously that "in times of excitement or restlessness, . . . when men in a frenzy of anger are looking about for someone to lead them, those who have been trained in this party may do great damage."⁴

Ely and others greatly exaggerated the terrorist nature of anarchism. In the period from Haymarket until World War I, anarchists were directly responsible for only three violent confrontations with American society. In 1892 Alexander Berkman, a young Russian Jewish immigrant, attempted without success to assassinate Carnegie Steel magnate Henry Clay Frick. Second, in 1901 Leon Czolgosz, a mentally disturbed and solitary figure with tenuous connections to the anarchist movement, shot and killed President William McKinley, an act which unleashed a wave of hysteria like that provoked by Haymarket. Finally, in 1914 a bomb exploded in a Lexington Avenue tenement in New York, killing a woman and three young anarchist men who had hoped to use it on John D. Rockefeller in retaliation for his part in the Ludlow Massacre in Colorado.⁵ In all, counting the seven policemen killed at Haymarket, anarchist terrorism in the United States was responsible for the deaths of twelve people, three of them anarchists themselves.

Since the actual terrorist threat posed by the anarchists was not serious, we must account in a different way for the panic they engendered. Americans viewed anarchists as the harbingers of chaos. The late nineteenth century was a period of upheaval: strikes, labor violence, and rural unrest underlined the severe tensions that accompanied industrialization and urbanization. The incredible variety of reform proposals, which ranged from socialism through farmer-labor coalitions to Henry George's single tax and beyond, served to emphasize the confusion that many people felt in the eighties and nineties concerning both the causes and cures for America's social and economic problems. While most Americans, including the majority of radicals and reformers, struggled to come to terms with the technological and economic forces that had transformed their society, the anarchists contemptuously refused to do so. They carried to extremes the doubts that others expressed in more moderate terms. At a time when others realized the ineffectualness of the government in solving the pressing problems of an urban-industrial society, the anarchists rejected the state absolutely. Just as many people wondered anxiously whether the family could remain intact in the face of increasing demands by women for roles that would extend or transcend their traditional domestic functions, the anarchists disdained marriage and traditional notions of family life. And finally, while many observant Americans worried about the magnitude of the industrialists' power and feared that such power had exceeded the ability of the society to control it, at least some anarchists called for the removal—by assassination if no other means worked—of capitalists like Frick and Rockefeller.

The anarchists were responding to the same social tensions as other Americans, and the excesses of the anarchist reaction shocked their contemporaries at least partly because many of them concurred with the anarchist assessment of the causes of society's ills, although they feared the anarchist idea of absolute liberty as a solution. Perhaps this explains the complex mixture of horror and fascination that Americans expressed toward the anarchists. Little did it matter, in the final analysis, that most anarchists never saw a bomb, let alone threw one; it was enough that they carried to its limits the sense of uneasiness that plagued the society in general during the last decades of the nineteenth century. Because the anarchists went to extremes, because they stood so conspicuously outside the mainstream, and because they did not try to conceal the depth of their hatred for modern society, they were ideal scapegoats who could be blamed for the unrest that gripped the society. The newspapers of the period reinforced such an interpretation of the anarchists and presented anarchism as a violent, secret, widespread, organized conspiracy, training itself to exploit the political tensions that existed in order to foment a revolution. Some editors denounced anarchism as "a murderous communist conspiracy," while an energetic reporter allegedly discovered a "dynamite college" in New Jersey where anarchists practiced marksmanship and took courses in assembling bombs. The *New York Tribune* frightened its readers by insisting that Haymarket was "simply the first gun in the revolution"; other newspapers expressed similar sentiments.[6]

Although the anarchists angrily denounced what they considered (often justly) their persecution by the police and the courts, they did not deny that their goal was to abolish the existing society. Just as it would be a mistake to view them with the exaggerated horror with which their contemporaries greeted them, it would be equally wrong to consider them as harmless eccentrics who teased but did not threaten existing institutions. In the late nineteenth century there were at least fifteen to twenty thousand committed anarchists in the United States, and perhaps an additional thirty to fifty thousand sympathizers. Because a majority of them were concentrated in urban centers, their numbers seemed larger; that concentration, and their often inflammatory rhetoric, made them a highly visible group.[7] The anarchists took themselves seriously, fully expecting to exert a powerful influence for social change. That they were unable to do so was partly a result of the persecution they faced, and partly because of their ideology itself.

At the core of anarchist ideology was the rejection of all forms of externally imposed authority, especially, but not exclusively, as it was embodied in government. Anarchists insisted on the right of each individual to absolute freedom, limited only by a prohibition against infringing on the liberties of others. This belief united anarchists who agreed on nothing else; for the anarchist movement, like the socialist movement, was faction-ridden and divided. In the United States the two most important factions were the Individualists and the Communist-anarchists,[8] who debated about the causes of political and economic tyranny, the most effective means of liberation from it, and the shape of the future society that would embody the anarchist ideal of individual liberty. The doctrinal disputes that separated the two groups were compounded by often insurmountable clashes of temperament and personality.

From the 1880s through the first decade of the twentieth century, Benjamin F. Tucker led the Individualists.[9] Born into a prosperous Massachusetts family and educated at the Massachusetts Institute of Technology, Tucker never quite managed to subdue his elitism. He began his anarchist career while in his teens, and in 1875, when he was twenty-one, became associate editor of *The Word*, Ezra Heywood's anarchist-feminist journal. In 1881 he founded *Liberty*, which quickly became the most important Individualist journal. Tucker derived his economic and political ideas principally from two sources: Josiah Warren and Pierre-Joseph Proudhon. Proudhon, the French printer whom all anarchists considered their intellectual father, developed an economic and social system that abolished government while it emphasized economic equality. Proudhon believed that such equality could be achieved only if individuals were left free to work out with each other the kinds of social and economic relationships most compatible with the autonomy of each. Josiah Warren was an American inventor who independently developed similar ideas. Warren spent most of his life devising social experiments in which his ideas could be tested, in the hope of proving that individuals could live together harmoniously without interference from the state.[10] Others before Tucker had begun to elaborate or synthesize the ideas of Proudhon and Warren: William B. Greene, the former minister and disciple of Proudhon; Stephen Pearl Andrews, the eccentric if sometimes brilliant sexual mystic who exerted considerable influence over Victoria Woodhull in the 1870s; and Ezra and Angela Heywood, the feminist publishers of *The Word*. Nevertheless, it was Tucker who brought their ideas together in *Liberty* and whose efforts attracted a solid core of followers and sympathizers.

Individualist ideology, as crystallized in *Liberty* in the early 1880s, included the following beliefs: abolition of the state; the creation of a society in which each person would choose freely how to live, with the single proscription against interfering with the liberty of others; acceptance of the costs and consequences of individual actions; the retention of a system of private property that restricted ownership to the amount of land which an individual would both occupy and use.[11]

The men and women who professed the philosophy of Individualism were sometimes known as Boston Anarchists because of the dominance of the *Liberty* circle among them. They came from a wide variety of backgrounds, but most of them were educated native Americans—former ministers, journalists, teachers, physicians, other professionals, farmers, and some skilled craftworkers, particularly in the printing trades. Among the women were the reporter Florence Finch Kelly, who eventually turned from anarchism to become a novelist and *New York Times* journalist; and Helena Born, who rejected a private income from her affluent family in England to become a union organizer, then came to the United States to find a place in which she could both express her beliefs and put them into practice independently of organized movements.[12]

Although it would be an exaggeration to say that all educated native born Americans who became anarchists chose Individualism, it is true that this wing of the movement proved more attractive to natives than to immigrants. Conversely, Communist-anarchism offered greater attraction to the foreign born. In a strict sense, the immigrant anarchism of the 1880s was more collectivist than communist, but the two are closely related and by the early nineties communism clearly dominated.[13] In the eighties the principal figure among the immigrant anarchists was Johann Most, the German bookbinder who arrived in New York in 1882. With a face deformed by a childhood disease, a bushy beard, and an unending store of violent rhetoric, Most quickly became the personification of anarchist malevolence. Indeed, he was probably the model for the stereotype of American imaginations. He once published a pamphlet containing detailed instructions for the making of bombs and suggested that his followers consider burglary, arson, and poison as useful weapons in the class struggle.[14]

In nearly every respect the sinister Most seemed the antithesis of the handsome, well-bred Tucker, yet in some ways they were alike; both possessed compelling personalities that brought them numerous followers, and both were men with such imperious attitudes and intransigent opinions that they ended up by alienating those who had once been devoted admirers. Naturally two men, at once so different and so alike, were bound to clash. Their conflict, and the factional antagonism that accompanied it, came after a brief period of harmony. Tucker and the Individualists had wanted initially to cooperate with the European anarchist movement. In 1881 the editor of *Liberty* hailed the creation of the anarchist "Black International," proposing that his paper serve as its English-language organ. He was equally enthusiastic about the arrival of Most and hoped for a working partnership with the German firebrand who already possessed an international reputation.[15]

These efforts at presenting a unified anarchist front failed less than a year after Most's arrival. In 1883 a group of Chicago anarchists and socialists invited "the socialists of North America" to convene in Pittsburgh in order to construct a platform on which anarchists and socialists, statists and antistatists, Marxists and Proudhonnists, Individualists and communists could stand. The followers of

Johann Most controlled the convention, and they alienated both the Marxists and the Individualists. The Marxists refused to accept the convention's rejection of a centralized organization in favor of the creation of a federation of autonomous local groups, while the Individualists would not support the delegates' endorsement of violence and sabotage as legitimate methods of social change.[16]

The Pittsburgh conference marked the end of organized collaboration between the rival anarchist factions, but it did not halt cooperation on a more informal basis among individuals and groups. Some anarchists never gave up trying to reunite the splintered movement. Until his death in 1893, Dyer Lum worked conscientiously though unsuccessfully toward that goal, and his protégée Voltairine de Cleyre continued his efforts. Nevertheless, after 1883 the formal breach was complete. The Individualists henceforth emphasized their ideological differences from the Communist-anarchists, which they had tried previously to mute. The chief area of disagreement between the two groups was over the question of property. The Individualists believed that the state was the chief obstacle to freedom, and they accepted the notion of private property. The Communist-anarchists, on the other hand, placed private property itself at the center of their analysis of social and economic oppression. Although both groups derived their ideas from Proudhon, the communists had been influenced as well by Marxian theories of class conflict.

From the eighties on, the chief theoretician of Communist-anarchism was the exiled Russian prince Peter Kropotkin. At the heart of Kropotkin's social theory was his belief that the essential characteristic of human beings was their desire to cooperate with others in order to secure the basic needs of life. Because of this quality, the individual was "essentially a social being who can achieve full development only in society, while society can benefit only if its members are free." Kropotkin and his followers saw no conflict between the interests of the individual and those of the community. Consequently, they felt no need for the preservation of private property and would abolish it along with the state. Instead, they wanted to create a system of federated but autonomous communes, producing and sharing freely. In these communes wages and payments for services, as well as private property, would be eliminated, because the community would provide equally for all of its members.[17]

In the United States Communist-anarchism appealed mostly to working-class immigrants or their children, who felt cheated by false promises of the American dream. Although some declassé intellectuals and American craftworkers joined the communists, the majority of the movement was composed of Eastern European Jews who worked in the sweatshops of New York's garment district, of Italian factory workers, and other immigrants with few skills and little hope of advancement.[18] The two most important figures among them were Emma Goldman and Alexander Berkman. Originally followers of Johann Most, they emerged from his shadow in the early nineties to become the foremost advocates of revolutionary anarchism.

No brief description can capture the ideas or the personality of Emma Goldman, the Russian Jewish seamstress whose criticisms of American capitalism earned her the epithet "Red Emma," whose free speech fights led to the creation of the American Civil Liberties Union, and whose refusal to bow to conventions of womanly social and sexual behavior brought her the admiration of young artists and writers struggling to make their own break from middle-class values and norms. Deported from the United States after World War I, she continued to the end of her life to wage, as her biographer Richard Drinnon has remarked, "an unrelenting fight for the free individual."[19] Goldman's chief collaborator in her work as publicist, publisher, and agitator was Alexander Berkman. The two conspired to assassinate Henry Clay Frick, although Berkman alone went to Pittsburgh for the actual attempt. It failed, Frick recovered almost immediately, and Berkman spent fourteen years in prison. After his release from prison he edited Goldman's *Mother Earth*, began his own short-lived newspaper *The Blast*, led demonstrations of the unemployed, and waited for the revolution. While Goldman took the anarchist message to middle-class audiences, Berkman retained his faith in the revolutionary potential of the working class. Deported to Russia with Goldman, he took longer than she to repudiate the Bolsheviks. Fleeing Russia, he remained in exile for the rest of his life, committing suicide in 1936.[20]

Berkman and Goldman personified anarchism to Americans who

read accounts of their speeches in the press or followed the news of their trials. The police persecution that they faced, the fear that they aroused, the relief with which the nation greeted their deportation—all testify to the sense of power and fierce determination that the two conveyed. And yet, during the first and second decades of the twentieth century, when the anarchists' notoriety was at a peak, their influence among American radicals was actually on the wane. Socialism, not anarchism, had become the dominant radical ideology, and some understanding of the reasons for the rejection of anarchism is necessary for any interpretation of its significance.

Anarchism had appeared during the late nineteenth century as one of a number of responses to the economic and social dislocations that attended the emergence of an increasingly centralized, urban-industrial society. Like socialism—and like other radical and reform movements such as Populism, labor unionism, or Bellamyite Nationalism—anarchism confronted the issues of the conflict between capital and labor, corporate centralization, the concentration of wealth and the creation of mass poverty, and rapid technological change. However, its voluntarist and decentralist ideology set it apart from all the others. By the 1890s the farmers who provided the core of support for the Populist movement of that decade had become convinced that the national government should act as the instrument of reform. The American Federation of Labor—the most important labor organization—accepted the large corporation as an ineradicable evil and directed its efforts toward obtaining the greatest benefits for workers within the existing system. Bellamyite Nationalists as well as other socialists looked forward to the nationalization and centralization of economic production.[21] The anarchists stood virtually alone. Their refusal to accept centralization and bureaucratization has sometimes been viewed as an indication of their shortsightedness in the face of modernization. Observers have discounted the views of the anarchists as antitechnological and therefore retrogressive, a position which is overly simplistic. Nevertheless, it is true that anarchists occupied themselves in trying to discover and put to use what they perceived as the elemental forces of the human spirit rather than in mastering the machine.[22]

The anarchists did not oppose technology in itself; but the dehumanization that accompanied technological progress in the nineteenth century appalled them, and justly so. They refused to believe that a large-scale, centralized system was necessarily more efficient than a decentralized one. Kropotkin, for one, welcomed technological innovation, arguing that in a decentralized society all communities would share in the benefits of technological progress. With the exception of Kropotkin and a few others, however, anarchists offered no clear accommodation to or rejection of technology; their primary goal was to exalt the human above the technological. In this they voiced a concern shared by other Americans, most notably in the nineteenth century Henry Thoreau and Henry Adams, who also proved unable to either reject the machine or come to terms with it. Perhaps better than either Adams or Thoreau, and certainly to a greater extent than any of the other radical and reform groups of the late nineteenth and early twentieth centuries, the anarchists understood the dangers inherent in centralized reform. Our contemporary conflicts over the role of the individual in an overweening bureaucracy, the issue of maintaining the environment in the face of dwindling energy sources, and the question of how to redirect technological progress so that human beings will feel less at the mercy of impersonal forces than they do at present, suggests that the anarchists, rather than being romantic reactionaries, predicted with foresight the problems of the modern bureaucratic state.[23]

The anarchists were separated from the other radical and reform groups ideologically because of their decentralist views; and as the nineteenth century came to an end they had also become more isolated in a practical, political sense. Earlier in the century—until the late seventies or early eighties—the anarchists, sharing with other radical and reform groups a common hostility toward established institutions, joined with those others in various projects. They participated in a coalition with socialists and radical feminists in order to found the New England Labor Reform League. In 1871 this organization became the American Labor Reform League, with anarchist William B. Greene as president and feminist Elizabeth Cady Stanton as vice-president. As tenuous and limited as such alliances were, they connected the anarchists with the larger radical community. But by the mid-seventies the isolation that later would seriously damage the anarchists had begun to become apparent. At this time the mainstream feminists withdrew from collaboration because of the increasing identification of anarchism with free love. Other reform groups also shied away, particularly after the introduction of revolutionary anarchism in the late seventies.[24]

As a result, by the early eighties cooperation had become difficult for the movement as a whole, although individual anarchists, particularly among the women, continued to move in wider radical circles. Perhaps their most serious break, in terms of their revolutionary potential, was their rupture with the Marxian socialists, which in the United States came conclusively at the Pittsburgh Congress of 1883. Like Proudhon and Marx themselves, their followers could not work together. George Woodcock's assessment of the two leaders, that is, that they possessed "not merely a complete divergence of theoretical outlook, but also—and perhaps this was more important—an irreconcilable opposition of personalities," might stand for the movements as a whole.[25] Despite the uneasy coexistence of the followers of Marx and Proudhon in the First International, and despite their concurrence that capitalism with its system of property lay at the heart of the political, economic, and social malaise in Europe and the United States, their disagreements over both revolutionary tactics and the future role of the state proved too strong to overcome.

In the United States, as in the more industrialized countries of Europe, radicals increasingly chose socialism for several reasons: its ideology reinforced rather than resisted the trend toward political and economic centralization; its reliance on political techniques allowed for organization and integration into an already existing governmental process; and its attitude toward technology as an unqualified blessing that would ultimately provide all members of society with material comfort contained none of the anarchist ambivalence toward a process that many in the nineteenth century revered as evolutionary progress. As a result, socialism in the United States grew until the presidential candidate of the Socialist Party of America polled nearly a million votes in 1912. By that year anarchism, while still attracting some youthful idealists, had ceased to be a powerful political force.[26]

Yet we should not dismiss them. The fear that they inspired among the conventional bears witness to their intellectual, if not political, potency. Moreover, as individuals they aroused admiration among many less conventional Americans. Goldman, for example, was the personification of personal rebellion to young urban writers, artists, and intellectuals who were themselves in revolt against authority. Although for the most part these young admirers of Goldman ultimately rejected anarchism as a political idea, they often took with them to socialism the anarchists' skepticism of all creeds, as well as their enthusiasm for direct action. Floyd Dell, among others who made the *Masses* the liveliest, most entertaining, and most irreverent socialist periodical ever published in the United States, had first been attracted to anarchism. On a different level Margaret Sanger, also not an anarchist herself, enjoyed the support of the anarchists who had begun the birth-control movement. Her later suppression of the anarchist origins of her crusade notwithstanding, Sanger was indebted to them.[27]

The anarchists did not generate a mass following. What they did was to announce that political remedies, however radical, were insufficient. That announcement was threatening enough.

2
True Freedom: Anarchist Womanhood

> Only in a society where no human being will rule over another can there be true freedom.
>
> *Mollie Steimer*

The central beliefs of anarchist ideology—individual liberty, the responsibility to refrain from limiting the freedom of others, and the rejection of all nonvoluntary authority—provided a unique opportunity to women who felt restricted by conventionally defined gender roles. After all, a political movement that claimed as its principal tenet the primacy of personal autonomy ought to have had no place for a subordinate group. This special appeal for women existed despite the fact that the men who developed anarchist theory did not usually apply the doctrine of individual liberty to women in the same way as to men.

Proudhon had considered the patriarchal family as the fundamental social unit in his society without laws. He also disapproved of divorce and expected that women would always fulfill domestic functions. Kropotkin, while expecting women to engage in active political work, expressed impatience with those women who put feminism ahead of their devotion to the (male) working class. His own family relationships were almost stereotypically conventional.[1] Proudhon, Kropotkin, and the other anarchist theorists who viewed women in such conventional ways argued that certain behavior patterns were natural for each sex. Since nature provided woman with a dependent personality, a nurturing instinct, and a desire for motherhood, to have her act in accord with those feelings would not violate her freedom because they would be an expression of her natural self. Many anarchist women, from Emma Goldman to the unassuming Helena Born, disagreed with this notion of woman's nature. Dismissing the interpretations of the male theorists, they appropriated for themselves the dogma of absolute individual liberty, reminded their male comrades of their responsibility not to infringe on the liberty of women, and rejected patriarchal as well as governmental authority. In their lives, perhaps as much as in their work, they gave evidence of their determination to apply anarchist tenets equally to men and women.

The task of defining anarchist womanhood is a difficult one, largely because anarchism appealed to women who, political philosophy aside, were quite different from one another in terms of class, education, and geographic background. Although American newspapers of the late nineteenth and early twentieth century routinely anathematized the anarchists as the "offscourings of Europe," with the staid *New York Times* suggesting that "it is highly improbable that there is a single native American anarchist in the United States," the categorizing of the movement was not so simple.[2] Anarchist women as well as anarchist men came from more than one class or ethnic group. Although Communist-anarchism drew much of its strength from the men and women who held the dirtiest, worst-paid jobs in America's urban centers, it also attracted some upper-middle-class women. Individualist anarchism appealed to rebellious young middle-class women, but also to some who had grown up in poverty. The picture presented by anarchist womanhood is more like a shifting kaleidoscope than a portrait. A single set of socioeconomic variables does not provide an adequate definition. One can, however, distinguish three broad categories of women who were drawn to anarchism, with certain characteristics common to all three groups. The first category included teachers, physicians, and journalists, educated in colleges or seminaries for women, who rebelled against their conventional backgrounds as they developed feminist consciousness. Their feminism led them to anarchism rather than to the organized women's rights movement because the latter did not satisfy their need for personal autonomy and sexual liberation, nor did it adequately speak to their dissatisfaction with the inequities of capitalist society. Most, but not all, of these women became Individualists, and many were active in the Boston anarchist circle of Benjamin Tucker.

The second category contained women who were markedly different in a socioeconomic sense: working-class immigrants or daughters of immigrants. Few of these women attained more than a rudimentary education, and they often began their working lives in the sweatshops of New York's Lower East Side or in similarly dismal circumstances. Given their place at the bottom of the social scale, it may seem surprising to find them as activists at all. But it is less surprising to see them as anarchists than as socialists. Throughout the Western world, anarchism in the nineteenth and early twentieth century often had special appeal for the peasantry and what the Marxists would call the "lumpenproletariat." An investigation into the socioeconomic backgrounds of anarchist women compared to socialists or labor activists suggests that a similar phenomenon took place in the United States. Labor activism drew from the daughters of the skilled working class, while socialism possessed a strong appeal for middle-class women. Those from the ranks of the less skilled, if they became politically active at all, responded to the ideology of anarchism.[3]

The last group of women attracted to anarchism was characterized more by the nature of its rebelliousness than by class, education, or ethnicity. These women—adventurers, bold sexual experimenters, determined convention-breakers—came to anarchism not because of its social and economic philosophy but because the movement seemed to offer them a chance for psychological liberation under the guise of political radicalism. Among this group were both disaffected daughters of the well-to-do and products of rural squalor or urban poverty. Whatever their backgrounds, they had two things in common: their anarchism was personal rather than political, and when it failed to provide for their psychic liberation, they rejected it.

The women in all three categories, despite their differences, had some things in common. First, with only a few exceptions, anarchist women accepted the inevitability of violence as a tactic for social change, even if they did not all approve of it enthusiastically.

Nevertheless, even those who did not endorse acts of violence against the state argued that working-class violence was to be expected in a capitalist society and ought not to be condemned. Second, anarchist women, to a remarkable extent, defied conventional habits of behavior regarding sexuality and marriage. Their unconventionality varied from divorce or marital separation, which constituted a relatively mild deviation from the norm, to sexual promiscuity or open homosexuality. Despite the difference in degree, their various behaviors all reflected nonconformity to accepted values of chastity and fidelity to spouse. In those terms, anarchist women were not conventional.

Because anarchist philosophy depended on individual autonomy, and because the movement itself was held together by only the rudiments of organization and order, we can appreciate fully the complexity and diversity of anarchist womanhood by supplementing collective description with individual portraits. The six women whose lives are sketched below were broadly representative of the movement's rank-and-file. Florence Finch Kelly and Helena Born belonged to the circle of Individualists who gathered around Benjamin Tucker's *Liberty*. Kelly's anarchism had been a product of youthful radicalism that did not outlast her twenties. Born, having become involved in the movement in her thirties, brought to it a steadfast commitment and mature reflection. Mollie Steimer and Marie Ganz were Communist-anarchists from New York. Steimer endured years of imprisonment and torture in various countries because of her beliefs yet never recanted them. Ganz abandoned radical causes altogether after her street-corner oratory earned her a brief jail sentence. Margaret Anderson, founder and editor of the *Little Review*, was perhaps the most flamboyant example of that group of literary and artistic rebels who gathered around Emma Goldman during the years before the United States became involved in World War I. Finally, there was Marie L., the subject of Hutchins Hapgood's *An Anarchist Woman*; neither a street-corner prophet nor fervent disciple, she participated fitfully in the movement for a few years, then withdrew into working-class respectability.[4]

Although in many ways Florence Finch Kelly and Helena Born differed from one another as well as from the other women considered here, both were representative of the kinds of women drawn to Individualist anarchism. Kelly (1858–1939) grew up on a succession of farms in Kansas.[5] The youngest of eight children, she later remembered herself as a sturdily independent young girl whose mother encouraged her to develop her strengths while her father attempted to stifle her. Conflicts with her father punctuated her childhood and adolescence. They disagreed heatedly over the question of female education. Kelly eventually acquired a high school education and a university degree without paternal approval or support. In her autobiography she recalled that as an adolescent she had never considered that because she was a woman she would have less opportunity to seek her fortune than her six brothers. Her subsequent disillusionment made her an implacable feminist.

Armed with a degree from the University of Kansas and ten dollars, Kelly left home—first for Chicago, then for Boston—determined to have a career in journalism. In the early 1880s she worked on the *Boston Globe* with Benjamin Tucker and became an anarchist. When Kelly wrote her autobiography she carefully played down her commitment to anarchism, presenting herself as skeptical and detached, two qualities that contemporary sources belied. Kelly contributed frequently to *Liberty* during the mid-eighties, particularly on the Woman Question but also on various social issues of general concern. She also wrote *On The Inside*, an avowedly anarchist novel. Her memoirs contained no mention of these, nor of *Frances*, her fictional tribute to free love. Although the older Kelly was embarrassed by the intensity of her earlier anarchist involvement, it nevertheless had been an important part of her life.

Kelly's conversion to anarchism rested on two things: her determined feminism and an imprecise but powerful sense of social justice. She recalled in her seventies that "the chief attraction of Tucker's anarchistic philosophy was that it recognized so strongly the rights of the individual and visioned a world that was not a man-made world, for men, but a world made up of equal individuals, regardless of sex."[6] When Kelly became an anarchist her intense desire to participate actively in a masculine world (journalism was then a field that rarely welcomed women) was the moving force in her life. That her frustration with sexual inequality drew her to anarchism rather than to the suffrage movement was significant. She was not unaware of the mainstream feminists; while in Boston she knew and admired Lucy Stone and formed a friendship with Alice Stone Blackwell. But Kelly could not accommodate herself to a belief in innate intellectual and psychological differences between the sexes. By the 1880s some suffragists had come not only to accept this notion but to make it a virtue. Kelly felt little attraction for a movement that championed her rights on the basis of woman's alleged superior moral instincts or her special aptitude for reform.[7] As she interpreted anarchist ideology, on the other hand, it provided for like freedoms and offered the same opportunities to both sexes. It also encouraged sexual liberation for both women and men, in contrast to many suffragists' increasing emphasis on social purity. With her keen competitiveness, her religious skepticism, and her sexual openness, the young Florence Finch found the suffragists worthy but dull. Conversely, the anarchists who gathered around Tucker were extremists without losing their gentility, and their ideology as she perceived it offered limitless possibilities for the development of the individual, regardless of sex.

Kelly's frustrations over the inequities of industrial America, although evident, were less well-defined than her feminist views. She castigated the state for its encouragement of corporate concentration and its oppression of the working classes, but she unthinkingly acquiesced in the standard anarchist answers, failing to come to grips on her own with such issues as poverty and violence. Eventually she came to believe that these anarchist remedies did not offer workable solutions to the problems of industrial society. As her belief in its ultimate success faded, her interest waned.[8]

Kelly later explained her disenchantment with anarchism as a natural part of her intellectual maturity, a statement that both minimized the extent of her commitment and oversimplified her own reactions. In part, the anarchists themselves, particularly Tucker and his friend Victor Yarros, disillusioned her. Their amused belittling in the pages of *Liberty* of the economic demands of women caused her to doubt the extent of their commitment to a liberated humanity.[9] Further, her temperamental and intellectual nature was pragmatic; she had been willing since her childhood to experiment with unconventional solutions to any problem, but she needed to see results. Anarchism could not provide her with tangible evidence of success. Perhaps the final element in her withdrawal from anarchism was her gradual retreat from full-time work in her profession by the late 1880s. Her marriage to fellow journalist Allen Kelly had not ended her career, but the birth and then early death of their first child reduced her to part-time work. She withdrew for a while from the world of masculine competitiveness and did not resume a full professional career until she and her husband separated when she was in her forties.

Despite her rejection of anarchism, Kelly never became a conventional middle-class woman. She worked as a freelance journalist and wrote several novels during her marriage. She traveled considerably, at one time living on a ranch in New Mexico and engaging in a strenuous outdoor life. At forty-eight she resumed full-time journalistic work at the *New York Times* and retired thirty years later to write her autobiography. She had entered the mainstream, but her years as an anarchist affected the ways in which she viewed American society. She met it on her own terms and never accepted the conventional solution to a problem unless she found it reasonable. She always believed that the anarchists had helped her to develop tolerance, skepticism, and a lack of reverence for tradition. All of these qualities, she believed, had allowed her to fulfill her own ambitions.[10]

Florence Finch Kelly and Helena Born (1860–1901) shared some of the same characteristics. Both women belonged to the Boston anarchist group, although Born entered it after Kelly had withdrawn from the movement; and both were well-educated women dissatisfied with traditional roles. But while Kelly had embraced the movement with youthful impetuosity, Born had become a convert after mature deliberation and years of feminist, socialist, and labor activism in her native England. Born grew up near Bristol, the only child of affluent parents. Her family provided her with a proper education at a girls' academy but refused to allow her to attend a university or train for a profession. She had no financial need for self-support since her father provided her with an ample private income.[11]

The reasons for Born's refusal to accept a role of feminine gentility are not clear. As early as her adolescence, she had begun to keep a scrapbook of newspaper clippings that focused with increasing intensity on questions of women's rights and labor reform.[12] While in her twenties she became active in the Bristol Women's Liberal

Association, a feminist organization. In the mid-eighties her friend Miriam Daniell introduced her to socialism; the two women forsook their middle-class feminist co-workers and moved into a working-class neighborhood in Bristol. There she became secretary in 1889 of the Bristol Gas Workers and General Laborers Union. Giving speeches, collecting funds, and walking the picket line during the strike of that year, Born fully expected to continue in Bristol as a labor organizer. Although criticized by her friends in the Bristol Women's Liberal Association for abandoning the women's cause, she insisted that she retained her feminist views. At one point she argued that her "union is one of the few unions organized by men which accords women full representation . . . and has included among its objects the obtaining, wherever possible, the same wages for women doing the same work as men."[13] Perhaps stung by the criticism of the women's rights activists, Born next turned her attention to organizing a union of Bristol's seamstresses, who worked in one of the most exploitative and poorly paid occupations of the late nineteenth century. She failed; dispirited, she allowed Miriam Daniell to persuade her to emigrate to the United States in 1890.

Daniell's child Sunrise and her lover Robert Nicol shared a home with Daniell and Born in Cambridge, Massachusetts. Despite their nominal socialism, the two women soon drifted into the Boston anarchist group, Daniell almost immediately becoming a contributor to *Liberty*. Although Born's career in England had been characterized by political activism, she did not return to such activity in the United States. It is uncertain whether her unhappy experience in attempting to organize the seamstresses deterred her, or whether she simply felt at a loss to find a direction for her energies in a new country. Her life in the United States was marked by a greater effort to define herself as a radical by living in keeping with her principles. She saw less need to convert others. Because she came to believe that "our ideal will never be met with in life unless we have first achieved it within us to the fullest extent of our power," such things as labor organizing became secondary.[14] For this reason she felt much more at home with the anarchists than with the American socialists. In England she had been a disciple of William Morris, who called himself a socialist even though his ultimate dreams for social regeneration were more in accord with those of many anarchists. (Indeed, Morris's utopian novel, *News from Nowhere*, made him a hero to American anarchists.) The American socialist movement had less room for dissident romantics. Born rejected socialism and embraced anarchism because, as her friend Helen Tufts later put it, she refused "to sacrifice individuality to a system."[15]

Born's anarchist dream was not markedly different from Kelly's, but in some ways it was more defined. Kelly had chosen anarchism largely because of its implicit feminism; Born, already a committed feminist, wanted to live her life in a world not circumscribed by her gender. Instead of articulating a feminist principle, she planned a life of feminist practice. Anarchism provided a theoretical rationale for goals she had already espoused. She gave up her private income and became a typesetter, but this did not entirely satisfy her desire to separate herself from a political and social system of which she did not approve. In 1893, therefore, she and Daniell moved to a rural commune in California, where they built a house and hoped to settle permanently. Tragedy beset them; their house was destroyed by fire, then Daniell fell victim to terminal illness. Daniell died in 1894, and Born returned to Boston. Unwilling to abandon her dream of a self-sufficient life, she and another woman friend attempted in 1898 to start a farm in New Hampshire. For reasons that are not entirely clear, but may have included the harshness of the winter climate, a feeling of isolation, and loneliness for her lover back in Boston, she abandoned the idea of subsistence farming after a year's experiment.

Although she had not succeeded completely in severing her ties to the larger society, Born never became tempted to make her peace with conventional views; she quite deliberately held herself outside the mainstream of American values. In her attitudes on marriage, nature, dress, and the future of anarchism, she greatly resembled Voltairine de Cleyre, although the two probably did not know one another.[16] Like de Cleyre, Born dressed unconventionally and was an ardent outdoorswoman with a Thoreauvian love of nature. She was also similar to her more famous comrade in her distaste for systematizing; both showed little concern about the actual structure of the coming anarchist society. Born refused to commit herself to any long-range vision:

> In bringing about the new order, I am willing to further any of the various plans that commend themselves to diverse adherents of the various

schools of thought, if they are born of a love of liberty, if I find myself in accord with the spirit in which they are conceived, and if I can do so without being bound.[17]

Born held the views common to women anarchists on the issues of marriage and sexuality. Although her lover William Bailie was married, she lived with him openly. She expected her anarchist friends to approve of their living arrangements and hoped that her nonanarchist ones would understand. She was not unconcerned with public opinion. Nevertheless, as one of her friends observed, "She lived her own life naturally, without straining for effect, and gave full expression to her individuality. [If this conflicted] with conventional forms and customs, so much the worse for conventionality."[18] In her relationship with Bailie she demanded to be treated as an equal, having castigated those "who . . . glory in an idea of equality restricted to one-half the race." Her insistence on having a life that included sexual equality was also reflected in her determination to share fully the responsibility for the small restaurant that the two operated together.[19]

Born died of cervical or uterine cancer in 1901, before she could attain her personal dream of creating a life that did not need the support of capitalist society. In an important sense, however, she personified the life-affirming qualities of anarchism too often submerged in a rhetoric of destruction. Helena Born became an anarchist, after years of other kinds of political activism, because its philosophy fulfilled her requirements for a movement that would encourage the ultimate realization of the three goals that dominated her adult life: the attainment of total equality for women based on their shared humanity with men; the free choice of individuals to determine their own lives without having to worry about social ostracism for eccentric or unconventional behavior; and the destruction of the capitalist economic system, the abolition of which would release the essential goodness of the human spirit. Despite her own setbacks, she continued until her death to act on the belief that her most useful contribution to political activism was her continuing refusal to cooperate with a system that she found repressive and confining. Her life and work demonstrated a consistency which marked her as one of the most successful of the anarchist women.

Helena Born and Florence Finch Kelly—well-educated, independent, and free to accept or reject the conventions of middle-class womanhood—were typical anarchist women, as were Mollie Steimer and Marie Ganz, who to all appearances were otherwise very different from Born and Kelly. In terms of their backgrounds and early experiences, Mollie Steimer and Marie Ganz were extraordinarily similar; but in terms of consistency of practice, Steimer resembles Born most closely, while Ganz was like none of the others. In some ways Ganz (1891–19[?]) exhibited complexities and contradictions not found in most of the other figures. At the height of her anarchist involvement some observers called her a ghetto Joan of Arc while others castigated her as an insincere headline-grabbing preacher of violence. Both Emma Goldman and the editorial board of the *New York Times*, who agreed on nothing else, characterized Ganz as a reckless and irresponsible young woman who attempted to incite others to violence and cared little for the consequences. Yet, during her brief period in the public limelight, she had scores of devoted admirers who considered her a tireless advocate of the immigrant Jews.[20]

Ganz was born in Galicia in 1891, immigrating to the United States with her mother and brother in 1896. Following a pattern usual for Eastern European Jewish immigrants, her father had preceded the family by two years, establishing himself as a pushcart vendor on New York's Lower East Side. Ganz's childhood resembled that of most ghetto children. Her father died in 1899, leaving a family of four: Marie, her mother, and two brothers. Mrs. Ganz tried to support the family by taking in piecework, and until she was old enough to leave school Marie spent her evenings and weekends helping her mother. At thirteen she began to work full-time, struggling in the city's sweatshops to help support the family. Like many other young men and women who tried desperately to eke out an existence in New York's Lower East Side, Ganz found comradeship within the Jewish radical movement. She had first come into contact with it in 1904, a year of exceptional political ferment. Beginning about 1902 and climaxing in 1904, the residents of the ghetto protested against high food prices, the conduct of absentee landlords, and the treatment of sweatshop workers by staging meat strikes, rent strikes, and demonstrations. Their anger reached such a pitch of intensity during 1904 that even child workers struck.[21] Countless individual crises had spurred the united action of the immigrant Jews, and the Ganz family was among those victimized. Both Marie Ganz and her mother were unemployed and desperate. Ganz later noted that this year marked a turning point in her political development: "Those days of suffering put a bitterness into my heart that never left it . . . the furies of hatred flamed in me then—hatred of the bosses, . . . of the landlords, . . . of the rich, . . . of the whole world, a world so black and hopeless."[22]

Ganz's rage was shared by the other members of her radical circle, a group of socialist and anarchist young men and women who met together to discuss literature, attend lectures, and plan for the overthrow of capitalism. Her anarchist convictions survived the next ten years, as Ganz drifted from job to job, largely responsible for the support of her mother and two brothers.[23] Her radical beliefs occasionally cost her a job, but on the whole her life was centered on her family and her circle of anarchist and socialist comrades. In 1914 all that changed, and overnight she became a notorious figure. The economic hardships of that year—one of grim unemployment for hundreds of thousands of garment workers—reminded her of the similar crisis of a decade earlier. Unable to find work because of her tendency to disrupt factory discipline and her avowed anarchist beliefs, she felt cornered, desperate, and determined to take revenge. She later recalled that "wild impulses surged in me bidding me to revolt, to stir others to revolt, to destroy and kill if necessary."[24] During the winter of 1914 she followed her resolve with action, becoming a major speaker at the demonstrations of the unemployed, which drew support from socialists and from the Industrial Workers of the World, as well as from anarchists. Her success as a speechmaker brought her into intimate contact with New York's anarchist leadership, and she became one of Alexander Berkman's youthful protégées.

The spring of 1914 brought the infamous Ludlow Massacre in Colorado, in which the state militia first shot at, then set fire to, a tent camp housing the wives and children of striking miners. Thirteen persons were killed. In New York the protest against the incident took the form of attacks directed at John D. Rockefeller as the head of the corporation that had provoked the violence. Caught up in the spirit of outrage, Ganz publicly threatened to assassinate Rockefeller. Perhaps inevitably, her promised *attentat* had the qualities of a farce; brandishing a pistol, she led a crowd to Rockefeller's New York office only to find her quarry absent. Thereupon she left a message with his secretary that she had come to assassinate the head of the firm, then left.[25] The threats against Rockefeller finally brought about Ganz's arrest and conviction on disorderly conduct charges. Released after serving half of a sixty-day sentence, she promptly turned her back on the anarchist movement.

Not the least mystery about Marie Ganz is her relative immunity from the kinds of police harassment with which other anarchists regularly contended. For months Ganz uttered threats that would have earned prison sentences for Emma Goldman. She finally forced the police to arrest her by her extraordinarily open attempt on Rockefeller's life; yet she was charged only with disorderly conduct. Such impunity probably stemmed from two sources: her friendship with Nat Ferber, the Hearst journalist with extensive police contacts who later became her husband, and her relative ineffectualness as an agitator. Newspapers like the *New York Times* feared Emma Goldman and Alexander Berkman, recognizing their speeches as serious threats to the status quo; but they thought of Marie Ganz as a caricature of an anarchist, and reported her activities accordingly. Ganz confirmed this assessment by her peremptory dismissal of her former beliefs upon her release from prison. She later said, in her autobiography, that a sudden realization of her comrades' insincerity had prompted her renunciation of them.[26]

Although Ganz's career as an anarchist agitator was brief, she was not an isolated figure. Rather, she represented an important element within the movement. She and others like her became anarchists because of a powerful but unfocused resentment of their own oppressed position within the industrial order. Ganz felt a genuine sense of outrage over the condition of New York's Jewish immigrants, but she also saw an opportunity to gain recognition for herself. Ganz used the anarchist movement to call herself to the attention of the newspapers and through them to the public, but she was not prepared for the consequences of her notoriety. Attracted to the image rather than the substance of anarchist ideology, she failed to consider whether it suited her own views of social justice. Sobered by her arrest and imprisonment, she quickly moved away from radicalism. During World War I she actively supported the preparedness campaign and later United States involvement, and after the war she dropped into obscurity.

There is a sharp contrast between Marie Ganz's brief and flamboyant career in the anarchist movement and the sustained dedication of Mollie Steimer (1897–1980).[27] Steimer emigrated with her family from the Ukraine in 1912. One of six children, she described her life in a New York ghetto as typical of "most poor Jewish immigrants."[28] Her father was a laborer, her mother took in boarders, and she worked in various factories. Her formal schooling having been limited by her poverty, Steimer, like Ganz and numerous others, received her education in the radical youth groups where literature and philosophy received almost as much attention as ideas for the creation of the new world. Inspired by Kropotkin's *Conquest of Bread*, she joined the anarchist group Freedom in 1917.

She could not have chosen a more unpropitious time to become an anarchist. The United States, having recently entered World War I, was increasingly intolerant of radicals. In August 1918, when Steimer and six of her comrades distributed leaflets supporting the Bolshevik Revolution and denouncing the Allied intervention in Russia, they were arrested for violation of the espionage act. While Marie Ganz had been sentenced to sixty days for brandishing a pistol in the offices of John D. Rockefeller, Mollie Steimer was sentenced to fifteen years for proclaiming: "The tyrants of the world fight each other until they see a common enemy—WORKING CLASS ENLIGHTENMENT. As soon as they find a common enemy they combine to crush it."[29] One of her indicted comrades, who had not engaged in the leaflet distribution, was acquitted; one turned state's evidence and received a light sentence; a third died in prison as a result of injuries inflicted by interrogating officers; and the remaining three were given twenty-year sentences.

After the Supreme Court refused to overturn the decision of the lower courts, Steimer began her prison sentence. Refusing to participate in a pardon campaign that was initiated on behalf of her and the others, she explained to her lawyer that "aside from the fact that I am against petitioning a government official, I consider it against

Helena Born, on vacation in Massachusetts in 1898. During this period she was engaged in an unsuccessful attempt to separate herself from capitalist society through agricultural self-sufficiency. She later returned to Boston. (Courtesy of New York University Libraries / Tamiment Library, New York.)

Mollie Steimer was deported to the Soviet Union in 1921, after serving three years of a fifteen-year sentence for violation of the Espionage Act of 1917. (Courtesy of Mollie Steimer.)

Marie Ganz, who came to prominence as an anarchist speaker during the winter of 1914, abandoned the movement after her threat on the life of John D. Rockefeller earned her a brief jail sentence. (Courtesy of the Library of Congress, Washington, D.C.)

Emma Goldman in 1911. During this period Goldman made a conscious effort to convert to anarchism the rebellious sons and daughters of America's middle classes. (Courtesy of the Library of Congress, Washington, D.C.)

Emma Goldman in 1919, shortly before she was deported to Russia. (Courtesy of the Library of Congress, Washington, D.C.)

Lillian Rubell, Becky Edelsohn, Louise Berger, and Alexander Berkman at the funeral of Berger's half-brother and two other comrades who were killed when a bomb, with which they intended to assassinate John D. Rockefeller, exploded prematurely. Berger, a participant in the plot, was not indicted. (Courtesy of the Library of Congress, Washington, D.C.)

Voltairine de Cleyre in 1897, during her first European tour. This trip enhanced her reputation at home and brought her into contact with the leading figures of European anarchism. (Courtesy of the Rare Books and Manuscripts Division, University of Florida Libraries, Gainesville.)

Voltairine de Cleyre at home in Philadelphia, where she spent most of her adult life. (By permission of the Houghton Library, Harvard University, Cambridge, Mass.)

my principles to ask for the release of four individuals while thousands of other political prisoners are languishing in the U.S. jails."[30] Despite her disapproval of the attempts to gain her release, Steimer and the others were removed from prison and deported to the Soviet Union in late 1921. At first welcomed by Soviet officials, Steimer soon earned the enmity of the Russian government. As an anarchist she had few illusions about her status among the Communists. Emma Goldman and Alexander Berkman had already fled Russia at the time of her arrival, and Steimer understood that dissenters paid stiff penalties. Nevertheless, animated by her principles and by the support of the Russian dissidents who had managed to stay out of prison, she continued her anarchist activities. While in Russia she had met and grown to love Senya Fleshin, an anarcho-syndicalist active in the movement to free Russian political prisoners, many of whom were anarchists. She and Fleshin were jailed, beaten, and tortured; whenever out of prison they remained under constant police surveillance. In 1923 the Soviet Union deported both of them.

For the next two decades Steimer and Fleshin endured ill health, privation, and government persecution. During the twenties they lived in France and Germany. Having the misfortune to be German residents when Hitler came to power, they fled to France again in the 1930s. While living this rootless existence, they witnessed the crumbling of what had remained of the international anarchist movement, and the devastation of their remaining hopes for the vindication of anarchist principles when Franco triumphed in the Spanish Civil War. On the heels of that defeat came World War II and the German occupation of France. Steimer was arrested in May 1940 and sent to a concentration camp at Gurs; Fleshin had escaped detention. Steimer remained in the camp for six months, after which she escaped to the unoccupied part of France. From there she and Fleshin fled to Mexico, where she lived until her death.[31]

It is difficult not to be overwhelmed by Mollie Steimer's fidelity to principle throughout decades of persecution. Whether such constancy is a virtue or a flaw may be argued; nevertheless, despite an almost identical sociocultural background to Marie Ganz, Steimer was inspired by intellectual, social, and psychological forces that profoundly distinguished her from the more changeable Ganz.

Steimer's conversion to anarchism derived less from an emotional response to a crisis situation than from her acceptance of the basic tenets of anarchist ideology. As a disciple of Kropotkin, Steimer possessed an intellectual and moral vision of the future. Ganz, on the other hand, consistently disclaimed a constructive image, insisting that destruction of the old order was her only object. Further, Steimer's prison experiences hardened her against democratic society. Although Justice Holmes, in his dissent against the conviction of Steimer and the others, argued that "the defendants were deprived of their rights under the United States Constitution,"[32] the majority of the Supreme Court thought otherwise, and Steimer remained convinced that constitutional safeguards of freedom were a sham. Finally—and this is a much more elusive argument—having endured imprisonment, torture, and exile for a cause, not once but three times, Steimer may have chosen simply not to question anarchist ideology in her later years. Whatever her reasons, she did not abandon her faith in anarchism. In her eighth decade she wrote: "I hold fast to my convictions, being certain that only in a society where no human being will rule over another, can there be true freedom."[33]

Despite the marked differences in the nature and duration of their commitments, Kelly, Born, Ganz, and Steimer were alike in that the anarchism of each rested on some sort of social ideal. The last two women considered here represent another type of anarchist woman, drawn to anarchism because of its immediate, direct, and transitory relevance to her emotional needs. Both Marie L. and Margaret Anderson, unlike their more socially aware sisters, were impelled by private dreams and singular visions, for which they found temporary support within the anarchist movement.

Marie L. was a young working-class woman from the Chicago slums who attracted the interest of the journalist Hutchins Hapgood during his investigation of the labor movement there. The anarchists fascinated Hapgood—he was to remain a long-time friend of Goldman and Berkman—but he was never an uncritical admirer. In 1909 he published *An Anarchist Woman*, an account of Marie L.'s adoption and ultimate renunciation of the anarchist cause.[34] Marie's background in some ways resembled that of Mollie Steimer and Marie Ganz. The daughter of an immigrant machinist who had serious drinking problems, she spent her childhood in poverty. After two years of formal schooling, she began a series of short-lived factory jobs, deciding at fifteen to exchange factory work for domestic service supplemented by occasional prostitution. Her introduction to the anarchists occurred when she had an affair with the brother of her current employer at age seventeen. Terry Carlin, nearly forty when he and Marie met, was a member of the anarchist circle in Chicago, to which he introduced the young woman. Carlin's attraction for her was "partly the fierce charm of a social experiment, the love for the proletarian and outcast; for I felt Marie was essentially that."[35]

Marie L. became an anarchist under Carlin's tutelage, discovering that its philosophy offered an intellectual justification for her hostility toward society. She told Hapgood that "I was filled with rebellion at the powers that were crushing me. . . . [W]hen he . . . pointed out to me the cruelty and tyranny of my parents and all society . . . I began to understand. . . . My conceptions of freedom were crude, but I began to feel that my revolt was just."[36] Anarchism not only provided her with an explanation for her rage but also offered a supportive social milieu and an opportunity for education. Her new comrades introduced her to political and economic debate, as well as to art and literature.

After remaining with the anarchists and Carlin for seven years, during which time she was primarily interested in sexual self-expression and liberation through the use of drugs and alcohol, Marie L. rejected both the man and the movement for respectability and a housekeeper's job in San Francisco. Her anarchist career seems atypical of the activists studied here; although she empathized with those men and women who were moved to violence by social conditions, her principal concern was immediate emotional gratification. Hapgood romanticized this quality in her, but his understanding of her position was essentially accurate. He argued that as long as anarchism "added to the fullness of her life, she saw its meaning and use; when it finally tended to sterilize her new existence, its 'pragmatic' value was nothing."[37] Nevertheless, Hapgood's analysis did not emphasize the intrinsic superficiality of her commitment. Never did Marie appear to be fully aware that anarchism was a philosophy of social rather than purely psychological rebellion.

She had used it as a device to explain her deviance from accepted patterns of social and sexual behavior. It was therefore easily abandoned as she outgrew her youthful rebelliousness and desired a more settled and secure existence.

Unlike Marie L., Margaret Anderson (1886–1973) never desired a secure and settled existence. In other ways as well she seemed far removed from the profane and promiscuous young woman whom Hapgood chose as the embodiment of anarchist womanhood. Margaret Anderson was one of the early bohemians, part of that group of middle-class youth, often from the Midwest, who later made Greenwich Village the symbolic center of social and intellectual rebellion. Born in Ohio, one of three daughters of a successful businessman, Anderson graduated from college, then broke away from parental restraint by moving to Chicago's bohemia and immediately becoming caught up in the youthful artistic revolt there.[38] Anderson's name is most familiar for her editorship of the *Little Review*, which she began in Chicago in 1914, moved to New York in 1917, and continued to edit until 1923, when she left the United States permanently. The best of the early "little magazines," the *Little Review* published the imagist poets, the realists, and—most notably—Joyce's *Ulysses*.

Anderson's privileged and indulged childhood contrasted sharply with Marie L.'s life in Chicago's slums. Yet neither could tolerate authority in any form, be it parental or societal. Both were emotional, impulsive creatures who gloried in their unpredictability and inconsistency. Moreover, of all the anarchist women studied here, they were the most unconventional sexually; while Marie L. was openly promiscuous from her early teens and occasionally took to prostitution, Margaret Anderson was homosexual. In embracing anarchism, both responded to an immediate and intensely personal attraction.

The quality in the anarchists that Anderson found most appealing was their explosive individualism, a trait she shared. Deliberately, provokingly, and often charmingly outrageous, Anderson never concerned herself with public opinion. Her unconventionality in this regard endeared her to Emma Goldman, who had begun to enjoy the attention and homage of the young middle-class rebels who formed the core of the new bohemia. Anderson's anarchism in fact stemmed directly from her friendship with Goldman. Anderson remained an anarchist for three years. Her drift away from the movement was actuated by her realization that Goldman and Berkman were human beings with frailties as well as strengths, not superbeings whom she could worship uncritically.[39]

Anderson never entered the mainstream of the movement. Despite her later assertion that during her years as an anarchist she found "people in clean collars uninteresting" and that she "even accepted smells, personal as well as official," since "everyone who came to the studio smelled of machine oil or herring," Anderson actually spent most of her time with the movement's leaders.[40] An elitist, she was simply drawn to people who emanated powerful individual strength or who seemed to her unique. Further, anarchism for her had all the romanticism of a lost cause. Involved with the movement between 1914 and 1917, during its decline, Anderson believed herself a member of an elite community, not a participant in a rebellion of the masses. In one sense, Margaret Anderson can be viewed as the personification of the alienated artist or intellectual attracted to radical causes as a by-product of her aesthetic rebellion. While others who had a greater sense of social purpose turned to socialism, her wildly emotional individualism led her directly to the anarchists. As long as the anarchists as individuals retained their fascination for her, she immersed herself in their cause; when they exhibited human weakness, she became disillusioned. Needing to worship, she was not content merely to participate.[41]

When Anderson abandoned anarchism, she turned first to literary rebellion in order to reestablish her intellectual bearings. Ultimately that too proved unsatisfactory. After World War I, at loose ends both mentally and emotionally, Anderson "didn't know what to do about life—so I did a nervous breakdown that lasted many months."[42] In 1923 she moved to Paris, never returning to live in the United States. She became a follower of the Western mystic Gurdjieff, one of the early figures of the human potential movements. Gurdjieff proved an enduring deity, for she remained a devotee throughout her long life. In her first autobiography Anderson had casually remarked: "In the natural course of events I had naturally turned from anarchism."[43] The disarming simplicity of that statement reveals the nature of the affinity between Margaret Anderson and Marie L. Both discovered in anarchism a temporary haven within which they were able to experiment without censure, to confront if not solve their own emotional crises. The anarchists, who were remarkably tolerant of all forms of eccentric or unusual behavior, provided them with a supportive community framework for their individual self-seeking. But these women did not find in anarchism a workable social philosophy because they were interested exclusively in their personal development. Since anarchism for them served no larger purpose, they could not sustain their interest in it.

The biographies of these six women offer compelling evidence of the complicated and diverse nature of the anarchist attraction for women. Nevertheless, a few general conclusions emerge from this complex and sometimes contradictory portrait of anarchist womanhood. First, anarchism appealed to both native-born Americans and immigrants. Communist-anarchist women were usually either immigrants themselves or the children of immigrants, often Jews from Russia or Eastern Europe. Their fathers worked as poorly paid manual laborers or kept small shops, while their mothers often took in piecework. Communist-anarchist women rarely attended school for more than a few years, economic necessity restricting their opportunities. After leaving school most of them lived in urban areas, finding work in factories, sweatshops, or domestic service. On the surface the Individualists seemed rather different; they were predominantly native-born Americans of varied socioeconomic backgrounds. But despite these superficial differences, the two groups also had striking similarities. The Individualists, although they had received more education, were usually as unable to support themselves comfortably as were their immigrant sisters; they often eked out wages as country school teachers, itinerant lecturers, or private tutors.

Since the initial involvement of the women discussed here spanned a forty-year period, during which time anarchism in the public mind ceased to be regarded as a legitimate albeit violent radical alternative and receded to the status of an extremist fringe group, it is necessary to consider the significance of this change upon the kinds of people likely to become anarchists. For the most part it appears that later converts, such as Marie Ganz, Marie L., and Margaret Anderson, were not committed to social change in the way that earlier activists—even those who ultimately turned away from the movement—had been. Nevertheless, there were exceptions: Mollie Steimer, for example, resembled Emma Goldman or Voltairine de Cleyre in the strength of her commitment more than she did Ganz or Anderson.[44] Although most of the women remained active in the anarchist movement for a period of two or more years, not all were long-term revolutionaries. Some of the women became disillusioned when the movement failed to confront the social and political problems that had spurred their initial involvement. Others for whom anarchism was a manifestation of post-adolescent rebellion outgrew their infatuation with radicalism and came to terms with conventional society. For still others, anarchist ideology was an intellectual fad to be abandoned in due course for other philosophies.

Because of the amorphousness of anarchist organization and its lack of a systematic program for social and political change, it attracted women and men from a wider variety of backgrounds and with more disparate views than did socialism, labor activism, or mainstream feminism, all of which were movements with more specific programs. As a result, it is not surprising that anarchist women differed among themselves by class, ethnicity, and education almost as much as they differed from other women radicals and reformers. Yet such distinctions serve only to make their similarities more striking. In general, anarchist women shared two intellectual characteristics that cut across socioeconomic boundaries: their consciousness of an experience of immediate and direct oppression based upon sex and their fierce insistence on remaining economically independent. The existence of these two widely shared patterns suggests that in spite of the looseness of anarchist thought, these women discerned an underlying coherence within anarchist philosophy, their exploration of which led to the development of anarchist-feminism. This constituted a vigorous and cogent challenge both to traditional notions of woman's place and to the organized women's rights movement.

3
No Purely Feminine Women: Anarchist Feminism

> There is no wholly masculine man, no purely feminine woman.
>
> *Margaret Fuller*

In some ways anarchist women were remarkably similar to nonradical women. They represented a cross-section of American society: their backgrounds were middle class and working class, urban and rural, immigrant and native, rich in culture and intellectually impoverished. Yet from such ordinary environments emerged a group of women who defied contemporary norms of womanly behavior, advocated a political doctrine that was anathema to a majority of Americans, and launched a stinging feminist attack on marriage and the nuclear family, an assault that alienated them not only from the mainstream of society but also eventually from the organized women's rights movement.

Anarchist-feminism, an ideology created and elaborated during the last third of the nineteenth century, developed directly from the cornerstone of anarchist philosophy: the primacy of complete personal liberty over all else. Although the factions within the movement disputed endlessly and vehemently about the proper methods for attaining such freedom, they all agreed on its fundamental importance. For the anarchist-feminists, this individualistic premise led to the conclusion that woman's inequality stemmed primarily from her dependence on man, particularly within the family structure. Thus far the anarchist-feminists were squarely within the tradition of the early feminists who ratified Elizabeth Cady Stanton's "Declaration of Sentiments" in Seneca Falls, New York, in 1848; but their further contention that the existing institutional framework made equality impossible took them beyond those pioneers. They believed that if women truly intended to be equal, their first step must be a declaration of economic, psychological, and sexual independence from men and from male-dominated institutions, beginning with marriage. While the belief in free love was not limited to the feminists within the anarchist movement, the emphasis was different. Although nonfeminist anarchists hoped for the replacement of state-controlled marriage contracts by consensual free unions, they intended no substantial changes in the nature of the family structure. Anarchist-feminists, on the other hand, wanted very much to alter traditional forms of household organization. They agreed first that women must be self-supporting in order to be free. Secondly, many of them also argued in favor of sexual "varietism"—that is, nonexclusive sexual relationships—on the grounds that exclusivity implied a form of property right. Such insistence on sexual and economic independence stemmed from a belief in the essential sameness of men and women. Anarchist-feminists believed in individual differences, but they refused to accept the prevalent view that intellectual and psychological distinctions were gender-based. Their unequivocal demand for economic independence from men, coupled with their frank avowal of female sexuality (not necessarily of a monogamous or heterosexual kind) placed the anarchist-feminists, therefore, in a unique position in late-nineteenth-century America.[1]

By this time the organized feminist movement had arrived at different conclusions about the nature of womanhood. (The terms "organized" and "movement" are used somewhat reluctantly, because both of them suggest a greater degree of structural unity than actually existed.) When referring to feminism, nineteenth-century Americans often used the less precise term Woman Question to describe the issues raised by demands for sexual equality. It is an appropriate phrase, evoking a sense of uncertainty and reflecting an inability to specify the exact nature of the unrest among women.

Feminism was not a set of specific beliefs and demands, despite the tendency of a later generation of scholars to subsume the whole movement into the drive for suffrage; it was a vast, complicated, and often contradictory movement.

Regardless of the many contradictions, however, some theoretical territory was common to all feminists. They all believed that American society had institutionalized certain inequities for women and that these inequities required remedy. As Kathryn Kish Sklar noted in her biography of Catharine Beecher, feminists agreed easily that women had a right to participate in and to influence the societal processes. Beyond that agreement, however, lay a dilemma. Articulated as early as the 1830s, it is a problem that continues to plague them: Should women exercise their power by emphasizing their differences from men or their common humanity? Increasingly in the nineteenth century, the organized feminist movement resolved the dilemma by arguing that while women had a right to equal access to the political, legal, and educational institutions of the society, they also, by reason of their maternal and reproductive roles, differed from men intellectually and psychologically.[2]

Antebellum feminism, especially as manifested within the environment of Garrisonian abolitionism, had been radical, compounded of the same blend of political outrage and moral fervor that fueled the extreme wing of the antislavery movement. The early feminists repudiated the notion of wifely obedience, refused to remain silent in public debates, insisted on access to educational institutions, and in 1848 demanded the right to vote.[3] The radicalism of the early feminists stemmed from their integration of a recognition of the inherent inequality of economic dependence, a reexamination of the marriage relation, and an insistence that women had a role to play in public life. Carrying this argument somewhat farther, another historian has declared recently that in itself the demand for suffrage was radical, because "to women fighting to extend their sphere beyond its traditional limitations, political rights involved a radical change in women's status, their emergence into public life."[4]

This is a compelling argument for the antebellum years because feminists clearly viewed suffrage as an escape from their restrictive private and domestic spheres. But by the last quarter of the nineteenth century perhaps a majority of the rank-and-file suffragists, as well as many of their new leaders, no longer saw suffrage as the first step in the liberation of women from the home. Some of them were at pains to express the view that voting women would not cause any disruption in the society. And even Elizabeth Cady Stanton, although it must have been hard for her, occasionally felt compelled to deny publicly that she advocated changes in marriage and family life.[5] Not only was the original radicalism of the demand for suffrage muted, but feminists often went further and invoked women's traditional roles as a justification for their right to vote.

As the feminist movement developed over the course of the nineteenth century, as it changed from a movement dominated by women who had held extremist positions on the question of slavery and therefore found radicalism congenial, to one that encompassed a broad range of women without the unifying coherence of a radical tradition, it became of necessity more conservative. As a result, by the last quarter of the nineteenth century, mainstream feminism—including the suffrage organizations, the women's clubs, and reform groups such as the Woman's Christian Temperance Union—had chosen to exploit the idea of inherent differences between women and men as a justification for granting women civic and legal equality. Many feminists supported the Social Purity crusades that swept the nation in the mid-seventies and periodically thereafter, contending that if only women were allowed to express their superior moral sense at the ballot box, they would be able to alleviate social ills like drunkenness and prostitution. Suffragists argued that "the state is but the larger family, the nation the old homestead"; hence, by extending their nurturing functions from the family circle to the larger society, women would not abdicate their traditional domestic role. Even Susan B. Anthony, who insisted that women needed the power to control their own lives through the vote and through economic opportunity, believed that the lack of both encouraged immorality, rendering woman "utterly powerless to extract from [men] the same high moral code that she chooses for herself."[6]

William O'Neill has argued that during the last years of the nineteenth century the organized women's rights movement capitulated to a "Maternal Mystique." What O'Neill has termed capitulation may have been in part a tactical move on the part of suffrage leaders to attract a mass following. Many feminists as well drew strength from the idea of the superiority of women as nurturers and guardians of morality, a concept that fostered a belief on their part that women ought to control public policy on all issues concerning women and children. In terms of actual feminist practice, the motives and ultimate goals of the feminists were probably less important than their immediate behavior. Mainstream feminist leaders (with the exception of the aging Elizabeth Cady Stanton and the younger Charlotte Perkins Gilman) muted the earlier criticism of sexual and familial relationships in favor of concentration on legal and political issues. Whether they shifted their emphasis because of ideological considerations or as a tactical move was in one sense irrelevant; in the eyes of both its own rank-and-file and the larger society the movement as a whole became less radical, less threatening, and hence less likely to effect fundamental changes.[7] The anarchist-feminists refused to accept this solution to the dilemma. Rejecting outright any notion of significant inherent intellectual or psychological differences between the sexes, they continued to insist on absolute equality based on a shared humanity. This approach had the strength of continuing to confront the vexing questions of domestic and economic equality. Those, however, were questions that an increasingly family-centered society was unwilling or unable to answer.

The anarchist-feminists' denial of gender-based distinctions precluded their use of many of the arguments for equality utilized by the mainstream feminists during the late nineteenth and early twentieth centuries. For example, the followers of Catharine Beecher could demand access to the teaching profession on the grounds that the female nurturing instinct made women biologically better suited than men to educate the young. Elizabeth Blackwell sometimes used similar arguments in her attempts to open the medical profession to women. Less generally remembered is that even Charlotte Perkins Gilman, who almost alone among the younger generation of mainstream feminists stressed the similarities between men and women, also on occasion found it necessary or expedient to exploit the concept of a special relationship between woman's biology and her drive for equality. In 1912 Gilman wrote: "We are the makers of men, and because we are the makers of men, it is requisite that we should be citizens of the world we live in."[8]

Because the anarchist-feminists' rejection of a belief in inherent differences between the sexes automatically barred their use of feminist arguments that relied on the reinterpretation of conventional feminine stereotypes in the interests of equality, they were forced to revert to a simpler polemical position. Deriving their analytic framework from the work of an earlier generation of feminists, particularly such singular rebels as Mary Wollstonecraft and Sarah Grimké, the anarchist women insisted that the humanity of women was all the justification their cause required. For them the issue was uncomplicated: "Woman's emancipation means freedom, liberty . . . pure and simple." And when the Individualist Marie Louise announced that what women needed was "Liberty to act; Liberty to live; Liberty to feel that our own acquired emancipation and happiness are not soiled by the aid of jealous proxies," her words were strikingly similar to the appeals to a common humanity voiced earlier by the Grimké sisters and Margaret Fuller. Anarchist-feminists would have concurred with Sarah Grimké's simple plea: "I ask no favor for my sex. . . . All I ask our brethren is that they will take their heels from our necks and to permit us to stand upright on that ground which God designed us to occupy."[9]

In basing their demands on a claim of justice—women are human beings; therefore they ought to possess all the rights and privileges of human beings—the anarchist-feminists refused to make any extravagant claims for social and political benefits that would flow from equality. But they thereby lost an opportunity to appeal to men on the grounds most likely to gain their attention, those of self-interest. The early feminists had faced the same problem and their arguments also had failed to win masculine support. As a result, the suffragists at the end of the century often felt it necessary to exploit their womanhood in an attempt to render feminism more palatable to men. Such tactics were unacceptable to the anarchist-feminists, but a few of them did try to persuade their male comrades that women's equality was essential to a radical platform. Gertrude B. Kelly, for example, argued that a successful revolution would depend on a commitment to feminism, contending that unless radical men began to take steps to end the oppression of women, their attempts to remake the world would end in failure. She agreed with her male comrades who said that there was "properly speaking no *woman question* as apart from the question of human right and human liberty." But men often used such statements to try to persuade women to mute their demands for sexual equality until after the liberation of the "people" had been accomplished, implying that while the concerns of male revolutionaries were by their very nature universal, those of women were at best parochial. Kelly, on the other hand, insisted that without sexual equality no liberation could take place. Men hurt themselves as well as women by their refusal to recognize this: "No wrong can be done to any class in society without part at least of the evil reverting to the wrongdoers."[10]

Gertrude Kelly's earnest attempt to enlist male support through appeals to self-interest was unusual. The anarchist-feminists recognized for the most part that women must seek their own emancipation. They placed (accurately as it turned out) little faith in the enlightenment of radical men. The significance of their approach may be seen most clearly by an examination of the anarchist-feminists' proposals for the reorganization of society based on the premise of economic and psychological independence from men.

Anarchist-feminists were preeminently interested in promoting economic self-sustenance by altering the structure of the nuclear family. Two general proposals were offered to accomplish that goal. The first, which was adapted from communitarian principles, suggested the construction of large cooperative households or communities in which lovers would have the option of living together or maintaining different apartments in order to preserve physical and psychological separateness. In such communal institutions children would be cared for by adults who chose the rearing and education of children as their life's work, and women as well as men would have the opportunity and responsibility to engage in productive labor. This vision was principally the creation of the Communist-anarchists, although support of it was not limited to that wing. Dyer D. Lum proposed the creation of "co-operative homes," and Voltairine de Cleyre later elaborated the idea: "I would destroy the individual 'home' with its waste of forces . . . and have instead magnificent palaces, spacious grounds . . . swimming rooms, bathrooms, everything on a large scale," yet with private rooms for every individual whenever he or she desired to be alone. In the early twentieth century, *Mother Earth* gloried in "the passing of the family," with Ada May Krecker sounding a premature death knell for the nuclear family: "'Home, sweet home' ties may appear beautiful today. But as our ideals socialize they will seem narrow, crude, savagely isolated and cold and confining," particularly for women. In the communal society of the future women "will not be set apart as mothers by profession any more than men will be set apart as fathers by profession. . . . [T]heir relations with their children will be relieved of kitchen and nursery service." Women, like men, would be free to be themselves.[11]

The Communist-anarchists chose to place their faith in the community, but most Individualists detested the notion of communal homes or cooperative communities. The ideal of many feminist Individualists was "independent men and women, in independent homes, leading separate and independent lives, with full freedom to form and dissolve relationships, and with perfectly equal opportunities to happiness, development, and love." Parenthood posed substantial difficulties, but these women averred that woman's chances for equality remained far greater if she were expected to provide for herself and her children than if she relied on a man. It was assumed that in the coming anarchist society childcare facilities would be available, which would solve some of the problems. The father might also want to contribute to the support of his children, though such assistance, while desirable, would not be considered an obligation on his part. The Individualist anarchist-feminists therefore, because of an ideological inability to accept the necessity of cooperation as an essential step toward economic liberation, accepted the idea of a double burden for the woman who chose motherhood.[12]

The crux of the argument for women's freedom, whether in communes, cooperative communities, or independent homes, was the demand for economic independence through self-support. Anarchist-feminists believed that all women—not only those who desired a career or were forced to work from necessity—needed to earn their own incomes. Florence Finch Kelly expressed the common view when she condemned "the idea that a woman is entitled to support from the man to whom she grants herself. . . . It is this idea that must be knocked to pieces before women can be free. . . . [W]omen must learn to be self-supporting. Else they will always be slaves."[13] This extreme position set the anarchist-feminists apart from others in the women's rights movement and may have been attributable in part to personal experiences of financial insecurity. The lives of many anarchist women were colored by impoverished childhoods or confrontations with economic discrimination in early adulthood. Among the Communist-anarchist women, for example, there was ample demonstration of the failures of male providers. The mothers of these women were often forced to take in boarders, engage in dreary and ill-paid factory labor, or work at even worse-compensated piecework at home to supplement their husbands' meager wages. And although the Individualists on the whole had been less deprived as children, as young adults they often found it equally difficult to maintain a comfortable income.[14]

The belief in the fundamental importance of economic independence cut across factional lines. Kelly's argument was not limited to the Individualists:

> I cannot see that much advance toward individualism in the relations between men and women is possible until the economic freedom of women shall have become an established fact. . . . Not until woman becomes a self-supporting, independent creature who has ceased to beg alms of [man] and who can and does support herself as easily and with as much comfort as he does, will he respect her as an equal and lose the last remnants of that old spirit of tyranny which made him get everything under his thumb that he could.[15]

Other anarchist-feminists agreed. Voltairine de Cleyre linked female submissiveness to economic discrimination and connected both to the erotic exploitation of women. Lois Waisbrooker, herself forced to give up her children because of inability to provide for them, urged women to unite into self-supporting cooperatives. And Gertrude B. Kelly asked, "Do not the lower wages paid to women in all departments of work force her into accepting support at some man's hand, and as a consequence surrendering all right to herself?"[16]

Anarchist-feminists found it difficult to persuade their male corevolutionaries to take the Woman Question seriously. De Cleyre publicly castigated anarchist men for their ambivalence and sometimes outright hostility to demands for equality: "So pickled is the male creation with the vinegar of Authoritarianism, that even those who have gone further and repudiated the State still cling" to a belief in male supremacy. Gertrude Kelly berated them because she believed that by ignoring the demands of women radical men were actually retarding the revolution, and Florence Finch Kelly damned the whole sex as tyrants, including "the best of men and the most imbued with a desire for justice and equity."[17]

The anarchist-feminists did not err in their assessment of their male comrades. While most anarchist men claimed to believe that once anarchism had been achieved, sexual equality would eventually follow, very few felt that immediate action was wise or desirable. Both Communist-anarchist and Individualist men joined in urging that the Woman Question be subordinated to other economic and political issues. For the Individualists, Victor Yarros demanded that the anarchist woman "join her strength to that of man . . . in *his* effort to establish the proper relations between labor and capital. And only after the material foundations of the new social order have been successfully built, will the Woman Question proper loom up and claim attention." Similarly, Peter Kropotkin counseled American women radicals to be more concerned with the liberation of "workers" than of women, since "it was by working to liberate the Russian people that [Russian women revolutionaries] have prepared the way for their own liberation."[18]

Perhaps more important than their unwillingness to accord to women's issues the same significance that they gave to other economic and social questions was the belief of most anarchist men that equality for women would not include a fundamental alteration in the relations between the sexes, even after the triumph of anarchist principles. Anarchist men seemed to fear possible changes in the domestic relationship. In an illuminating essay, part of a series on the Woman Question, Victor Yarros truculently asserted, "When I speak of a man and woman's making a home, I mean that he is to provide the means and she is to take care of the domestic affairs." Although he obviously felt threatened by the demands of anarchist women for "material and pecuniary independence," he took comfort in his belief that "nature is . . . bent upon preserving the dependency of both mother and child upon the father." Yarros was simply expressing a view common to anarchist men, most of whom despite their advocacy of free love retained conventional attitudes regarding woman's place in the family structure.[19]

Recognizing the interrelationship of domestic and economic dependence, anarchist men resisted stoutly the demands of their female comrades for equal pay. Georgia Replogle, by trade a compositor, coedited a small anarchist periodical, *Egoism*, in which she argued that equal work deserved equal pay. Nonsense, retorted Benjamin Tucker in *Liberty*: "Apart from the special inferiority of woman as printer . . . there exists the general inferiority of woman as worker." Even skilled women, he insisted, demonstrated "a lack of ambition, of self-reliance, of a sense of . . . responsibility."[20] The Individualists, at least, despite their assertion that at some point in the future the issue of sexual equality would "loom up and claim attention," were unable to conquer their own conventional conceptions of woman's role in either the domestic or economic arena. Since these two interrelated areas were precisely where the anarchist-feminists insisted that immediate changes were necessary, a meeting of the minds was unlikely. Sexual egalitarianism was almost as rare among the communists. Certainly the position of Johann Most tended toward outright misogyny. The rank-and-file in both factions of the movement seemed in agreement that woman's equality was an issue not worthy of immediate consideration.[21]

A few anarchist men rejected the dominant viewpoint. Hugh Pentecost (who edited *Twentieth Century* in the early 1890s and during that time worked closely with the anarchists) and John Beverly Robinson both contended that women were entitled to equal economic and educational opportunities. Pentecost was convinced that differences in upbringing and adult environment caused the supposed intellectual inferiority of women: "When we . . . consider the intellectual differences between men and women . . . I think there is good reason to believe that if women were as free as men . . . no such differences would be perceptible."[22] The most important male feminist among the anarchists was probably Moses Harman, who, despite an air of sentimentalism, transcended conventional attitudes about women. He dedicated his journal *Lucifer* to the "emancipation of women from sex-slavery"; although its primary target was the erotic exploitation of women by men, throughout the nineties *Lucifer* remained the only anarchist journal consistently denouncing the oppression of women. Perhaps inevitably, neither *Lucifer* nor Harman was taken very seriously by most anarchist men.[23]

Like the male former abolitionists who in the late 1860s stood firmly behind the suffrage amendment that enfranchised black men only, and like the socialist men of the early twentieth century who urged patience upon women comrades who wished to make an issue of sexual inequality, anarchist men persisted in believing that masculine concerns were universal concerns, while the demands of the women were at worst selfish and at best of secondary importance. The abolitionist men, pleading that it was "the Negro's hour," perhaps forgot that half the former slaves were women, doubly cursed by their race and sex. Socialist men proclaimed adherence to the ideal of sexual equality but allowed women little power within the party, and in many cases they were more traditional in their domestic arrangements than the most ardent capitalist.

Because the abolitionists were reformers and not revolutionaries, their inability to surrender their assumption of the preeminence of masculine goals is understandable. That the socialist and anarchist men were similarly incapacitated, despite their radical philosophies, indicates that a belief in the naturalness of female subordination extended even to those men who scorned conventional American society. Anarchist men were incapable of ridding themselves of the notion of distinct spheres of concern for men and women, with women confined to the domestic and personal, hence less important, sphere. If the anarchist-feminists could not convince their own comrades, their chances of reaching a larger audience were considerably diminished.

The anarchist-feminists never wavered in their belief that the source of woman's oppression was rooted in the domestic relationship, specifically in monogamous marriage and the nuclear family, with its interlocking elements of financial, psychological, and social dependence. Nor did they abandon their belief that liberation would come only with the abolition of marriage and the conventional family structure, the acceptance of female eroticism, and full economic independence. Nevertheless, anarchist-feminists as participants in the larger society could not ignore the legal, civic, and social questions that engrossed the organized women's rights movement during the last quarter of the nineteenth century and the early years of the twentieth.

Mainstream feminists during this period sought economic and educational opportunities, agitated for suffrage, and participated in (and sometimes led) crusades for temperance, social purity, and the abolition of child labor. The anarchist-feminists responded to these issues, with the exception of suffrage, in a united and predictable way. They heartily endorsed the drive for equal economic and educational opportunity, believing that such parity would help to undermine the nuclear family. One of *Liberty*'s female correspondents submitted an agenda for women's emancipation that included the following: freedom to enter any trade or occupation; access to birth control; the development of a single sexual standard that would provide greater sexual freedom for women rather than less for men; and the eradication of traditional marriage. Because economic and educational equality held a central place in anarchist-feminist ideology, anarchist women, in particular the Individualists, supported the organized women's rights movement on these issues. Most concurred with Ellen Dietrick's assertion that "any man who wants to curb the intellect, to check the freedom of vocation-choosing, to retard the pursuit of knowledge . . . is a most pestiferous enemy of society, *especially* when his efforts are directed against such development in women."[24]

The enthusiasms of the social feminists—for example temperance, protective legislation for women and children workers, and social purity—usually drew a negative response from the anarchist-feminists, both communists and Individualists. Although like the more conventional feminists they abhorred prostitution, anarchists believed it to be a predictable result of both capitalism and societal repression of sexuality that could only be removed by the overthrow of both. The Individualist Gertrude Kelly argued in 1885 that social purity advocates possessed the evidence to show "that destitution is the chief cause of prostitution" but that they refused to follow the logic of their findings. "When we come to examine the remedies proposed, we find not a word on the subject of . . . making their wages equal to those of a man for the same work." Emma Goldman, the leading Communist-anarchist of the early twentieth century, expressed an identical view more than twenty years later: "Whether our reformers admit it or not, the economic and social inferiority of women is responsible for prostitution."[25]

Temperance movements also failed to attract anarchist-feminists, who believed that personal habits were the concern of the individual; as long as vices caused no direct harm to others in the society, they were not seen as a matter of public interest. Similarly, the drive for protective legislation for women and children elicited more hostility than sympathy; anarchist-feminists believed that any regulation singling women out for special treatment amounted to economic discrimination. Most also felt that the state had no right to intrude into the question of child labor. Marie Louise, who contributed both to *Alarm* and *Liberty* in the 1880s, gave voice to a widespread view when she asserted that "no one has a right to dictate as to whether *certain* or *all* labor is undecorous for women and undesirable for children under fifteen years of age. In such cases, let the woman judge about decorum and the parents of the child about the undesirability of factory or other work for their offspring."[26] Anarchist-feminists did not argue that children should work, but neither did they believe that legislation could act as a palliative. Since capitalist society perpetuated the horrors of child labor, the only remedy could be the overthrow of industrial capitalism and the authoritarian state that supported it.

The question of woman suffrage caused anarchist-feminists the most difficulty. As anarchists they were committed to an ideology that repudiated majoritarian democracy, but as feminists they abominated a society that denied to women any form of power or influence that was granted to men. They solved this dilemma in one of two ways. Either they scorned the ballot as a tool of capitalist society unworthy of serious consideration by committed radicals, as Voltairine de Cleyre demanded when she argued that "the ballot hasn't made men free and it won't make us free"; or they chose to view suffrage as an intermediary goal on the road to the ultimate creation of an anarchist society. The former position was more characteristic of the Communist-anarchists, who tended in general to be both more consistently revolutionary and more alienated from the larger society than the Individualists. While de Cleyre had argued that the ballot served no useful purpose for either men or women, Emma Goldman went further and called it absolutely harmful: "Suffrage is an evil, . . . it has only helped to enslave people, . . . it has but closed their eyes that they may not see how craftily they were made to submit."[27]

Individualist feminists, on the other hand, often took the position that "the use of the ballot will educate women, as it has already educated men, in knowledge of the imperfections of human government." Unlike many suffragists, who throughout the eighties and nineties and into the twentieth century insisted that women would reform and purify the society once they achieved the vote, those anarchist-feminists who supported woman suffrage did so because they believed that women were entitled to have an equal share of whatever power the current society allotted to men. Ellen Dietrick, in protest against shutting women "off from all participation in the common affairs of society," insisted that "a vote is simply a voice, simply an acknowledgement that the individual has a right to speak in behalf of his or her interests." By the late 1880s and 1890s none of the anarchist-feminists expected that women would purify politics by their participation, although in 1868 Lois Waisbrooker had argued that "we must have a moral side to politics; or if it pleases you better, a feminine side." Waisbrooker's differentiation between men and women was not a common view, and she herself modified her statement by a refusal to believe that men and women should have different spheres of influence; she believed in "diversity in the same sphere, and not the separation that indicates different spheres."[28]

Nonfeminist anarchists like Victor Yarros and Benjamin Tucker castigated their comrades who supported woman suffrage, however lukewarmly, as reactionaries bent on preventing the development of anarchy. Yarros expressed this view: "Anarchists and Individualists oppose woman suffrage simply and solely because they are convinced that woman's political activity would be directed tyrannyward and would arrest the political emancipation of all of us." Nevertheless, those anarchist men among the Individualists who usually agreed with their female comrades on other aspects of the Woman Question also supported them on the suffrage issue. Ezra Heywood had argued in 1877 that "to rule adult citizens against their will is tyranny; women are adult citizens, hence those who deny them the ballot are tyrants." With similar sentiment, if less vehemence, John Beverly Robinson declared in 1894 that although "for the ballot itself I care nothing," whatever freedoms men enjoyed, including the right to vote, women also had a right to possess, "on the ground of their common humanity and as equal individualities."[29]

Because they were split among themselves on the issue of suffrage and disagreed with the organized women's rights movement on reform questions, anarchist-feminists did not participate extensively in the larger feminist movement. Nevertheless, individual anarchist women sometimes joined nonanarchist feminist organizations, or, though less commonly, actively aided the suffrage movement. Lois Waisbrooker served as a suffragist lecturer and pamphleteer for a time during the late 1860s and early 1870s. Voltairine de Cleyre, Mary Herma Aiken, and Lillie D. White were among the anarchists and anarchist sympathizers who became founding members of the Women's National Liberal Union.

The Women's National Liberal Union was a short-lived, self-styled "radical woman's society" that came into existence in 1890 under the direction of Matilda Joslyn Gage, a suffragist and friend of Elizabeth Cady Stanton. Gage believed that "existing woman suffrage societies have ceased to be progressive," since they chose to concentrate narrowly on winning the vote, ignoring other issues that she considered crucial to the achievement of sexual equality. The purpose of the Women's National Liberal Union was to provide a feminist forum to consider the issues of marriage and divorce reform, show sensitivity to the plight of working-class women, and counter the influence of religion on women. (Gage believed that the churches, both Protestant and Catholic, were the primary oppressors of women.)

Anarchist-feminists agreed with Gage's antagonism toward religion. Further, several resolutions congenial to the anarchist viewpoint passed the convention, including the following: "That the centralization of power, whether in the Church or in the State, is dangerous to civil liberty and to individual rights, and . . . must be constantly and firmly opposed, . . . that the first duty of every individual is self-development," and "that morality is not theology, . . . that right is right and wrong is wrong, not because any being in the universe so declares, but in the nature of things, the origin of right being in truth and not in authority." Unfortunately, the Women's National Liberal Union did not long outlast its first convention; Gage was unable to muster sufficient support from within the mainstream feminist movement. In any case, it is probably an exaggeration to consider anarchist participation in the Union as evidence of cooperation with the larger women's rights movement. Because the Union came into existence as a result of Gage's dismay over the growing conservatism of her fellow suffragists, it was itself on the fringe of organized feminist activity, rather than part of the mainstream.[30]

Voltairine de Cleyre's experience with the Union may have motivated her own attempt at feminist organization, for it was in the early 1890s that she became instrumental in the creation of Philadelphia's Ladies Liberal League. The League, which remained in existence for nearly a decade, belied its genteel appellation by its attempts to bring together the various radical and reform constituencies in the city through controversial forums and lecture series. It was originally conceived not as a feminist organization but as a women's branch of the Friendship Liberal League; its male sponsors had envisioned a ladies' auxiliary that would raise money for liberal causes. De Cleyre captured the spirit of those early intentions when she noted that "bed quilts done up gorgeously with silks and raffled at ten cents a ticket may have been distantly in view." But the women—freethinkers, anarchists, socialists, and feminists—rebelled. Their early sessions, which were remarkably similar to the consciousness-raising groups of the feminist movement in the 1960s and 1970s, evolved into an ambitious program of self- and public education.[31]

Like the Women's National Liberal Union, the Ladies Liberal League was not a part of the mainstream feminist movement, but existed on its periphery. Nevertheless, the participation of some anarchist-feminists in such organizations that were explicitly feminist though not anarchist suggests that these women sought a sense of solidarity or sisterhood extending beyond the confines of a single radical movement. Unfortunately, that solidarity was always short-lived and difficult to attain.

Despite the fact that many nonanarchist feminists would have agreed in part with the major contention of anarchist-feminists—that economic dependence subordinated women to men—the ideology of anarchist-feminism as a whole elicited little serious attention outside the anarchist movement during the late nineteenth and early twentieth centuries. It appealed neither to mainstream feminists nor to most women radicals, who turned instead to an equally unsatisfactory socialist movement. The reasons for this rejection lie partly in the changing nature of anarchism and feminism during this period, and partly in the inappropriateness of an individualistic ethos in an organizational age. From the mid-seventies onward, organized feminism had become increasingly decorous. Matilda Joslyn Gage, after all, was forced to go outside the organized movement to find a platform for her anticlerical views, and the venerable but always irreverent Elizabeth Cady Stanton found herself outflanked and outvoted by her more conventional sisters. While feminism moved toward respectability, anarchism, at least in the public view, became increasingly radical. Partly because of the fiery rhetoric of Johann Most and his admirers, and partly because of antiforeign sentiment, the anarchist came to be viewed as a symbol of irrational violence. The public image of the anarchist was that of a deranged terrorist. Alliances between anarchists and reform groups grew more difficult to achieve. As anarchism became more revolutionary, and as feminists became ever more determined that working within the existing legal and political framework offered their best hope for achieving equality, the community of interest between the two groups vanished.[32]

Although the negative public image of anarchism may have prevented some potential adherents from an investigation of the ideology of the anarchist-feminists, that is an insufficient explanation for its limited impact. The primary reasons for its relative lack of influence lay in the nature of the ideology itself; for the anarchist goal of complete personal freedom, limited only by the proscription against interfering with the liberty of others, precluded organization, except in the most rudimentary sense. Although there was widespread agreement on the answers to the Woman Question among anarchist-feminists, there was little coordination among them in promoting their ideas, and they worked mostly as isolated individuals. Their writings were scattered, almost haphazardly, throughout the anarchist press. The only major anarchist journal concentrating on the subject of women was *Lucifer*, which increasingly after 1895 dealt almost exclusively with issues of sexuality. Emma Goldman did not begin *Mother Earth* until 1906, too late to exert any influence for change in the by then pragmatic, almost totally suffrage-oriented feminist movement. At the more personal level of intellectual interaction among peers, the anarchist-feminists do not appear to have developed any social forms comparable to the homosocial interpersonal relationships that were so successful in providing a support network for both suffragists and social feminists.

In an organizational age, the insistence on the part of the anarchist-feminists that equality was based on individual refusal to participate in an unjust society seemed anachronistic to many radical as well as conservative women. In addition, their conviction that the assertion of personal independence was necessarily connected to a rejection of marriage and the nuclear family structure further alienated them from many who may have agreed with other aspects of the anarchist argument. As Richard Sennett has pointed out, the last quarter of the nineteenth century was a particularly infelicitous period for attacks on family structure. Such attacks directly threatened the emergent belief that the family offered the most secure refuge from a chaotic, unstable, constantly changing industrial society. Finally, the anarchist-feminist contention that one of woman's first steps toward equality should be complete self-support not only offered even greater insecurity but also contravened a growing national trend toward sentimentality about the family. Women who were disastisfied with contemporary economic or social conditions had other choices, particularly socialism, which did not threaten explicitly the existing family structure. In fact, much American socialist literature declared that socialism would purify marriage. As a result, anarchist-feminists could not hope to gain the support of most radical women.[33]

Despite its inability to influence the direction of mainstream feminism in late-nineteenth- and early-twentieth-century America, anarchist-feminism was not simply a *divertissement* in the drama of the struggle for sexual equality. Although to a certain extent the anarchist-feminists appear to have been almost reactionary—they were undaunted individualists in an organizational age, antifamily in an era of family romanticism—the developments in twentieth-century attitudes about women's roles suggest their particular strengths. Their insistence that the roots of inequality lay in the domestic relationship has resurfaced as modern feminists recognize the inability of legal and political reform to assure complete equality. The attempt to create a balance within sexual and familial relationships is one of the major problems bequeathed to the feminists of the late twentieth century. Finally, the anarchist-feminists refused to be shaken in their belief that the most important thing about men and women was not their difference from each other but their common humanity. This premise, a truism for the early feminists, appeared to have been left behind by a generation of pragmatic suffragists and social feminists who utilized their womanhood as a tactic in their drive for political and legal rights. In the short run, the organized suffragists seemed to have been following the most assured path to equality. In the long run, however, American society still struggles with the issues abandoned by them but kept alive by the unsuccessful, unpragmatic anarchist-feminists.

4
A Ring of Gold: Love, Sex, and Marriage

A ring of gold with the sun in it?
Lies. Lies and a grief.

Sylvia Plath

By the late nineteenth century, conventional American views of marriage and family life included the pervasive belief that the family offered (or at least ought to offer) a refuge from a hostile and chaotic world, that childhood was an age of innocence to be preserved and protected from encroachments by the adult world for as long as possible, and that woman, because of her reproductive role, was more suited biologically than man to understand and control the processes of family life. These conventional views did not necessarily exclude feminism; for many women participation in the larger society was essential if they were to fulfill adequately their maternal and familial duties. Nevertheless, despite widespread acceptance of such views, alternative values and prescriptions for behavior existed among the anarchists, who articulated a sexual theory that offered women an opportunity to repudiate conventional patterns of behavior.

Anarchist sexual theory, as it developed within American culture, was neither an alien importation nor a simple aberration. The anarchist sexual alternative served two important functions. First, for those men and women whose sexual beliefs and habits defied convention, it provided a subculture that tolerated unconventional behavior. More important was its role in offering a forum in which to introduce and debate unorthodox views. An analysis of anarchist ideas concerning sexuality and domesticity enables the historian to understand better the degree to which self-proclaimed revolutionaries are capable of developing a vision of a future society that transcends conventional norms, hence to comprehend the limits of radical disaffection from contemporary values.

Romanticization and idealization of the domestic circle had come to dominate popular fiction and the public imagination by the last third of the nineteenth century, the result of a process of response and adaptation to economic and ideological transformation.[1] Industrialization, or the entire complex of processes usually grouped under the heading of modernization, has most often been mentioned as the precondition for changes in family life. Although modernization as an explanatory device has sometimes been stretched beyond the point of usefulness, the transformation of the United States into an industrial nation, and the concomitant upheavals in the rhythm of work and leisure, brought about substantial changes in the nature of family life and in the position of women in the family. As the locus of production shifted from the home or small shop to the larger industrial unit, the ties of economic interdependence that had heretofore bound the family no longer sufficed to keep it intact.

Kathryn Kish Sklar, in her biography of Catharine Beecher, has referred to an "ideology of domesticity" that began to take shape in the 1830s. Middle-class women, without the economic functions that had occupied their grandmothers, began to conceive of their roles in different terms. Economic productivity gave way to emotional productivity. Catharine Beecher and her followers attempted to direct the attention of Americans toward the home, the domain where women predominated. While they insisted on the maintenance of separate spheres for the functions of men and women, they attempted to establish the significance to the larger society of the roles women played within their defined sphere.[2]

The ideology of domesticity and the feminist movement developed during the same period, and both were responses to the same phenomena. But they offered fundamentally different models of behavior for women who wished to be active in the larger society. If the choice had to be made, most women chose the Beecher model, influence from the domestic circle rather than power in the society, privileges instead of rights. Feminists realized that if they wanted to succeed in creating a mass movement, they could not ignore the domestic reformers. In some areas their task was easy; they were in accord on the issues of temperance and prostitution. Other questions were more problematic. On the crucial question of the proper role for women within the family and the larger community, the two groups seemed at odds. But even here the disagreement was less sharp than appearances suggested. The domestic reformers wanted women to exercise influence over their husbands and children from the fireside, while the feminists urged them to move into the public arena.

Despite their belief that women need not be confined to the home, many of the first generation of feminists accepted the idea that at certain stages of a woman's life the responsibilities of homemaking and motherhood would become paramount. Notable women's rights advocates, including Lucy Stone and Antoinette Brown Blackwell, retreated temporarily from active participation in the movement in order to devote their energies to their children. These women believed not in separate spheres for men and women but in overlapping ones. Still there remained some tasks, such as childbearing and childrearing, which continued to fall to the lot of women. They saw the sexes as "equal but complementary halves of the human family." Not all antebellum feminists agreed with Stone and Blackwell, and those who did agree also insisted on the need for more egalitarian marriages with shared responsibilities; but after the Civil War, as more conservative trends emerged within the movement, interest in altering the marriage relation abated, while the idea of special functions for women remained intact.[3]

By the 1870s some of the domestic reformers had come to accept the idea of woman suffrage, to which they had heretofore been opposed. This allowed them to join with, and to influence, the women's movement. As a result, by the last quarter of the century there developed a kind of popular feminism that might be described as follows, in terms of its significance for relationships between men and women and the development of the family: Women and men are equal, but they have different functions in life. A woman's proper role is to marry, keep an orderly and pleasant household, and bear the primary responsibility for the spiritual and moral development of her children. Nevertheless, she should take an interest in the outside world, especially in areas of her particular concern, such as the oppression of children under the factory system, the working conditions of poor women, temperance, and the evil of prostitution. Since the remedy for such concerns lay in the public rather than domestic sphere, she should agitate for suffrage. If she were unable or unwilling to marry, she ought to train for a profession—as a teacher, a physician treating women, or (by the late nineteenth century) a worker in one of the helping professions such as social work or nursing. The incorporation of some of the most important aspects of the domestic ideal into the women's rights movement progressed rapidly. By the 1870s many feminists viewed questions about childrearing, parenthood, and sexuality as women's concerns. For that reason alone, it is difficult for the historian to separate domestic and sexual issues from the larger Woman Question—which included questions of economic, legal, and civic equality as well—that preoccupied much of the middle class during the last half of the nineteenth century. Nevertheless, it is important to do so, if only because organized feminists increasingly chose not to challenge publicly the domestic ideal in their quest for equality.

Although the family had been sentimentalized and romanticized almost to the point of idolatry by the 1870s, much of the rhetoric seemed to have an element of desperation surrounding it. Because middle-class Americans perceived the family as a refuge from a hostile world, the members of the family must have felt intensely pressured to love one another, and conversely not to seek stability or happiness outside the familiar circle of home and loved ones. Richard Sennett has argued that although the family did serve as a bulwark against hostile outside forces, stability came at a very high price. The middle-class families that Sennett studied in Chicago were unable, because of their isolation within the nuclear family structure, to prepare their children to function in industrial society.[4]

There is other evidence of disquiet. During the 1870s the idea of Voluntary Motherhood began to reach a broadened and receptive audience. Believing that women should have the right to choose when to conceive children, advocates of Voluntary Motherhood were among the first to proclaim the right of women to control their own reproductive systems. Yet they remained unwilling to endorse abortion or "mechanical" birth-control devices for fear that separating sexuality and reproduction would result in unbridled license. Voluntary Motherhood was therefore seen as a way to limit offspring without endorsing sexuality for its own sake. Despite their essentially conventional views on sexuality, the proponents of Voluntary Motherhood were viewed with alarm in the belief that endorsement of artificial contraception would be a logical, if frightening, next step. Because of that fear, the Comstock Law, the first enforceable legislation directed against the use of contraceptive devices, was passed in 1873 as part of the social purity crusade; it forbade the sending of "obscene" materials through the mail. During this period as well laws against abortions proliferated, and those who held unconventional sexual viewpoints came under increased attack.[5] The Voluntary Motherhood movement, for all its sexual conservatism, reflected a growing opposition to the traditional view of woman as sexually subordinate to her husband. The opposition to the movement, as well as to more radical sexual viewpoints, underscored the fear that respectable women would be attracted to aberrant sexual ideas unless the society resorted to a powerful legal means of suppressing those ideas. Because many feminists held conventional views of sexuality, they endorsed Voluntary Motherhood while condemning contraceptive devices. Although there were some notable exceptions, the majority of mainstream feminists refused to separate reproduction from sexuality.

The anarchist view of sexuality differed in several respects from that described above. Anarchists began with the premise that men and women were erotic beings, both needful and desirous of an outlet for their sexuality. They further argued that sexual relationships concerned only the people involved and that neither the state nor the church was required to license or bless such unions. Commonly calling themselves free lovers, anarchists believed that adults could decide what type of sexual association they desired and were capable of choosing the nature and the duration of that association. However, beyond their agreement on these questions, anarchists divided on the issues of monogamy or varietism, on birth control, and on the roles and functions of women in free unions.

It was during the early 1870s that the issue of free love and its connection to anarchism began to receive widespread public attention. Victoria Woodhull in 1872, at that time espousing the doctrines of the native American anarchist Stephen Pearl Andrews, announced from a New York stage that she both believed in and practiced free love. Because she chose to raise the theoretical issue of free love during a speech in which she revealed that New York's most popular minister, Henry Ward Beecher, had engaged in an affair with the wife of his close friend Theodore Tilton, Woodhull ensured herself a wide audience. One immediate result of her public affirmation of the anarchist position on sexuality was the alienation of several prominent feminists who had heretofore supported her. Susan B. Anthony led the suffragists in denouncing "the Woodhull," and Elizabeth Cady Stanton, whose sympathies with liberal sexual notions were more pronounced, reluctantly joined in. But although the Woodhull scandal caused a breach with the organized feminists over the issue of public propriety and private morality, it was in fact merely a public examination of a viewpoint that the anarchists had been developing for about two decades, and which by the 1870s had matured into a full-fledged article of the anarchist faith.[6]

Josiah Warren, known as "the first American Anarchist," did not consider free love to be a cornerstone of his antistatist philosophy. Nevertheless Modern Times, his community on Long Island, New York, attracted free lovers, and anarchism became associated with its doctrine. In the fifties and sixties Stephen Pearl Andrews was representative of a number of anarchist writers who turned their attention to the question of sexuality, coming to the conclusion that marriage was a vestige of an earlier civilization best left behind. As Woodhull's mentor in the 1870s, Andrews heavily influenced her views on sexuality.

Woodhull is an apt symbol for the free-love controversy of the 1870s because she espoused three causes that were often united until that decade: anarchy, free love, and spiritualism. Most anarchists were not spiritualists during the period preceding the spread of

Marxian materialism within the movement, but many spiritualists were attracted to anarchism. In a sense, both anarchists and spiritualists were engaged in a struggle to comprehend and come to terms with the chaos and uncertainty of mid-nineteenth-century life: the rupture of the secure religious doctrine of orthodox Protestantism; the urbanization and industrialization of the East and Midwest; the growth of national corporate and governmental power and the subsequent sense among many Americans that their most important decisions no longer rested in their own hands.

The spiritualists came to terms with questions of morality and evil, earthly success or failure, by concluding that death did not exist; consequently, the individual never had to admit to final loss of control. Spiritualists developed a contempt for government that complemented their belief in eternal existence. Government after all had no control over the spirit-world, which to the spiritualists was just as tangible as corporeal life, and more important. It was not that government had to be overthrown, it was simply irrelevant. The anarchists, who in the sixties and seventies welcomed any allies they could get, sometimes found the spiritualists trying, but the spiritualists' opposition to both government and organized religion lent credibility to the view that the two groups were natural allies in the fight against dogmatism. The anarchist position in the 1870s is connected to the issue of spiritualism since during this period anarchists welcomed most nonorthodox thinkers. Later, when anarchists became more self-consciously revolutionary, they would show less tolerance for those whose views coincided only partially with theirs.

The nature of the anarchist argument for free love and its involvement with other social philosophies in the 1870s may best be understood by looking at the work of two free-love propagandists of the time, Ezra Heywood and Lois Waisbrooker. Heywood, an eclectic radical who was best known for his sexual iconoclasm but was also interested in labor reform and in the broader women's rights movement, published *Cupid's Yokes* in 1876, three years after founding the New England Free Love League. *Cupid's Yokes*, an argument against the institution of marriage, was banned from the mails and earned its author a two-year prison sentence at hard labor for violation of the Comstock Law. In it Heywood declared,

"The Free Love faith proclaims the fact that persons recognized in law as capable of making a sexual contract are, when wiser by experience, morally able to dissolve that contract; and that passion is not as depraved as to be incapable of redemption and self-government."[7] Heywood insisted that free love would not lead to excess or debauchery since a corollary of liberty is "non-invasiveness." "In claiming freedom for myself," he declared, "I thereby am forbidden to encroach. When a man seeks to enjoy woman's person *at her cost,* not a lover, he is a *libertine,* and she a *martyr.*"[8] His argument centered on two points: marriage laws as constituted were an unwarranted and unjustified invasion by the state into individual lives; and under the sanction of this law women were rendered powerless to protect themselves against sexual abuse by their husbands.

In addition to these two major theses, Heywood's tract included four other subsidiary themes. First, he concluded that celibacy was physically unhealthy and that variety in sexual partners was conducive to a full and rich life. Second, although celibacy was unhealthy and unnatural, sexually active men and women should consider parenthood carefully. "What graver act than to give life to a human being? What clearer right has a child than to be well-born?"[9] Parenthood ought to be voluntary and undertaken only after serious consideration for the child's future. Nevertheless, Heywood did not approve of artificial contraception, condemning condoms, pessaries, and even withdrawal. He approved of "male continence," which was intercourse without ejaculation. Vaginal douching was acceptable, although less strongly recommended than the rhythm method. (Unfortunately, general medical knowledge then placed the safe period for intercourse during what we now know to be the time of ovulation.)[10] Third, Heywood argued that prostitution was a by-product of marriage and that men were responsible for keeping women in such a dependent position "that [a woman] consents to sell the use of her person for food and clothing." Finally, anticipating later socialist arguments, he argued that "having, through property in land, interest on money, rent, and profits, subjected labor to capital, recipients of speculative increase keep working *men* poor; and by excluding women from industrial pursuits and poisoning their minds with superstitious notions of natural weakness, delicacy, and dependence, capitalists have kept her wages down to very much less than men get for the same work."[11] Although Heywood recognized that limited economic opportunities for women made them susceptible to the lures of prostitution, he did not in *Cupid's Yokes* make economic independence for women a central part of his free-love doctrine. He was primarily concerned with the invasion of the state into private matters, the evils of unwanted children, sexual abuse of women, and the personal misery that followed from marriages maintained by legal force.

Heywood sought to base his free-love argument on rational or "scientific" grounds, and despite his rather unsuccessful attempt to turn Jesus into an advocate of free love, the tone of the work clearly suggests that the religious references provided embellishment or offered at most an attempt to persuade his readers that he did not defame Christianity. They were not central to his argument, which he based loosely on a progressive-evolutionary view of human development. The spiritualist wing of the movement did not greatly influence his position.

Lois Waisbrooker, on the other hand, came to anarchism through spiritualism, and the mystical and at times nearly incomprehensible mixture of Christianity, evolutionary themes, and spiritualism reminds the reader of the prose of Stephen Pearl Andrews, who probably influenced her. In her free-love tract *The Plain Guide to Naturalism*, published in 1879, Waisbrooker promulgated a free-love creed based on the belief that sexuality would ultimately provide human beings with a key to immortality. Twentieth-century readers would no doubt find her views eccentric; nevertheless she remained within the mainstream of the anarchist movement until her death in the early twentieth century. In the 1890s she edited *Lucifer* while Moses Harman was in jail for violation of the Comstock Law, and in the early twentieth century she was president of the anarchist colony at Home, Washington. Two things, however, marked Waisbrooker as an anachronism, a representative of an earlier generation of free-love anarchists: first, her foundation of quasi-Christian mysticism; second, her occasional reference to female superiority.[12]

Waisbrooker's novel *Nothing Like It*, while lacking literary merit, is interesting as an indication of Waisbrooker's antipathy toward marriage and organized society and her belief in the moral force of women. The novel concludes with a dream in which the narrator is confronted with a group of women in bondage—to their fathers, to their husbands, or to the state. The vision stunned the narrator: "The rule was that a man could take a woman from the state, if she chose to go with him, upon condition that he bound her to himself; and, because women had this right to the choice of masters, I heard a song of rejoicing, the burden of which was 'Freedom.'" To the narrator it seemed a strange freedom, but those who chose to defy convention "were the scorn of all, and had the rights of none." Realizing that it would be futile to ask men for help, the dreamer believed there was no solution, until a disembodied voice prodded her: "I looked, and there was none to help, and I wondered . . . ; then my own arm brought salvation."[13] Women would have to free themselves, the narrator concluded, echoing the sentiments of the novel's heroine, Minnie Morris, who had earlier devised a scheme for the economic independence of her "reformed" fellow prostitutes: "Man controls the purse while in the plan I propose, woman does it, or enough, at least, to make her independent of him."[14]

Waisbrooker delineated in *Nothing Like It* the connection between free love and the economic independence of women. In the *Plain Guide to Naturalism,* she made sexuality the central force in human existence and the foundation for the development of both the emotions and the intellect, urging both men and women to develop their sexual natures. She began the tract by declaring that through the consistent, joyful, and loving use of sexuality human beings might literally become immortal, although she was unclear about the nature of that process. Her argument does suggest, however, that she wanted women, and men, to stop considering their sexual functions to be a matter for embarrassment. Sexuality becomes what we think it is, she argued; if we think it is brutalizing or degrading, it becomes so. She interspersed her bizarre religious views with admonitions to men to be gentle and tender with their wives or sweethearts, to seek reciprocity in sexual satisfaction. She also quite accurately noted the connections between religious and sexual ecstasy. What is significant about Waisbrooker's tract is that it represented an obvious struggle on her part to connect Victorian notions of feminine moral superiority with post-Victorian ideas about the beneficial aspects of a joyful sexuality. If the modern reader were to take her ideas of "Re-generation" through sexuality figuratively rather than literally, they would not seem entirely foreign.[15]

On the whole, however, Waisbrooker's sexual-religious mysticism cut her off even from most of the free lovers of the next decade. Both she and Heywood were of an older generation of free lovers whose roots were in the individualist ethos of earlier nineteenth-century America. Heywood was antiurban and anti-industrial, and Lois Waisbrooker, despite her radicalism, had been deeply influenced by the Victorian exhortation that women purify men, even if she did want to purify them through sex. Neither could speak compellingly for or to the new generation of anarchists. Nevertheless, elements of both their philosophies remained central to the anarchist approach to sexuality and marriage.

In the 1880s younger, more urban-oriented anarchists, attuned to the contradictions of the concomitant idealization of womanhood and her exploitation in the new industrial society and not yet irreconcilably separated over the issues of violence and communism, evinced a compelling concern over questions of sexual morality. For this revolutionary group of anarchists—which included native Americans like Dyer D. Lum and Albert Parsons as well as many immigrant radicals—the issue of free love began to take on new dimensions. There were three important elements to this new theoretical direction: first, in terms of the definition of the role of women within sexual relationships, a clear difference emerged between male and female free-love advocates; second, these young anarchists placed greater emphasis on contraception; third, the analysis of the evils of marriage stressed more heavily the unhappiness that was caused by incompatibility, where the earlier generation had been more concerned to encourage variety for its own sake. Later, in the early twentieth century, anarchists became acquainted with sexual theorists like Havelock Ellis and Ellen Key, who brought a greater sophistication to these issues. By the second decade of the twentieth century, anarchists were in the forefront of such drives as the agitation for access to birth control and the right to free sexuality of all types, including homosexuality.

English speaking anarchists in the eighties and nineties could rely on two journals to discuss the sex question, Benjamin Tucker's *Liberty* (which he began to publish in 1881, when he was twenty-seven years old) and Moses Harman's *Lucifer*. Albert Parsons's (later Dyer D. Lum's) *Alarm* was far more preoccupied with the Labor Question than with the Woman Question, reflecting a difference of emphasis in the 1880s between the Communist-anarchists and the Individualists. To a certain extent *Lucifer*, edited by a man whose ideas about sexuality had developed during the same period as those of Ezra Heywood and Lois Waisbrooker, continued the ideas of the older sex radicals, although the influence of Lillian Harman and her husband E. C. Walker brought to it some of the more modern viewpoints. In practical terms, this amalgam of old and fresh ideas meant that Harman emphasized the right of voluntary motherhood without either endorsing or condemning contraceptives, although he expressed a preference for the rhythm method or male continence. He disapproved of abortion as a birth-control method, yet endorsed its use in rape cases.[16] *Lucifer*'s columns often featured horror stories about the sexual abuse of wives, and suggested that men were overly preoccupied with sex.

Beginning as the *Valley Falls Liberal* in 1880, and ending as the *American Journal of Eugenics* in 1907, *Lucifer* proclaimed itself dedicated to the liberation of women from "sex slavery."[17] In practice Harman was interested principally in the right of women to control their own bodies—which often boiled down to the "right of refusal"—and the right of children to be "well-born," meaning free from genetic disease. Harman abhorred the marriage laws not because he favored variety or promiscuity but because they denied woman control over her body. He never condemned those who married rather than face the opprobrium of a hostile community. In fact, when his daughter Lillian went through a marriage ceremony with E. C. Walker, he defended her action as the only practical course to take. The marriage prompted a storm of controversy in anarchist circles in the eighties, but the Harmans and Walker stood firm.

The Harman-Walker marriage was illustrative of the nature of *Lucifer*'s political stance. Harman never urged people to antagonize the state unnecessarily, although he encouraged them at all times to inform the state of its errors. Most male anarchists seem to have taken Harman lightly. Dyer D. Lum, for example, thought him a bit of a crank. Women anarchists, on the other hand, while they did not agree with all his theories, took him rather more seriously. Voltairine de Cleyre, in attempting to gain signatures on a petition to free Harman from prison in 1892 (he had been sentenced to five years hard labor for printing a letter that contained the word "penis"), referred to him as "my champion" and asserted that his service to women was that "he beheld every married woman for what she is, a bonded slave, who takes her master's name, her master's bread, and serves her master's passion; [and] who passes through the ordeal of pregnancy and the throes of travail at *his* dictation."[18] Harman's major theme was sexual exploitation within marriage; he was less concerned with developing new patterns of sexual relationships.

Liberty, on the other hand, while not dedicated to the "emancipation of woman from sex-slavery," as was *Lucifer,* did in the mid-eighties devote extensive space to the sex question as viewed by the young contributors to the fledgling journal. There was a relationship between the acquisition of other contributors (besides Tucker and a few close friends) at mid-decade, especially several women, and the heightened interest in sexuality. Because a significant number of these contributors were young—in their twenties or thirties—*Liberty*'s columns of those years reflected the sexual views of the new generation of Individualist anarchists.

Two elements of the *Liberty* positions on sexuality and marriage are striking. First, there was a clear difference of opinion between men and women concerning the purpose of free love, with the male writers emphasizing the importance of compatibility and the tragedy of personal unhappiness that resulted from unsuccessful marriages. The women, on the other hand, emphasized the belief that marriage precluded woman's economic independence and rendered her too dependent in other ways on men. The women argued that entirely different social and sexual arrangements must accompany free love, while the men foresaw no dramatic changes in the domestic roles to be played by a free couple. Second, there was a greater willingness on the part of both men and women to separate the concepts of sexuality and reproduction. Lois Waisbrooker differentiated between them in her tract of 1879, but she did not endorse sexual pleasure for its own sake. Rather, sexuality was a tool in her "Re-generation" theory. The *Liberty* columnists, on the other hand, with some exceptions, were approaching in the eighties a position in which sexual pleasure was a good in itself. The principal woman writer on sexuality and marriage in the 1880s was Sarah Elizabeth Holmes, who used the pseudonym "Zelm," with occasional articles by Florence Finch Kelly and her sister-in-law Gertrude B. Kelly. (In the nineties, when *Liberty* had become far less interested in sexuality and had lost most of its women contributors, the principal women writers were Lillian Harman and Miriam Daniell.) In addition to her writings in *Liberty*, Florence Finch Kelly also wrote two novels that espoused the free-love position: *Frances: A Story for Men and Women* (1889) and *On the Inside* (1890).

Zelm argued for the abolition of traditional marriage as well as free unions in which women and men lived together and engaged in traditional domestic responsibilities based on the defined sex roles. Her ideal was individual homes for men and women, for she believed that only physical separation could promote the economic and emotional independence so necessary to a free womanhood.[19] In a debate with Victor Yarros over the questions of sexuality, domesticity, childrearing and economic independence, Zelm contended that while she agreed that men and women should be free to form and dissolve liaisons, women could never attain full freedom if they continued to live with men, remaining primarily responsible for providing the domestic comforts of the home.

In proposing a free-love philosophy, Zelm was careful, much as was Ezra Heywood in the 1870s, to distinguish between sexuality and licentiousness. Whether through ignorance of contraception (which is unlikely, given the fact that *Liberty* writers mention mechanical birth control casually), or through a deliberate choice to ignore it, Zelm is careful to warn women of the dangers of too freely obeying their "'natural' sexual instincts," reminding her readers that they "know the consequences of following the simple sexual impulses to be more serious than any other." She tied the sexual appetite to other sensual pleasures:

All our life is a foregoing of what we are inclined to do for the sake of a future happiness we may thereby attain or a future pain we may thereby avoid. I do not always eat whenever I see appetizing food; . . . I sometimes get up when I am still sleepy. . . . I may consider many of nature's methods exceedingly wasteful and clumsy, and I may believe that, if I had made the world, I would have made it otherwise; that I would have made our simple, spontaneous, first, and most keenly-felt desires those which, if blindly followed, would result in the greatest conceivable happiness. But nature and the laws of the universe and of our own selves are facts which we cannot alter and to which we can only study to adjust ourselves.

While she did not specify that the adjustment must exclude contraceptive measures, she concluded with the warning that "for the woman, the consequences of simply obeying the sexual impulses is the bearing of children."[20] Sexuality and reproduction, therefore, were still connected.

Florence Finch Kelly, herself married, had been a reluctant bride and remained a theoretical free lover at least throughout the 1880s. Like Zelm, Kelly argued that the purpose of free love, as far as women were concerned, was to provide for the economic and psychological freedom of women. In *Liberty* she denounced "conventional marriage" as a "condition which could have given Dante points for his inferno," arguing that while "the separate individual existence of the man and the woman" was the desired goal of free lovers, such freedom was impossible "until at least relative economic freedom for women is realized."[21] In another article she denounced "the conventional code of morals on the sexual question." Kelly argued that sexual liberty was a woman's right, and that the nature and kind of sexual life chosen by a woman, be it celibacy or varietism, was her own choice; an externally imposed moral code should not inhibit a woman's sexual behavior. While claiming that sexual freedom was an absolute right, she contended that neither men nor women had properly analyzed the connection between sexual freedom and economic issues:

> The most important point . . . is that prostitution . . . and conventional marriage . . . stand upon the same principle, . . . namely the principle that a woman's sexual favors are rightfully a matter of commerce. The

only important difference between the two conditions is that prostitution gets better pay than marriage.[22]

In her novels, *Frances* and *On the Inside*, Kelly continued her defense of free love. *Frances*, which in its structure conforms to the romantic style of the popular domestic novels, has an improbable plot, characters who are either paragons of virtue or evil men and women who get their just deserts, and a happy ending. But it is iconoclastic compared to the conventional domestic novel in that the heroine lives in a brothel and the hero abandons a perfectly respectable wife for her. Kelly presents the reader with two morals: love is a higher law than conventional morality, and yet is a transient thing that should not be bound by promises of lifetime fidelity. The final scene of the novel shows the lovers Frances and Harris, with their two children (for love, however free, was not without its consequences), affirming their devotion to one another. Frances asks, "Shall we always love each other so much?" and Harris, free lover to the end, answers:

> I do not know, dear. We love each other now and that is enough. We will not lose the happiness of the present by being anxious about the future. As long as love lives of his own free will we will enjoy him and be as happy as we are now. But if he should ever wish to leave us, we would not try to force him to stay, for love compelled is not worth having.[23]

By 1890 Kelly had recovered from her early romanticism and *On the Inside* is more explicitly a novel with a social conscience. It contains among its characters women with independent lives and unconventional ideas. The plot, which revolves around a love affair between an anarchist called Harry Reberfell and a young woman whom he converts to anarchism, serves as a forum for presenting readers with a discussion of anarchism. While the author demonstrated her ties to Victorian society by her treatment of Reberfell as the mentor of young Isbelle and she as his devoted pupil, the character of Isbelle suggests nevertheless many of the strengths of the position taken by anarchist women on the questions of sexuality and marriage. When not serving as devoted pupil, she is a resourceful, independent young woman who came to New York alone from the Midwest to make her fortune. She is honest, open, and rarely coy in her behavior toward men. In addition to Isbelle, several other women, mostly anarchists, are portrayed as self-supporting, career-oriented, intellectually independent and worthy of emulation. A lack of subtle sexual moralizing also prevails in the novel: notably, children are not always a consequence of sexual indulgence.

The weakness of the story, considering its didactic purpose, is that Kelly could not show how anarchism or free love offered anything of substantial value to women. Indeed she discussed such standard Individualist remedies for social ills as the gradual abolition of the state, occupancy and use of the land as a prerequisite for ownership, voluntary taxation, mutual banks, the abolition of rent and interest, and the development of individual freedom limited only by the fact that one "does no injury to others."[24] But she failed to connect these remedies with the problems of sexuality and marriage. Reberfell, asked when anarchism will come about, could only say, "Perhaps in three centuries, perhaps in ten." As for the problems of the present, "For that there is no help. Absolutely none."[25] Perhaps this novel moved Kelly herself to a belief that anarchists offered no practical solution to the difficult questions of sexuality and marriage, for soon after this novel was published she left the radical movement.

In some contrast to the women who considered the issues of sexuality and marriage in the 1880s, the male contributors to *Liberty* usually emphasized the goal of sexual, rather than economic, liberation. The men were also more willing to condemn deviations from the free-love line by those who professed to believe in it, and they evinced a far greater concern with the emotional and spiritual gratification offered by free love than for the economic benefits derived from it. Further, they showed less willingness to consider alternative household arrangements to the traditional nuclear family (albeit without marriage). In some ways these male writers were more closely connected to the free lovers of the sixties and seventies, in terms of their position on household arrangement, than the women. During the early to mid-eighties, male commentators on sexuality and marriage in *Liberty* included Victor Yarros, J. William Lloyd, and the editor himself.

Lloyd, a utopian and a romantic, devised sexual theories in keeping with his belief that men and women were capable of self-regulation of their appetites. In 1888, in the midst of a debate over whether he would participate in antivice crusades, Lloyd affirmed:

> Yes, I am a purity and morality crank, and I tell you the people will never have liberty till they are worthy of it; could have it now if they were self-wise and self-free enough to be worthy of it. . . . Liberty, like charity, must begin at home. Reform vice thoroughly, and you have no crime to stop, for crime is also a vice, being always injurious to self. Perhaps it may be no good reason, because we are not all prudent, virtuous, and brave, that we are robbed and plundered, but it is a reason, nevertheless. It is very nearly *the* reason. Give us enough of the prudent, virtuous, and brave and we will very soon stop that work. . . . I am sure I don't know . . . whether I am a Malthusian or anti-Malthusian, or a Neo-Malthusian, or no Malthusian at all, but I believe in small families. I am a free lover, but I believe in . . . sexual temperance. I am no ascetic, but I believe in simple diet, non-exciting pleasures, slow living, and moderation in all things.[26]

Lloyd thought of himself as a social scientist seeking the means by which society could be made both virtuous and free. He was friendly with physicians such as E. B. Foote, Jr., one of the early advocates of birth control. Like Foote, Lloyd believed that once a woman bore a child with a man, that man influenced her physiologically, "so that subsequent children are liable to partake of his nature."[27] Likewise, Foote suggested the possibility, which Lloyd believed to be a fact, that even where childbearing did not take place, the physiological influence also obtained. Lloyd called this phenomenon "mental impregnation." However, while Foote used this theory as a rationale for sexual fidelity in a relationship, in order to "breed" better children, Lloyd did not fully accept that argument:

> By mental impregnation I mean that the spiritual or mental nature of the man . . . flows into her brain and nerves, and perhaps effects physical changes in their molecular arrangement, mode of action, and growth, but at any rate implants . . . germs of thought and feeling which will ultimately develop into full-formed ideas and emotions, such as the woman herself never would have had without such fertilization.

In keeping with the Victorian views of semen as a magical life force, and with female sexuality as passive and receptive, Lloyd did not believe that women affected men in the same way during the sex act, as "it appears to be the ordinary arrangement of nature that the woman should be chiefly receptive and impressible, the man mainly projective and positive."[28]

Despite his theory of mental impregnation, Lloyd was not at all sure that sexual fidelity was called for. He did believe that, if this theory were true, it served as an argument against promiscuity, by which he did not mean a variety of partners but rather "the careless and inconsiderate gratification of impulses toward the other sex." But, on the other hand, it did not necessarily imply exclusivity; rather, in the interests of herself and her unborn children, a woman "will naturally be eager to associate with those men whose mental nobility she admires, . . . peremptory in her refusal of men whom she doubts or fears, and wisely cautious in her relations with all." For Lloyd, to try to enforce an agreement of exclusivity on a woman, no matter what the greater good, was inconsistent with her liberty.[29]

Lloyd resembled Heywood and Waisbrooker in that his free love doctrines were part of a larger system of morality, which included temperance and diet control. He thought that women, by nature's decree, were more passive and impressionable than men. Perhaps because he strongly believed in the triumph of the natural, he argued forcefully against trying to impose any system on women, saying that they were capable of making their own decisions. In some respects he was more egalitarian in his views than either Benjamin Tucker or Victor Yarros. His vision of the future of free love in several ways resembled the recommendations that Charlotte Perkins Gilman proferred in the late 1890s, although she believed in monogamous marriage. Lloyd's ideal included "free love and free-homes," but he believed they would only be attainable under the following conditions:

> First, a grouping of human beings, either in contiguous houses or in large hotels; secondly, a freedom, division, and spontaneous organization of labor which makes it unnecessary for any human being to labor more than half the daylight hours, at the most, and which takes cooking,

laundry work, and housekeeping, out of the hands of the home-holder, and the care and education of the child (to any desired extent) out of the hands of the parents.[30]

In the 1880s neither Benjamin Tucker nor Victor Yarros were concerned with developing a communal focus for anarchy. Unlike Lloyd, they were not utopians. Instead, they argued from a materialist standpoint that liberty in the personal sphere meant the right to complete personal autonomy. When applied to sexual relations, this argument provided women with the right of free sexual choice. They based their views on the anarchist repudiation of marriage as an institution that rendered women the property of their husbands; free love was the remedy. Nevertheless, unlike Zelm and Florence Finch Kelly, they were unable to connect their condemnation of "women as property" with the realization that the domestic relationship that made women economically dependent was at least partly responsible for their social, legal, and civic inequality. The views of Yarros and Tucker on the sex question were quite similar. Yarros, in his debate on marriage and sexuality with Zelm in 1888, argued that one of the reasons for abolishing marriage was that "women are subjected to the misery of being the property, tool, and plaything of man; her slavery is sanctioned by custom, prejudice, tradition, and prevailing notions of morality and purity." His solution? "Intelligence is the cure for this. Man's brutality and cruelty will be buried in the same grave in which his own and women's superstitions will be laid away."[31]

From this beginning, Yarros turned to a discussion of female sexuality, assuming that woman's sexual instincts and her desire for maternity were inextricably connected and insisting that women were therefore naturally and inevitably at a disadvantage. According to him, a woman becomes sexually involved with a man "in order to gratify one of her strongest natural desires." But

> while man's part in the relation is pleasurable throughout, woman purchases her enjoyment at an enormous price. Up to the moment of her contracting to cooperate with man in the production of offspring, a woman may be considered as man's equal. . . . Economic independence, education, culture, and refinement,—all these would be fully within her individual reach. But let her enter into love relations with the young man

and *resolve upon assuming parental obligations and responsibilities* and all is changed. . . . She has to depend upon the man whom she made the father of her child, and who suffered no inconvenience from the new relation. . . . With the equality of powers for self support vanish all other equalities.

This was inevitable, and advocates of economic independence for women, according to Yarros, too often overlooked "this cruel, illusion-breaking fact of *natural* inequality . . . resulting from the wide difference in the consequences which reproductive sexual association entails respectively upon partners to same."[32] To those who would suggest that smaller families offered an obvious solution, Yarros contended that in the new society, which would be free from poverty and the fear of poverty, large families would be "a joy and a blessing." And while he discussed birth control, which he termed "artificial checks and preventives," his attitude was ambivalent; contraceptive devices were "methods that nobody would recommend except as necessary evils, but which should never be resorted to in the absence of serious reasons."[33]

Yarros consistently emphasized the relative freedom of men in sexual relations but assumed that women, for whom he deemed maternity instinctive, would always be less free because of that instinct. His failure to endorse a goal of small families, let alone childless sexuality for women, flowed in part from this belief in a maternal instinct and in part from a nagging fear that women were themselves attempting to separate sexuality and reproduction. While he granted the right of women to sexuality without maternity, he attempted to negate this awful possibility by stating that women have a biological urge for motherhood and that this urge in fact fuels their sexual drives. Therefore, for women sexuality and a desire for children were inseparable. Despite his conviction on this point, he betrayed some insecurity by noting that "assuming sexual passion to be no stronger in women than in men (some are of the opinion that it is much stronger), there will always be a preponderance of forces and tendencies in favor of men." Later he asked anxiously, "Why should not love relations remain much as they are today? . . . Why a man should not make a home for the women he loves, I am unable to see. While he is providing the means, she is educating the children and surrounding him with comfort. When they cease to be happy together, they separate." In other words, according to Yarros, the Victorian ideal of domesticity would prevail under anarchism.[34]

When Zelm, in her reply to Yarros, accused him of analyzing the situation from a purely masculine viewpoint, he reminded her of woman's natural inequality, and used the indisputable statement that under existing conditions it was extremely difficult for a woman to support children independently as an argument for the inevitability of female economic dependence. It never occurred to either of them that parents could care for children jointly, with each partner retaining comparable economic independence. It was not a case of Yarros's misunderstanding Zelm's position, for he noted succinctly that "Zelm . . . insists upon the mother's material and pecuniary independence." For Yarros, that was simply an impossibility. He believed that under free love the woman would find security "against brutal intrusion and unwelcome assiduity in attention on the part of the husband," since "in family life under freedom" there would be "peace and respect" between men and women. But that was as far as he could go. He still insisted that the traditional "division of labor and functions in a family" were natural and therefore that anarchism would not alter them. Moreover, both the mother and children would continue as dependents of the father. "There is no help for it, if men and women are to continue to live and love and reproduce their kind."[35]

In this controversy between Zelm and Victor, Tucker remained neutral, yet his comments on the sex question in the eighties indicate that his views were much more in tune with those of Yarros than with Zelm's, as far as the relationship between free love and the economic independence of women is concerned. The chief difference was that Tucker, at least in the early eighties, was an outspoken proponent of birth control. Throughout the eighties Tucker's comments on free love ranged from simple assertions that marriage rendered women slaves and playthings to attacks on the prohibition against sending birth control information or devices through the mail, to denunciation of those people who believed in free love but became legally married because of societal pressure. His abhorrence of legal marriage was unequivocal. When Lillian

Harman and E. C. Walker were married, they prefaced their signing of the marriage contract with the statement that in marrying they did not surrender "any natural right of man, and especially of Woman." Tucker, urging all anarchists to "STICK TO THE PLUMB-LINE" of anarchy, demonstrated that his main concern was not to grant freedom to women under free love, but to refuse to abide by legal contracts. Harman and Walker had clearly stated that they married under protest. Tucker condemned them for acceding to the marriage rites, yet he admitted to paying taxes and in other respects obeying laws.[36]

Liberty's concern with sexuality and marriage diminished at the end of the eighties. Thereafter *Liberty* only occasionally printed sketches, letters, or essays on the subject. By 1890 Tucker began writing most of *Liberty* himself, having alienated or insulted many of his former contributors. His comments grew more waspish, his denunciations more sweeping, his presentations more one-sided in many areas, including sexuality. Jo Labadie had warned *Liberty*'s readers in 1889 not to be concerned with free love and sex relations but to concentrate on changing the control of the means of production.[37] And indeed, although discussions of questions of sexuality still appeared sometimes, the tone was far more moderate. Even the very few women who wrote for *Liberty* in the nineties no longer argued stridently for "independent homes."

John Beverly Robinson was the only male columnist to develop a theoretical framework for the abolition of marriage. Robinson, who wrote for *Liberty* during the 1890s, was genuinely concerned about the subordinate position of women under the contemporary marriage laws, and he argued that "marriage was not instituted to maintain the rights of the wife and children, it was instituted and is still upheld to maintain the privileges of the man." The abolition of those privileges was one of his major demands, especially the husband's right of possession of his wife's body. Like Heywood, he attempted to refute the charges of licentiousness often levied against free lovers:

> It is commonly felt that all who urge the abolition of marriage particularly wish to free themselves to lead a reckless life sexually. In my opinion it is chiefly those who are happily married who have reason to desire the

abolition of marriage, because, the fact of possessing any power of coercion continually comes up as a little drop of bitterness.

Robinson believed that as more women trained for professions, marriage would not be the only career to which they might aspire. Since women, once "the equalization of men's and women's wages" became an established fact, would have a choice between marriage and remaining single, Robinson hoped that women would refuse to vow obedience and that men, realizing the independence of women, would fear to demand it. Sexual equality and independence might then result. Nevertheless, Robinson did not go so far as the women anarchists of the 1880s when they asserted that at all times women ought to support themselves. He seemed to assume that women would retire to domestic cares upon pregnancy and continue at home during the period of childrearing, but that if thrown upon their own resources they could return to the marketplace.[38]

Five years later Robinson reiterated his views, beginning his article with the claim that for innumerable centuries "the essence of marriage has been the subordination in some sort of the woman to the man. Such is still its essence." Robinson wished to respond to any signals that pointed to the eventual abolition of marriage, such as the refusal of young women to agree to the vow of obedience, or the increasing popularity of divorce. Alone among the men who wrote about free love, he predicted that only when women are able to support themselves would marriage be unnecessary. "What does the money-freedom of women mean, as far as the future of marriage (as an institution) is concerned? Simply this: that as it grows more difficult for men to support women, and easier for women to support themselves, the odium against non-marriage will disappear." Still, he assumed that a woman would support herself and her children only if her relationship with the father proved unsatisfactory. Robinson favored birth control, although he expressed himself with delicacy and argued firmly for a woman's right to choose whether, and when, to bear children.[39]

With the exception of Robinson's essays, discussion of marriage in the nineties more often took the form of fictional sketches. In one sketch R.S.U., the winner of a dialogue concerning the merits of free love, argued that:

Marriage or no marriage, a woman is not and cannot be *free*, unless she is economically independent. Unless she can provide for her own needs, she is a man's slave in some form or degree (it might be in a very civilized form, by the way), be he her legal or illegal lover or husband. The majority of women are not awakened to the real cause of this slavery.

R.S.U. stated that American society offered no possibility of real freedom for women. Disapproving of this line of reasoning, Tucker retorted in the same issue that when a woman enters into sexual relations with a man, she chooses willingly to abdicate certain freedoms. If a woman loves and accepts the consequences of that love, then she herself has chosen. For the woman who fears losing both the man she loves and the possibility of attaining worldly success, Tucker had little sympathy. "Her real choice was between the freedom of celibacy without Peter, and the slavery of marriage with Peter. The case of Mary Jane . . . may be stated in these simple words: she wanted Peter more than she wanted freedom."[40] Tucker spared no compassion for women who chose sexuality over celibacy.

Tucker's acerbic retort to those men and women who wanted a society in which both sexes could have independence and erotic lives cut to the center of woman's dilemma in the late nineteenth century. During the nineties women writers who appeared in *Liberty* did not demand—as had Zelm, Florence Finch Kelly, and Gertrude Kelly—that women must be self-supporting in order to be free; rather, they asserted that if women chose to remain in the home, their domestic duties should command the same respect as the work of men outside the home. Miriam Daniell, in one of her sketches, had a husband say, "Remember, I support this house by my earnings and will always regulate its affairs." The wife, having recently come to the realization that her husband considered her a subordinate, retorted, "I might earn as good a living as I desire if I spent my time and strength in printing or teaching, instead of in bringing forth and rearing our children and in doing the housework, etc. This is not to be taken as the equivalent of your labor?" It undoubtedly came as no surprise to the readers that the man's response was, "No, of course not." Daniell concluded that the problem was unresolvable.[41] A woman must accept male domination, or she must support herself, or she must use the threat of self-support, as Robinson would have her do, to compel her husband to allow her freedom. After over a decade of analyzing the issues of sex and marriage, the men and women who wrote for *Liberty* remained in disagreement over the question of woman's freedom within the free-love relation.

The men, while they began to comprehend by the 1890s the interconnections between domestic relationships and economic dependence, often naively stated that woman's wages would very soon equal those of men and that she could therefore coerce men into treating her with respect and dignity by threatening to take the children and support herself. Alternatively, like Tucker, they callously told woman to make her choice, then live with it. Neither way was very satisfactory. In fact, the emphasis of individualist anarchism on each person's right and duty to provide for him/herself, coupled with the absence of strong communal support, offered scant hope for women in the 1890s. This may explain the decline of women contributors. Zelm had disappeared from *Liberty*'s columns, Florence Finch Kelly had abandoned the movement, and the other women whose pseudonyms abounded in the pages of the journal in the 1880s had also left.[42]

Of course, there are other dimensions to sexual liberation besides the question of the extent to which a freer sexuality contributes to the independence of women. *Liberty* stood consistently behind the campaign to eliminate the sexual double standard and to remove any social stigma from those women who chose to exercise their sexual freedom. To that end it reported with horror the attempt on the part of nonanarchist reformers to have laws passed that would raise the age of consent to eighteen or twenty-one. Lillian Harman, in her comments on the proceedings of the Age of Consent Symposium, noted that many reformers argued that women who did not adhere to conventional notions of chastity were socially valueless. Such a view implied, according to Harman, that nothing about a woman "is worth a moment's consideration but her conformity to a sexual code which man has invented. . . . What would be left to the world of the achievements of men, if their sexual unorthodoxy had cancelled all their intellectual and ethical services?" By 1895, all that was left of *Liberty*'s sex reform was its continued fight against the double sexual standard and its affirmation of the woman's right to sexual pleasure. In itself, such a position may be as conducive to inequality as to equality.[43]

Since the 1880s anarchist-feminists had searched for a way to make sexual equality compatible with eroticism. Moving tentatively toward the advocacy of birth control, demanding access to sexual freedom, and refusing to accept the domestic ideal, they faced enormous difficulties, not only in society at large but also among many of their male comrades. Both *Lucifer* and *Liberty* in the 1890s reflected the inability to devise a solution to the problem. However, by the turn of the century anarchist-feminists found assistance in the works of some of the new sexual theorists, particularly Edward Carpenter and Havelock Ellis, both of whom had begun to reach American audiences. The decade before World War I witnessed a growing public discussion of sexuality, brought on, in James Reed's words, by "the recognition that conventional standards of sexual conduct were somehow inadequate." Middle-class Americans, beset by the expanded role of women in the work force, by female encroachments into politics, and not least by the rising divorce rate, now questioned seriously their code of sexual morality.[44]

The anarchists extended their understanding of sexual behavior by exposure to and participation in the public discussion of sexuality. But their goals remained different: while most Americans looked to an enhanced eroticism to strengthen marriage ties, anarchists continued to urge the abolition of marriage, and anarchist-feminists still demanded the destruction of the nuclear family. As a result, in the early twentieth century anarchist-feminists forged an explicit link between sexuality and self-realization. Just as the anarchist free lovers of the 1860s and 1870s, such as Ezra Heywood and Lois Waisbrooker, had claimed that sexual varietism led to the development of higher moral standards, and those who gathered around Moses Harman in the eighties and nineties professed that free love would end sexual excesses and produce happy, healthy, and wanted children, so the anarchist women of the early twentieth century spoke about the relationship of sexuality to the liberated personality. Although not all free lovers agreed, there was a common emphasis on the need to safeguard one's individual identity, and a fear that marriage stifled each partner's intellectual and psychological growth.

In 1907 Voltairine de Cleyre gave a speech to Philadelphia's Radical Liberal League entitled "They Who Marry Do Ill." Moses Harman and Lois Waisbrooker would have approved of the title, but de Cleyre's definition of marriage would have shocked and dismayed them. By marriage she meant "the permanent relation of a man and woman, sexual and economical, whereby the present home and family life is maintained," be it polygamous, monogamous, polyandrous, legally constituted, or free union. "It is the permanent dependent relationship, which . . . is detrimental to the growth of individual character, and to which I am unequivocally opposed." De Cleyre argued that once a man and a woman became bound together, they lost the freedom to follow their own ideals, their own paths to intellectual as well as emotional self-fulfillment: "People will not, and cannot, think and feel the same at the same moments, throughout any considerable period of life, and therefore . . . moments of union should be . . . of no binding nature." Individual growth, said de Cleyre, was inevitably stifled by marriage, and therefore marriage was wrong.[45]

De Cleyre did not view sexual expressiveness as the only sign of a liberated personality but as part of a larger scheme of social, psychological, and economic liberation. However, Hutchins Hapgood, a journalist who befriended anarchists and other radicals in New York and Chicago during the first two decades of the twentieth century, found American anarchists preoccupied with sex. Hapgood believed that Marie L., the subject of his journalistic examination of the world of anarchism, was typical of anarchist women—wild and sexually promiscuous. Even those whose sexual tastes were less catholic than Marie L.'s, noted Hapgood, were "extreme rebels against sex conventions," and he claimed to have witnessed "many an 'orgie' . . . , sexual and alcoholic," among the Chicago anarchists. He saw this as natural since he was convinced that "the rebellious temperament instinctively takes as its object of attack the strongest convention in society. Anarchism in Europe is mainly political; in America it is mainly sexual, for the reason that there is less freedom of expression about sex in America than in Europe."[46]

Anarchist-feminists openly advocated the use of birth control in the first decade of the twentieth century, adding to the old *Lucifer* argument that frequent childbirth injured the health of the mother and produced sickly children the new one that women had a right to freedom of sexual expression, a right which they could exercise fully only if they possessed the means of preventing pregnancy. Although the dissemination of contraceptive information dated back to the 1830s, the Comstock Law of 1873 and other efforts by the advocates of social purity had succeeded in suppressing much of the literature in the last quarter of the nineteenth century. A handful of radicals, mostly anarchists, had kept the question alive, several earning jail sentences of varying lengths for their publication or distribution of "obscene" material. The anarchists who publicly advocated birth control in the early twentieth century were therefore both continuing and extending the work of Ezra Heywood, Moses Harman, and Lois Waisbrooker. Further, they gained the attention of a general public that had become increasingly aware of sexuality and paved the way for the ultimately more acceptable efforts of Margaret Sanger to promote birth control.[47]

Among the anarchists, Emma Goldman was the most important propagandist for birth control. As early as 1908 she gave lectures and provided technical information. When Margaret Sanger made birth control her crusade with the publication of the *Woman Rebel* in 1914, Goldman supported and encouraged her, selling copies of Sanger's journal on her lecture tours and marshalling the radical community after Sanger fled the country in 1914 following her arrest for violation of the Comstock Law.[48] Sanger eventually muted and then abandoned her radicalism in order to gain acceptance for birth control from the medical community. But in the early years she was in accord with the anarchists of Goldman's circle in their belief that along with political liberation must come psychological and sexual freedom. Goldman, among others, argued that contraceptives were as necessary for single women as for those who were married. She believed that working women in particular, in whose "drab and monotonous existence the only color left is probably a sexual attraction," should not be compelled to stifle their sexuality, nor to face the consequences of abortion or unwed motherhood. Estelle Storey agreed with Goldman, contending that for single as well as married women sexuality without fear of pregnancy promoted mental health.[49]

Such ideas attracted sexually unconventional rebels who might otherwise not have been drawn to anarchism. Convention-breakers like Margaret Anderson and her friends among the literary bohemians in Chicago and New York became Goldman's admirers and brought their own sexual views into the anarchist movement. Margaret Anderson not only openly championed birth control but also suggested that homosexuality might be a more normal form of sexual behavior than heterosexuality. She and her friends represented the link between the anarchist-feminist idea of sexual liberation as one component, albeit an essential one, of a society of freely cooperating individuals, and the bohemian idea of sexual liberation as the sole means to self-realization without a corresponding social vision. For a while Anderson believed that the two were identical, and Goldman's friendship encouraged her in that belief. When she realized her error, Anderson, like other convention-breakers, left the anarchist movement.[50]

It is on this issue—the role of sexuality in the larger society—that the differences between the anarchist-feminists and the other advocates of an enlarged sexuality become clear. For the anarchist-feminists sexual liberation was one element of a total reconstruction of woman's role, a reconstruction which also included the abolition of the nuclear family, economic independence, and psychological self-sufficiency. But they were in the minority. William O'Neill has argued that by the 1920s it had become "possible to take a radical stand on sex and a conservative one on women's social role," because erotic liberation, shorn of its political and economic context, might just as easily strengthen as undercut conventional domesticity. Indeed, sexual fulfillment became in the twenties a substitute for participation in the larger world. The idea of an erotic, pleasure-seeking, economically independent woman was simply too overwhelming for most Americans to accept.[51]

Given the fact that at least one school of thought among the anarchists—that of Moses Harman and his followers—relied heavily on the argument that free love would ultimately result in happier, healthier, more intelligent children, it may seem surprising that on the whole anarchist-feminists devoted far less time to questions about childrearing than they did to the issue of sexuality. Whether because of lack of interest or because they sensed the difficult and perhaps insoluble issues that children posed, many anarchist-feminists ignored the subject. Whenever the question was raised, however, it provoked storms of controversy, suggesting that here was an area in which they could not reach agreement. While the theories and attitudes toward sexuality and marriage followed definable and often sex-differentiated patterns, no such consistency obtained with regard to theories relating to childhood. Only on one issue, that of voluntary motherhood, did anarchists concur: that every woman has the right to choose when, or whether, she should bear a child. As this chapter has made clear, however, such a unified viewpoint did not suggest a widespread belief in artificial contraception, particularly in the nineteenth century. Voluntary motherhood meant one thing to Lois Waisbrooker and quite another to Voltairine de Cleyre or Emma Goldman.

Children presented a profound theoretical problem for many anarchists, particularly among the Individualists. Because their view of the coming anarchist society left little room for those unable to provide for their own welfare, the Individualists were uncertain how to accommodate children and their needs. In a society of sovereign individuals, whose only social responsibility is a negative one—that is, to refrain from invading the rights of others—who bears responsibility for the children? Obviously, since children cannot look after themselves, to consider them as sovereign individuals was impossible. This led many Individualists to conclude that because children were not sovereign individuals, they had no rights under anarchism. For Benjamin Tucker, for Georgia and Henry Replogle, among others, the child was the "labor product" of the mother and hence the property of the parents.

Tucker and Henry Replogle argued that under anarchist theory the parents had the right to treat children in any way they saw fit, short of murder, and that parents bore no responsibility for nurture or support unless they chose to do so. Georgia Replogle even went further, asserting that children, when grown, had contracted a debt to their parents for food, clothing, and any education they received. If they refused to repay, then the society should ostracize them or they should commit suicide. She believed that:

> A child upon whom its parents at great cost to themselves have conferred . . . life, is, on reaching maturity, under an obligation . . . to

either make good to the parents the cost incurred by its production and maintenance, or else show, by committing suicide, that there has been no value received; failing in which obligation, the child should be subjected, by all decent people, to the . . . boycott.[52]

Neither Henry Replogle nor Tucker was willing to go quite that far; nevertheless, both declared that others had no right to interfere with a child's upbringing unless the parent "starves, tortures or mutilates his child"; and in unspecified other cases, Tucker calling them "sufficiently serious," other people may intervene if the parents "neglect to provide food, shelter, and clothing" for the child. They may, but they need not feel obligated to do so. In less severe instances, however, such as when "a parent willfully aims to prevent his child from reaching mental or moral . . . maturity," or when parents refuse to allow their children to be educated in even a rudimentary sense, Tucker contended that others could not interfere under anarchism.[53] Henry Replogle even went so far as to define the limits of acceptable parental abuse as "all but death or permanent disablement." Tucker drew the line at mutilation.[54]

Not all Individualists agreed with Tucker or the Replogles in providing for an almost absolute power of parents over children. Some, mostly men, argued that Tucker's basic premise—that children were property—was wrong. Others, mostly women, took issue not with the notion of children as property but with the problem of whose property they should be. Most women concluded that the child was the mother's property, and nearly all of them skirted the problem of abusive mothers. Only rarely did anyone, man or woman, argue that both parents shared equally in parental responsibility. In most cases, theoretically at least, it appears that children were a nuisance, an unavoidable hitch in the doctrine of complete personal liberty. Indeed, how can one's liberty be complete if he or she has responsibility for another human being? That, indeed, was the heart of the Individualist's dilemma.

Three women, Clara Dixon Davidson, Florence Finch Kelly, and Zelm contributed to the debate on children. Davidson expressed the problem of children under anarchy succinctly. "Children, because of their ignorance, are elements of disharmony." Her solution was "to quicken the processes of their growth as to contribute toward the equilibrization [sic] of social forces. Then, liberty being essential to growth, they must be just as free as is compatible with their own safety and the freedom of others." There, of course, lay the problem. Davidson concurred with Tucker in his belief that parents have no obligation to support their children, but she dismissed the likelihood of child neglect and abuse under anarchy with her belief in "the certainty that increasing intelligence will more and more incline individuals to face the consequences of their own acts (i.e., the bearing of a child); not for duty's sake, but in order to establish and preserve that social harmony which will be necessary to their happiness." She then disposed of the entire discussion of the obligation of parents to care for their children as "purely abstract and rather unprofitable, since no one will refuse to do so." In other words, once freed from the fears of poverty, or from the stigma of unwed parenthood, parents would take pleasure in children, raise them lovingly and in freedom, and restrain their whims and desires as little as possible. Davidson did not wish to consider the potential difficulties in childrearing. She was more interested in adults. As she concluded, "The life of a child is usually incident to the pleasure of its parents." For her, the liberty of the adult was always more important than the needs of the child.[55]

Unlike Davidson, who carefully refers to parents in the plural, Zelm tackled with relish the question of which parent would assume control of the offspring. As one of the staunchest advocates of "individual homes," Zelm argued that children belonged to their mothers. Her dismissal of the possibility that women would abuse their children was, like Davidson's, based on the concept of maternal instinct. "Only a wholly world-corrupted mother, an unnatural mother, even can think of anything but the delight of feeling the clinging of the baby lips and the pressure of the little head against her heart." But the maternal instinct was not the mother's only justification for her right to the child; in fact, "a child is nonetheless a product for which a price has been paid. Suffering endured [in childbirth] is cost. . . . And this forever establishes the claim, this product is not *anyone's* or *everyone's* only the *mother's*." Zelm maintained that the benefits of maternal control over the children included the use of a single standard in upbringing so that the child would have a clear understanding of what was expected and a single authority figure.[56]

Some of *Liberty*'s columnists disagreed with Zelm; J. William Lloyd and A. Warren both complained that children were not slaves and that fathers had some rights.[57] Nevertheless, neither of them challenged the belief in the incorruptibility of a mother's love.

Zelm was unaware of the dangerous edge to her emphasis on maternal rights. As middle-aged cynic Dyer D. Lum pointed out, the only people to benefit from the practice of sole maternal responsibility would be irresponsible fathers. In a letter written to Voltairine de Cleyre shortly after the birth of her son, protesting her contention that women should bear the sole responsibility for childrearing, he argued vehemently that "the father has no right to shirk responsibility. . . . If you mean . . . that woman shall assume the whole burden . . . I disagree. . . . Your logic . . . plays into our hands."[58] De Cleyre apparently was amenable to persuasion against the idea of maternal duty, for her son did not live with her until his adolescence.

The Communist-anarchists as well as some anarchists who refused to accept a label, like de Cleyre in her later career and Lizzie Holmes, were less concerned with defining the child as a non-sovereign individual. Unlike the Individualists, the Communist-anarchists did not accept the idea of private property, so the question of children as property never came up. Because they planned to create cooperative communities, they expected that within those communities would be adults who would freely choose to devote their professional lives to child care. These anarchists proposed communal domestic arrangements as sensible alternatives to the isolated nuclear family in which sole responsibility for child care rested nearly always with the mother. The Communist-anarchists did not consider such questions as the possibility of child abuse; they expected the community as a whole to establish norms and the individuals within the group to acquiesce.[59]

On the whole, both Individualists and Communist-anarchists were more interested in questions of sexuality than in domesticity. For both groups, at least until the Communist-anarchists became involved in the free school movement toward the end of the first decade of the twentieth century, the center of ideological concern was the adult and children were at best of subsidiary interest. Despite the fact that as radicals the anarchists realized that their hopes for the development of an ongoing society based on their principles rested with the indoctrination of the young, they did not make a sustained attempt until the twentieth century to find a place for children within anarchist philosophy. Their failure in this crucial respect was indicative of an inability to translate radical commitment into practical action. It also suggests that the anarchists were primarily concerned, in the realms of sexuality and domesticity, with attacking the norms of contemporary society with regard to the behavior of men and women, rather than with creating a framework within which future generations could build a new society.

5
Successful Propagandists: Anarchist Activism

> Successful propagandists have succeeded because the doctrine they bring into form is that which their listeners have for some time felt without being able to shape.
>
> *Thomas Hardy*

Women anarchists were not successful propagandists, as success is commonly measured. Their creation and elaboration of an ideology that placed marriage and the nuclear family at the center of their analysis of feminine subordination received little favorable attention outside the anarchist movement and often generated hostility within it. Whether they were too far in advance of their time, too far behind it, or, as Juliet Mitchell has suggested about the anarchists in general, simply outside time, the fact remains that American society did not address seriously the concerns of the anarchist-feminists.[1] Reasons for this lack of attention on the part of non-anarchist-feminists included: the hostility of Americans in general toward anarchists; the tendency to idealize the family at a period when divorces were rising and many people believed the family was seriously threatened; and the increasing importance within the organized women's rights movement of social purity advocates who fought bitterly any attempts to challenge the sanctity of home and family.

The anarchist-feminists thus found it difficult to gain a serious hearing. But their difficulties extended beyond the question of the degree to which they were out of step with their contemporaries. A further problem arose from anarchist philosophy itself. Despite their provocative and original answers to the Woman Question, anarchist-feminists were unable to integrate their insights about the relationship between female powerlessness and sexual and economic repression into an overall framework for social change. In fact, they became trapped by their anarchism, and it is difficult to know how they could have avoided that trap. Anarchist-feminism required the anarchist belief in complete individual liberty; no other philosophy provided a theoretical rationale that allowed for unconditional self-expression. The right of unconditional freedom was the basis of the anarchist-feminist challenge to feminine dependence. Nevertheless, as anarchist women elaborated their feminist ideology, they found it exceedingly difficult to connect the problem of sex-based inequality with the standard anarchist solutions to social ills. While the anarchist ideal of personal liberty provided a foundation for the formation of a feminist theory, at the same time anarchism prevented anarchist-feminists from using that theory as a basis for the creation of an egalitarian society. In short, the anarchist-feminists were incapable of unifying their anarchist principles with their feminist views.[2]

Notwithstanding the claims of both the Individualists and the Communist-anarchists that they were engaged in the development of a scientific revolutionary theory based on the laws of evolution, anarchism was in reality more of an emotional response to oppressive social conditions than a philosophical system, scientific or otherwise. American anarchists, perhaps more than others, rejected the idea of systems-building; their primary task was the destruction of the existing order. The contrived, artificial, and confining society of the present would give way to a natural, spontaneous, and free community. "Discipline and restraint—are they not back of all the evils in the world?" Emma Goldman declared. "Slavery, submission, poverty, all misery, all social iniquities result from discipline and restraint." Such feelings do not easily lend themselves to the discipline of a program of revolution.[3]

Goldman, as activist agitator and articulate propagandist, brought anarchism—and a feminist viewpoint—to the attention of young urban intellectuals in the early twentieth century. Partly because of her own celebration of spontaneity and her refusal to advocate specific goals for anarchism, the young bohemians to whom she appealed tended to espouse her views on sexual liberation and to disregard their political context. That Voltairine de Cleyre, who was a better theorist and a more methodical thinker than Goldman, faced similar difficulties in attempting to unify her anarchism and her feminism, suggested that for the anarchist women of her time the dilemma was profound.

De Cleyre exemplified the anarchist fascination with spontaneous emotion, with feeling, with intuitive insight. She urged her hearers to eschew a purely intellectual commitment to the cause, to feel rather than think their way into anarchism:

> Turn cloudward, . . . let the dreams rush over one—no longer awed by outside powers . . . —recognizing nothing superior to oneself, . . . letting oneself go free, go free beyond the bounds of what *fear* and *custom* call the "possible"—This, . . . Anarchism may mean to you, if you dare apply it so.[4]

The reward for this emotional conversion was immediate psychological liberation from conventional society; the individual became free, even if political, economic, and social systems remained unchanged. Although de Cleyre suggested that the restructuring of institutions ultimately would develop from this initial emotional rebirth, it was never clear how such changes would come about.

While psychological liberation has its merits, it does not necessarily promote social change; and anarchists, after all, portrayed themselves as revolutionaries, not mystics. In late-nineteenth- and early-twentieth-century America this meant coping in some way with an urbanized, industrialized, and increasingly centralized state. After the turn of the century anarchists began to admit that they were ill-equipped to offer a program of change. De Cleyre bemoaned the "hopelessly and helplessly interdependent" nature of modern society, with its "correlative political tyranny," but she also realized that the anarchists could at best continue to "affirm the economy of self-sustenance, the disintegration of great communities, the use of the earth." She was not optimistic that affirming the value of such a future would bring it any closer: "I am not ready to say that I see clearly that this *will* take place; but I see clearly that this *must* take place if ever again men are to be free." Discouraged by the apathy of her fellow human beings, disgusted by their failure to see the necessity for radical social change, de Cleyre concluded that her only hope for revolution lay "in the blind development of the economic system and political oppression itself."[5]

The above quotes come from an essay widely regarded as the best American treatment of anarchist ideas, and they illustrate that anarchists themselves recognized by the turn of the century that their dreams of a stateless future had become not a certainty but an increasingly remote possibility. The Mexican Revolution briefly rekindled their flagging hopes, but there too they were disappointed. As social, economic, and political liberation loomed ever farther in the distance, de Cleyre in the early twentieth century concentrated on more immediate gains. She pledged to her readers psychological release—from political hypocrisy and from conventional standards of behavior.

In neither of her two most important theoretical essays, "Anarchism" and "Anarchism and American Traditions," did de Cleyre try to bring her anarchist and feminist concerns together. This is very significant because she suggested in both that the particular strength of anarchism was its ability to provide individuals with the psychological courage needed to wage their personal, isolated battles against society. In her essays on the Woman Question de Cleyre also stressed the importance of the solitary female warrior against convention, but nowhere did she directly link her theoretical treatment of psychic liberation with her analysis of feminism, although a careful reading of her work as a whole shows a connection between the two. Juliet Mitchell has expressed succinctly what de Cleyre perceived dimly: anarchism with its emphasis "on private liberation and individual freedom" possesses "a necessary randomness which aims a blow at anything in its way." Therein, argues Mitchell, lies the appeal of anarchism for women: "Privatized in their isolated family lives, individual freedom seems the natural horizon for which to strive. Liberation, in anarchist terms, expresses itself as a release of all one's damned-up psychic energies: probably no-one feels the need of this more than a woman." Although Mitchell disapproves of anarchism because she believes that it frees women from the "need to work out the whole oppression of women" and the "need to organize," nevertheless she defines, in a way that de Cleyre never did explicitly, the potential for a theoretical integration of anarchism and feminism.[6]

De Cleyre possessed one of the best minds among the American anarchists, and her essays, particularly in the early twentieth century, were sophisticated and subtle. On the other hand, the other anarchist-feminists who attempted to explain anarchist ideas tended to approach every problem as a separate issue without reconciling, or in some cases even noticing, disharmonies and contradictions. They espoused feminism and the standard anarchist remedies for social ills without troubling to look for connections. It almost seems as if they deliberately avoided those questions that would force them to confront anarchist ideology as a whole. Gertrude B. Kelly, for example, concentrated on questions of finance when she was not writing about women. She was enthusiastic about the innovation of checking accounts, which she viewed as the harbinger of the Mutual Bank, an institution that, for Individualists, was at the heart of anarchist economics. Yet she not only found it unnecessary to explain the effect of new bank practices on the overall power structure, but she also failed to connect monetary issues with questions about the redistribution of wealth or the economic role of women.[7]

Florence Finch Kelly, who in the 1880s contributed significantly to the anarchist-feminist response to the Woman Question, and whose later career outside anarchism revealed her to be an intelligent, shrewd, and practical observer of the American scene, did not connect the several aspects of her anarchist philosophy. Although her articles in *Liberty* dealing with feminist issues demonstrated a thoughtful grasp of the problem, once outside the Woman Question she faced serious difficulties. Where Gertrude B. Kelly had confined herself to specific details of anarchist thought without attempting an inclusive analysis, Florence Finch Kelly offered sweeping generalities without touching on their application. In her attempt at a definition of anarchist philosophy, she argued that "Anarchy means a slow growth of the principles of liberty and justice; the gradual dropping off of the thou-shalts and thou shalt-nots of laws and constitutions as men slowly learn that it is better to be governed by reasonable and intelligent conviction from within than by compulsion from without." Kelly never defined either the steps that had to be taken in order to create an anarchist society or the roles that men and women would enact once it had become a reality.[8]

The limited theoretical perceptions of most women anarchists not only hindered their attempts at the development of a comprehensive anarchist analysis but also contributed to the breakdown of anarchist-feminism itself. By the first decade of the twentieth century many of those women who called themselves anarchists had been drawn by its reputation for personal nonconformity. Anarchists—not entirely unwittingly—had made their movement a temporary haven for alienated youth. Emma Goldman, who misunderstood the nature of her appeal to young middle-class rebels, believed she had at last begun to convert the American intelligentsia to anarchism when what she had succeeded in doing was exciting their admiration for her courageous anticonventionality. Those whom she brought into the movement tended to be interested largely in anarchy as self-expression to the exclusion of its larger economic and social aims. Margaret Anderson, when she explained the raison d'être for her new magazine, expressed a typical viewpoint:

> *The Little Review* is a magazine that believes in life for Art's sake, in the Individual rather than incomplete people, . . . a magazine written for Intelligent people who can feel; whose philosophy is Applied Anarchism, whose policy is a Will to Splendor . . . , and whose function is—to express itself.[9]

Anderson and others like her did not completely misinterpret anarchist philosophy—Had not de Cleyre urged her listeners to discover their inner spirits through anarchism? Yet they attempted to make this single facet of anarchism its totality. This is what appealed to the literary bohemians who subscribed to and wrote for the *Little Review*; seeking a philosophy that would be radical yet not oblige them to make difficult sacrifices for the masses, they appropriated Emma Goldman—to the extent that anyone could appropriate her—as the mascot of rebellious intellectuals. Goldman, who genuinely believed she had finally gained for anarchism a following among the intellectual vanguard in the United States, encouraged their participation. Although she did not compromise her own political views and still preached to her admirers a philosophy of revolution against capitalism by and on behalf of the working class, she nevertheless seemed too fond of her new position as darling of the intellectuals to alienate them. They in turn, engaging in what a later generation would call "radical chic," enjoyed being harangued and insulted by a genuine revolutionary. Anderson trivialized Emma Goldman and displayed the limits of her own view of the latter's criticism of capitalist society when she said of Goldman, "She spoke only in platitudes, which I found fascinating."[10]

For many young women Goldman came to be viewed as the symbol of liberation. That Goldman herself was not insulted by some of the views of her admirers demonstrated the extent of her misunderstanding of her own appeal. One woman compared a Goldman speech to "a glass of fine, old wine," under the influence of which the listener grew "more and more excited and stimulated . . . until finally I feel I can sit quietly no longer, but just must give expression somehow to the surge of thought and feeling she awakens." Louise Bryant likened Goldman to "the other good things that come to us, like the spring and the rain and the sunshine," and referred to her lectures as "inspirational messages" of "healing and life-giving qualities."[11]

These women might have substituted with equal results a sermon of Billy Sunday, or a concert or play, for all the difference it made to the creation of a revolutionary movement. Goldman provided entertainment; perhaps her young admirers expected little more. Nevertheless, the relationship between Goldman and these young women had a more serious and more disturbing aspect. Goldman was a remarkable figure who may have given these women a sense of being included in "the Cosmic secrets of nature,"[12] but they misinterpreted emotional experience as revolutionary commitment. In return for their admiration, the young bohemians expected Goldman to shoulder for them the burden of the consequences of political activism. Nearly the whole of anarchist philosophy was reduced to hero-worship of those few individuals who were willing to do the things that others were prepared only to imagine—to endure the unwelcome attention of the authorities, to accept prison, to act as surrogates for those who wished to have something in which to believe but not necessarily to emulate.

Anarchism had lost some of its ideological force. While the anarchist-feminist inability to articulate a consistent theoretical congruence between anarchism and feminism was not the sole cause of its lessened impact, it does seem clear that the lack of a soundly interconnected ideological position left anarchist women with few choices. They could retreat into the narcissism of the worship of self-expression, or they could abandon anarchism altogether in favor of a feminism that offered less in terms of personal liberation, or they could (increasingly unsuccessfully) try to preserve both by ignoring intellectual consistency. None of these alternatives was altogether satisfactory.

Anarchist women, like anarchist men, shunned the traditional political process. They refused to vote or run for office because they believed that "the basis of all political action is coercion; even when the state does good things, it finally rests on a club, a gun, or a prison for its power to carry them through."[13] By its very nature, therefore, political action destroyed freedom. Anarchists substituted "direct action" for politics, claiming that they followed a practice initiated by the antebellum nonresistants, particularly William Lloyd Garrison and Henry David Thoreau. Emma Goldman referred to Thoreau as "the greatest American Anarchist" and quoted approvingly his antigovernment statements.[14] But anarchists—excepting some Individualists—carefully refused to limit themselves to the methods of the pacifist nonresistants. Although direct action might be peaceful, Voltairine de Cleyre warned her readers that it might just as easily be "the extreme of violence."[15] Not only civil disobedience, mass demonstrations, and strikes, but also terrorism and sabotage, were included under the rubric of direct action.

Because the anarchists laid the blame for violence on the state, because some of them—particularly among the Communist-anarchists—publicly encouraged terroristic retaliation against the state, and because nearly all refrained from condemning their comrades who engaged in violent action, Americans from the time of the Haymarket bombing in 1886 through World War I generally viewed the anarchists as fanatics and assassins.[16] Although the cartoon stereotypes typically presented a maniacal-looking male with dagger or bomb in hand, women anarchists were not exempt from that characterization. In fact, the idea of women revolutionaries could evoke responses that bordered on frenzy. Haymarket provides a case in point. *Red Ruin,* a sensationalist fictionalized account of the Haymarket incident, consolidated all of the fears that anarchists inspired into detailed descriptions of violence, greed, and hatred. Analogous to pulp adventure novels written today, *Red Ruin* was obviously intended for a predominantly male, poorly educated audience. Given those assumptions, it is significant that the anonymous author interrupted his narrative of the events leading to the bomb-throwing in order to deliver an extended diatribe against women as radicals, with particular emphasis on Lucy Parsons, the wife of one of the men convicted in the case. This attack on women was unconnected to the events in the story that preceded or followed it, but the author wanted specifically to warn his readers of the dangers that lurked when women stepped outside their assigned roles. Women radicals, he argued, were a threat to society in two ways. First, they supported male revolutionaries with their earnings, so that the men had more leisure to engage in violence. The second and more insidious danger was that women would tire of their roles behind the scenes and would not only incite men to greater violence but desire to engage in it themselves; once aroused, women revolutionaries would be far more dangerous than men. *Red Ruin*'s author ominously intoned, "Charlotte killed her Marat. Lucy Parsons married hers. And now that justice has wiped him out, she wants to get a whack at justice with a can of nitroglycerine and a detonating fuse."[17]

Red Ruin's hysterical response to women radicals seems extreme, but it did not present an aberrant view. The press reaction to the speeches of Emma Goldman in the 1890s and in the early twentieth century was equally irrational. And the *Brooklyn Eagle*, hardly a scandal sheet, said twenty years after the appearance of *Red Ruin* that the typical anarchist woman "seems redder than her destructive brother. . . . [N]othing limits the daring of the woman whose mind had yielded to the influence of the doctrine of violence."[18]

That the press and public responded to women anarchists with such vehemence immediately raises the question of whether anarchist women did in fact engage in acts of terrorism and violence. If Haymarket is included, anarchists were responsible for four violent incidents from 1886 through World War I. Even though no one ever proved that the Haymarket bombing was the work of anarchists, the evidence indicates that an anarchist (not one of those tried and convicted) did throw the bomb; it is clear, moreover, that at least one of the Haymarket "martyrs," Louis Lingg, made bombs, although he did not make the one that killed the Chicago policemen on May 4, 1886. And some of the others arrested apparently had participated in the "armed section" of Chicago's anarchist movement. For these reasons Haymarket is included in this tally of anarchist violence.[19]

After Haymarket, anarchists were responsible for the attempted assassination of steel magnate Henry Clay Frick in 1892, the successful assassination of William McKinley in 1901, and the bomb explosion in a New York City tenement on Lexington Avenue in 1914. In each case the violence was not the work of the movement as a whole but an act of spontaneous rebellion on the part of a single individual or a small group. Women played some part in two of the three. Emma Goldman had shared in Alexander Berkman's decision to assassinate Frick and had purchased his revolver. Her participation in the deed was not discovered until she herself admitted it in her autobiography nearly forty years later. In the Lexington Avenue bombing case, two women were suspected of involvement. In that incident three young men—Arthur Caron, Charles Berg, and Carl Hanson—died when they prematurely exploded a bomb that they were assembling in order to assassinate John D. Rockefeller. Louise Berger and Marie Chavez shared the tenement apartment with the three men. Chavez, who was apparently unaware of the conspiracy, also died in the explosion. Berger, a close associate of Goldman and Berkman, was at the office of *Mother Earth* when the bomb went off. Despite her steadfast denial to the police, who could never prove her complicity, Berger was involved in the plot. No women were connected with the McKinley assassination, although the police (falsely in this case) tried to implicate Goldman.[20]

In the case of Haymarket, two women were arrested in the aftermath of the bomb-throwing—Lizzie May Holmes, the assistant editor of the *Alarm*, and Lucy Parsons—but both were released without charge. It seems unlikely that either woman was active in the armed section of the movement; rather, they confined themselves to labor questions and for a time worked to organize Chicago's seamstresses. If Frank Harris, Emma Goldman's friend who wrote a fictionalized account of Haymarket, accurately portrayed the anarchist milieu in Chicago in the 1880s, there was little room for women except as helpmeets. Harris described an aggressively masculine world in which women subordinated themselves to men. Louis Lingg, who in later years was the most revered among the Haymarket martyrs, seemed almost a caricature of stereotyped masculinity. Although Harris's anarchist friends did not universally acclaim *The Bomb*, their complaints centered on his interpretation of specific incidents and not on his portrayal of the personalities involved. In that respect, Harris seemed to have characterized the movement accurately. Lizzie May Holmes and Lucy Parsons tended to take secondary roles, the former as assistant, the latter as wife. Perhaps because they were trying to attract working-class men, they preferred not to draw attention to themselves as women lest they court ridicule instead of respect. In any case, the anarchist men in Chicago during the 1880s possessed a revolutionary dream in which they were the heroes and women were devoted followers.[21]

Anarchist terror existed mostly in the realm of fantasy, and that realm was largely a male one. Women anarchists played a decidedly secondary role. This is not to say that women did not have to face the issue of violence. Emma Goldman, Voltairine de Cleyre, Mollie Steimer, and Marie Ganz were all accused of supporting revolution or fomenting violence. Goldman, although unsuspected of the Frick plot, nevertheless was the first to face arrest; in August 1893, during the first year of a four-year depression, she spoke to a mass meeting of the unemployed. Accounts of her speech varied; Richard Drinnon stated that "the gist of what she said was that the unemployed should distrust the state and labor politicians; she adjured them to stand up and demand what was rightfully theirs—and they could commence by demanding bread, an obvious first step for the starving." Voltairine de Cleyre rendered Goldman's words as follows: "Ask for work; if they do not give you work ask for bread; if they do not give you work or bread, take bread." Goldman insisted that she simply told the audience to "protect what belongs to you—what you yourselves have produced, and in the first place you ought to take bread." But the police officer who caused Goldman's arrest testified that she had told her audience to "take it by force," which convinced a jury to send her to Blackwell's Island prison for a year.[22]

Not all her comrades approved of Goldman's confrontational style—Voltairine de Cleyre once said privately, "I have never liked Emma Goldman or her speeches; I don't like fishwifery or billingsgate"—but after her incarceration on Blackwell's Island, Goldman continued to fight tenaciously for the right of all ideas to have a hearing. Despite numerous arrests and other forms of police harassment, she escaped conviction for more than twenty years. Her free speech fights inspired the creation of the National Civil Liberties Bureau, which eventually became the American Civil Liberties Union. And de Cleyre, despite her disapproval of Goldman, admitted that her more flamboyant comrade was unjustly accused of advocating terrorism: "I never heard her say, nor anyone of all I ever knew that heard her, that anyone could do any good by killing. All she has ever said is 'If your rights are attacked by force you should resist, by force if necessary.'"[23]

Goldman deliberately antagonized the authorities by calling "policemen names which they deserve but which it is neither dignified nor sensible to use," but she did not incite her hearers to riot. She used instead the tactics of nonviolent confrontation to assert her right to speak. After twenty-two years of using those tactics to discuss issues ranging from poverty and the violence of capitalism to the modern drama, in 1915 she began to use them to confront the question of birth control. Although she had lectured on the subject since 1908, she had never before deliberately set out to be arrested for it. In part she wanted to come to the assistance of Margaret Sanger, who had tried to challenge specifically the laws that prohibited the dissemination of information on contraceptive methods but was instead indicted on another charge. When Sanger fled the country, Goldman took up the issue and tried to provoke a confrontation in 1915. Drinnon noted that "arrest seemed so certain for this first public discussion of contraceptive methods that [Goldman] took a book with her to read in jail." But she was not convicted for her birth-control activity until over a year later, when she spent fifteen days in the Queens County Jail.[24]

Goldman's crusade for birth control suggests that the techniques of direct action—especially those of civil disobedience and nonviolent confrontation—could be used successfully in expressly feminist issues. But with this exception anarchist-feminists did not pursue such a course. Goldman believed that she was criticized because many radicals "look upon Birth Control only as a very small phase in a much larger social setting; namely the freedom of expression in life, labor, and art which is constantly being interfered with and curtailed by the reactionary forces." Rebekah Raney had a different objection; she believed that the most efficacious way to fight for contraception was through individual acts of "courageous defiance" of the prohibitions against birth control, rather than through confrontation with the legal system. Goldman disagreed with Raney. She felt that birth control was "a tremendously important phase, first because it is tabooed and the people who advocate it are persecuted. Secondly it represents the immediate question of life and death to masses of people."[25]

In short, Goldman argued for the importance of contraception, but she did so, at least in *Mother Earth*, from a viewpoint that emphasized its importance as a free speech question and its relationship to the despair of working-class mothers over frequent pregnancies. She was concerned only secondarily with contraception as a method of women's emancipation. Birth control was only one of Goldman's many interests, and on occasion she seemed to view it as simply a single aspect of the free speech issue, instead of an aspect of the Woman Question. She therefore failed to explore fully the potential uses of direct action in a feminist context. Nevertheless, her crusade on behalf of contraception was the closest that anarchist-feminists came to utilizing direct action as a means in their struggle for sexual equality.[26]

The career of Voltairine de Cleyre was less flamboyant than that of Goldman. For the most part de Cleyre avoided confrontational tactics, except as an individual engaging in a personal refusal to obey the dictates of society. Although in 1894 she defended Emma Goldman's action in urging the unemployed to demand relief, she refused to give such advice herself. She insisted that:

> I, as an anarchist, have no right to advise another to do anything involving a risk to himself; nor would I give a filip for an action done by the advice of someone else, unless it is accompanied by a well-argued, well-settled conviction on the part of the person acting, that it really is the best thing to do.[27]

When she made this speech she no doubt was anxious not to face arrest herself; throughout her life she remained more circumspect than Goldman. Despite her tempered rhetoric, however, de Cleyre overcame her unwillingness to advise on method. In 1908, at a demonstration of unemployed Italians and Jews in South Philadelphia, de Cleyre urged her listeners to unite with "all the workers" and by "straightforward, direct action . . . take the land, the mines, the factories as your own." Although she did not counsel violence, and probably had in mind the encouragement of general strikes, this speech led to her arrest on charges of conspiracy and inciting to riot. Unlike Goldman's meeting in 1893, this demonstration ended in a spontaneous march of about a thousand men on City Hall. A confrontation with the police ensued, four men were seriously injured, and de Cleyre was taken into custody.[28]

Arrested with de Cleyre on the same charges was Chaim Weinberg. Four Italian workers, who clashed directly with the police, were indicted and convicted on riot and assault charges, their sentences ranging from one to five years. De Cleyre insisted that she neither counseled the march on City Hall nor approved of it. When their case came to trial in March, both de Cleyre and Weinberg were acquitted, the prosecution's only witness having failed to appear. De Cleyre's son claimed in 1948 that Weinberg was so frightened of conviction that he bribed the state's witness to stay away, an action which infuriated de Cleyre because she believed that the evidence against them was totally insubstantial anyway.[29] This was de Cleyre's only arrest, and she had not urged her listeners to immediate violent retaliation against the state, however much she accepted some violence as an inevitable accompaniment to the revolutionary struggle.

Neither de Cleyre nor Goldman was cavalier about violence. Goldman became far less convinced of its efficacy while witnessing the ordeal of Alexander Berkman; his action not only did not advance the revolutionary cause, but it robbed Berkman of his youth and early manhood. De Cleyre accepted the necessity of judicious revolutionary violence, but she deplored its indiscriminate use. Mollie Steimer, who was harassed, imprisoned, and finally deported for her support of the Bolshevik Revolution, believed at the time that only through revolution could capitalism be overthrown. She later supported the equally direct, but less overtly violent, concept of the general strike as the most effective revolutionary tool.

It was the temporary radicals, not the lifetime anarchists, who took the most casual positions on violence. Marie Ganz threatened publicly to shoot John D. Rockefeller "down like a dog," and Margaret Anderson wondered in the *Little Review* "why didn't someone shoot the governor of Utah before he could shoot Joe Hill? . . . Or why didn't five hundred . . . get Joe Hill out of Jail? . . . For God's sake, why doesn't someone start the revolution?"[30] But whether anarchist women were nonchalant or prudent in their advocacy of violence, they were agreed on the primacy of direct action. They participated in strikes, they led demonstrations, and they urged individuals to engage in personal acts of rebellion against the state by refusing to participate in an unjust government. All of these activities except the last are organized responses. Yet, with the exception of Goldman's birth-control crusade, the anarchist-feminists for the most part did not consider adapting these techniques for feminist purposes.

Although direct action was the preferred means of bringing about social change among the anarchists, they also used techniques of propaganda and education, and the creation of alternative institutions that would promote anarchist goals on an experimental scale. Some anarchist-feminists took a considerable interest in the creation of anarchist communities and in the development of alternative educational structures. Obvious opportunities to provide a framework for a sexually egalitarian future existed in each case—to construct miniature societies in which the rules of the larger society would not fetter individual growth, or to fabricate a system of education in which children would be freed from traditional customs. Yet an analysis of anarchist involvement in community-building—both theoretical and actual—as well as in educational reform, further illustrates the difficulties that the anarchist-feminists faced in integrating their demand for sexual equality into their anarchist activism.

Anarchism had been connected to communitarianism in the United States since the days of Josiah Warren. After two years, from 1824 through 1826, at Robert Owen's utopian community of New Harmony, Indiana, Warren spent the next thirty-odd years in an effort to unite the ideas of individualism and co-operation. He planned to achieve the goal of a stateless society by creating communities that would test on a small scale his economic and social principles. Once his theories had proved workable, he hoped that the larger society would also put them into practice. Just as numerous other antebellum visionaries founded intentional communities as laboratories for social change, Warren began four communal experiments from the late 1820s through the 1850s. Three of them were in Ohio: Equity, which lasted for one year, Tuscarawas, which lasted for two, and Utopia, which struggled on for six. In 1850 Warren founded Modern Times on Long Island. Modern Times maintained its status as a communitarian experiment for over a decade before its residents began to be absorbed by the surrounding suburban environment.[31]

Warren's failures were the failures of a generation. Communitarianism as a movement was moribund by the 1860s. An urbanizing, industrializing society that was coming to depend on large-scale organization had little space left, physically or psychologically, within which men and women could secede from the larger community and at the same time believe that they were creating a new social order that would eventually dominate the entire society. Nevertheless, despite the disintegration of communitarianism in practice, the idea of communalism retained a powerful hold on the minds of many Americans. This was particularly true in the last decade and a half of the nineteenth century. Labor violence, including the great railway strike of 1877, Haymarket, and the Homestead strike; urban poverty, as exhibited in the immigrant ghettoes of all the major cities; and rural unrest, as manifested by the growing militancy of the Populists—these convulsions and upheavals provoked fears of impending crisis within the industrial order. Feeling unable to do anything concrete, many reformers and radicals took up their pens. Visions of ideal societies that had solved the problems of alienation, class conflict, and economic uncertainty were the result.

The last twelve years of the nineteenth century witnessed an unprecedented outpouring of utopian literature, spurred in part by the incredible success of Edward Bellamy's *Looking Backward*. Bellamy's novel described an America that had abolished poverty, labor unrest, and sexual inequality by means of socialized and centralized economic production. Although not all the utopian writers agreed with Bellamy's visions—indeed there existed considerable diversity among the proposed social and economic solutions—there was a definite trend in most toward the creation of a society that possessed a centralized economy, was directed by experts, and yet was in some (often very vague) manner subject to the wishes of the citizenry.[32]

Dreams of consolidation and centralization pervaded most of the utopias; to the anarchists they were nightmares. Nevertheless, anarchists were not immune to utopian reveries. And William Morris, who once referred to *Looking Backward* as "a horrible cockney dream," gave them *News from Nowhere*. Although Morris was nominally a socialist, his ideal society had no laws and consisted of small, nonurban, cooperative communities. To the extent that anarchists could conceive of a perfect society, William Morris's England of the future—curiously premodern despite its dependence on an unseen industrial base—most closely resembled their conception. Because his *News from Nowhere* received such high acclaim from both men and women anarchists (it was one of Voltairine de Cleyre's favorite books), Morris's views on the function of women in the society have particular significance. In tomorrow's England, as he saw it, women would discharge the traditional feminine duties, including waiting on men and performing household chores. Yet Morris insisted that sexual equality would prevail because women would choose freely to engage in such occupations. As one woman explained, "It is a great pleasure for a clever woman to manage a house skillfully."[33] Morris dealt with the searing question of defining new roles for women by re-creating the old ones and arguing that women, once freed from the artificial constraints of capitalist society, would return joyfully to their positions as nurturers and homemakers.

Morris, along with a host of other nineteenth-century men, obviously believed that to engage in the role of helpmeet, to cook, to clean, and to run a house were natural female functions. Therefore, women of his utopia did not consider such duties evidence of inequality. One wonders how the anarchist-feminists who admired Morris's book could find comfort in such a future. Perhaps they sometimes were nagged by a fear that a secondary role was indeed the natural position for women, and that without the economic pressures that compelled women to seek a husband or to face the uncertainty of self-support, women might still "freely" choose home and hearth. Given the articulate arguments of the anarchist-feminists against those ideas, it is hard to imagine that they consciously accepted such a view. Yet the fact that they not only failed to protest Morris's vision but, on the contrary, praised the book extravagantly suggests that at some level they might have been vulnerable still to masculine assertions about purportedly natural feminine qualities.

News from Nowhere was the only anarchist literary utopia. In addition to the realm of fantasy, however, anarchists also had access to two actual communitarian experiments during the late nineteenth and early twentieth centuries: Home, Washington, and Stelton, New Jersey.[34] Disillusioned veterans of an unsuccessful socialist colony founded Home in 1896. The *Independent* published a favorable article about it in 1903, and Home retained its character as a radical community until the late teens, subsequently becoming a typical rural community.[35] The *Independent* assessed Home's residents as temperate, kind, and nonviolent, deliberately contrasting them to the conventional anarchist image. The author, E. A. Slosson, was relieved to discover that they did not proselytize, "frankly acknowledg[ing] that their theory of individual liberty . . . is not suited for general adoption until a higher development of personal morality and self-control is attained." Their principal mission was rather "to furnish a living example of perfect liberty of thought and action and the coincident existence of happiness and prosperity."

Having emphasized the respectability of Home, the *Independent* was understandably loath to dwell on imputations of immorality deriving from the community's attitude toward sexual emancipation or women's roles in general. Slosson admitted that "as they are opposed to law and force of all kinds, they are, of course, believers in the theory of free love." Nevertheless, he further argued, "Yet this is said not to have resulted so far in any lewdness or laxity of morals."[36]

Had Slosson taken heed of the works of Lois Waisbrooker, who served as president of the colony for several years, he would have felt less assured of Home's adherence to conventional patterns of behavior. Waisbrooker, in her seventies, retained her militant feminism and her mystical eroticism. She continued to publish *Clothed with the Sun*, her small anarchist-feminist journal, at Home. In 1902 she was convicted in federal court on obscenity charges for an article in her journal advocating a liberated sexuality. Yet perhaps the *Independent* did not err in its refusal to take cognizance of Waisbrooker. Although Home's residents acknowledged Waisbrooker's views, her feminist philosophy did not pervade the colony. Feminism elicited tolerance rather than emulation. Home's residents accepted it as they accepted vegetarianism or transvestism. Women who refused to behave according to accepted feminine norms found a welcome at Home, but they did not necessarily find a community that fostered sexual equality.[37]

Stelton, near New Brunswick, New Jersey, was founded two decades later and differed from Home in several ways. Its residents were far more urban oriented, often commuted to jobs in New York, showed less interest in escaping from the larger society, and possessed the urbanite's lack of aesthetic understanding of the natural environment. But probably the most important difference was that Stelton had a mission: to provide a supportive social atmosphere within which to create an educational structure that would liberate children from the shackles of traditional society.[38]

Anarchists, especially but not exclusively women, had begun to advocate educational reform as early as the 1890s. In part, the interest stemmed naturally from occupational concerns; Lois Waisbrooker, Voltairine de Cleyre, Lillie White, and Lizzie May Holmes had all worked as teachers, and Holmes had articulated an anarchist critique of education in 1892. In *Twentieth Century* she condemned American schools because they fostered "blind obedience." Arguing that the proper goals of education were "the development of the human faculties, the rounding out of individual character, [and] the opening of the way to the freest and fullest activities," she offered specific suggestions for the implementation of these rather vague objectives. Her program included elimination of rote memorization and "set tasks," abolition of all threats of physical force, increased use of field trips, and reduction of class size to twelve students per teacher.[39] In the twentieth century de Cleyre and Goldman elaborated Holmes's ideas. Their views provided the theoretical foundation for the Modern School, the first full-scale anarchist educational experiment in the United States.

The anarchist educational philosophy is not without its ironies. In light of the indifference with which many of them approached the responsibilities of parenthood, their intense concern with education seems curious. But it might be argued that because they realized their shortcomings as parents, they considered their children's educational experience all the more significant. Although de Cleyre's years as a teacher helped to form her educational ideas, both she and Goldman became associated with the Modern School movement as a result of their involvement in the cause of Francisco Ferrer, a Spanish educator executed by his government for allegedly inciting the Barcelona uprising in 1909. Ferrer served as a symbol of educational radicalism for the American anarchists; they did not attempt to transplant his educational theories. Rather, they responded to a widespread interest in educational reform. Laurence Veysey has suggested that in progressive education some anarchists found "a cause deeply congenial to their own faith in human liberation."[40]

Goldman was the moving force behind the founding of New York's Modern School in 1911. Having contended as early as 1906 that American education destroyed the minds and spirits of children, she believed that "if education should mean anything at all, it must insist on the free growth and development of the innate forces and tendencies of the child. In this way alone can we hope for the free individual and eventually also for a free community, which shall make interference and coercion of human growth impossible."

Goldman wanted the Modern School to encourage the spontaneous development of the child; the teacher should not direct, but "should be a sensitive instrument responding to the needs of the child as they are at anytime manifested." Teachers should not discipline their pupils because "to discipline a child is to set up a false moral standard," which would inhibit the child from developing his or her own moral nature.[41]

The Modern School stayed in New York for four years. De Cleyre seriously considered Alexander Berkman's offer of a position in the venture but finally declined. Nonanarchist radicals and rebellious Greenwich Villagers became involved. Margaret Sanger sent her children to the school. Will Durant served as its principal and chief teacher for more than a year, while Robert Henri, among other artists and writers, offered classes for adults. The school derived its vitality from the city. Nevertheless, because its backers believed that the students' education had been interrupted by their extensive participation in the political activities of their elders, the school was removed to Stelton in 1915. Anarchist educational ideals reinforced this decision. Goldman had been impressed very favorably with Sebastian Faures's boarding school in France, La Ruche, and seemed to think that children could develop more freely if not constrained by the presence of parents. De Cleyre had argued in 1910 that:

> The really ideal school, which would not be a compromise, would be a boarding school built in the country, having a farm attached, and workshops where useful crafts might be learned, in daily connection with intellectual training. . . . In free contact with nature, the children would learn to use their limbs as nature meant, feel their intimate relationship with the growing life of other sorts, form a profound respect for work and an estimate of the value of it; wish to become real doers in the world, and not mere gatherers of other men's products.[42]

The founders wanted the colony to form the backdrop for such an education, designed not to fit children for industrial society but to teach them values that would at the least transcend that society, at the most encourage rebellion against it.

Judged by their professed goals, the anarchists at Stelton were not a success. Disagreement over political and educational questions brought about an estrangement between the colonists and the school, and after the first few years the community could no longer provide the supportive environment intended by the founders. Nevertheless, I would argue that in turning their attention to education, the anarchist-feminists for the first time came to terms with the implications of their ideology. Both de Cleyre and Goldman looked forward to a society in which gender did not form the basis for differences of personality, temperament, or intellectual interests. The ideas of the Modern School movement offered the promise of such a development. But World War I, the Red Scare, and the bitter disputes among radicals that followed the Bolshevik Revolution combined to help prevent their further development. In addition, because of the anarchists' insistence on providing for the free and spontaneous development of the child, they were loath to impose any system on the school. Finally, as the school and the colony found themselves often in disagreement, the anarchist experiment in alternative education faltered, although the school remained in existence until mid-century.[43]

The anarchist-feminists never controlled the Modern School movement, despite the extensive participation by Goldman. Nor did the Stelton community, any more than Home, provide positive community support for independent women. As a result, in the areas of education and community-building, anarchist women faced considerable difficulties, although they did experience a greater practical integration of anarchism and feminism than they had achieved in their advocacy of direct action. Nonetheless, in order for the anarchist-feminists to have successfully accomplished the integration of their sophisticated comprehension of the Woman Question with other anarchist concerns, they would have had to embrace a concept of systematic change, of planned and organized development. Their own insights regarding the condition of women had grown out of the connections between the anarchist tenet of absolute individual liberty and their own experiences of sexual oppression. To insist on inserting feminist principles into educational concerns or community-building in any systematic fashion would appear to trample on the freedom of others. The best they could expect, therefore, was that, given an atmosphere of freedom, individuals would choose to liberate themselves. A limited expectation, it finally resulted in the toleration of unconventional women within a circumscribed environment. Beyond that, anarchism could not take them.

6
No Illusions: The Anarchist Life of Voltairine de Cleyre

She fought without illusions, but she fought to the end.

Leonard Abbott of Voltairine de Cleyre

No single figure better represents the complexities and contradictions, the strengths and weaknesses, or the ambiguities of anarchist-feminism than Voltairine de Cleyre. Yet until recently we knew very little about the second most important woman in the American anarchist movement, in part because Emma Goldman—who had served as this country's symbol of anarchist womanhood during her and de Cleyre's lifetimes—eclipsed de Cleyre after their deaths as well. Goldman had earned prominence by her wide-ranging propaganda efforts that reached well beyond the confines of the anarchist movement. She was outspoken, independent, and free from the constraints of conventional society; her flamboyance captured the imaginations of rebellious sons and daughters of the middle class in the years before World War I. After her death she was rediscovered in the 1960s by a generation of feminists who celebrated her defiance of traditional womanly behavior.[1] By contrast, de Cleyre's career was marked by less notoriety and by a quieter, though nonetheless genuine, defiance of American norms of femininity.

To a degree, de Cleyre chose a comparatively less aggressive role than Goldman. Although during her early years as an anarchist propagandist she had participated in a wide variety of reform and radical activities, from the late nineties until her death she worked largely among anarchists. Second, for most of her adult life she lived in Philadelphia, away from the center of intellectual rebellion in New York. Further, since she, unlike Goldman, refused to accept payment for her service to the anarchist cause, she needed to earn her living; her work as an ill-paid private teacher of English to Russian Jewish immigrants took up a great deal of her time that might otherwise have been spent in writing or lecturing. Finally, her personality was reserved, so that she found it impossible to court public attention in the way that Goldman did. But the reasons for de Cleyre's comparative neglect outside the anarchist movement go beyond questions of temperament or style. Anarchists themselves have blurred her historical significance by creating around her a myth of secular sainthood. As a result, their memory of her life presents her as the embodiment of revolutionary virtue, rather than as a woman of loves and hates, passion and reserve, generosity and pettiness. Such sanctification can be more destructive to an understanding of her significance than obscurity.[2]

Paul Avrich, in his recent sympathetic yet unsentimental biography of de Cleyre, has rescued her from anarchist hagiography. In his analysis he emphasizes her role as an anarchist activist and theorist, with particular importance placed on the interconnections in her work between American and European anarchism. Although he includes a brief discussion of her feminist philosophy, for the most part the focus is on the anarchist movement.[3] This analysis is less concerned with de Cleyre as anarchist than with de Cleyre as a nineteenth-century American woman who needed to make choices about the direction of her life in Victorian America. Women born in that period could not fail to be inordinantly cognizant of gender. Both the ideology of domesticity and the feminist movement intensified their consciousness of maleness and femaleness; and both as well encouraged women to make decisions about their social roles. It is in this intellectual context that de Cleyre and the other women anarchists are examined here.

While socioeconomic variables do not serve as complete predictors of political affiliation, certainly not in the case of anarchist women, these women did share the experience of direct and immediately felt economic or social oppression as girls or young women, and they developed a consciousness of themselves as oppressed, either because of sex or class, or their families' social marginality. For example, Lois Waisbrooker was forced to earn her living as a domestic after the failure of her marriage; although later trained as a teacher, she was never able to earn an adequate income. Florence Finch Kelly, having chosen a male-dominated profession, found herself consistently earning from one-third to one-half the salaries of male co-workers. Such a sense of personal oppression is not enough in itself to create radicals, but it seems to have existed more extensively among those women who chose anarchism than among those who became socialists. This consciousness was combined with the intellectual decisions necessary for the formation of a political philosophy; it was that fusion which created the anarchist woman.[4]

Voltairine de Cleyre's childhood and young womanhood illustrated the interaction between experience and intellectual choice. The third and youngest daughter of Hector Auguste and Harriet de Claire, Voltairine was born on November 17, 1866, in Leslie, Michigan. The de Claire marriage was unsuccessful, and her parents separated before Voltairine entered school. Hector plied his trade of itinerant tailor in northern Michigan while Harriet, Voltairine, and her older sister Adelaide (the oldest child had drowned in a swimming accident) lived together in St. Johns, Michigan, until 1878. Harriet worked as a seamstress, occasionally receiving a little support from her husband, but the family was constantly poor. No doubt worry about money contributed to Harriet's bitterness, to her incapacity for warmth or affection.[5]

Voltairine left St. Johns at twelve to live with her father in Port Huron, sent by her mother ostensibly because fourteen-year-old Adelaide, having become ill, required Harriet's full attention. But it was also true that Harriet had lost control over her wild, free, intellectually precocious, and impulsive younger daughter. Hector's success was scarcely greater; failing to subdue her, he initiated stronger measures by enrolling Voltairine in a convent boarding school. The school (Our Lady of the Lake in Sarnia, Ontario) undoubtedly played a central role in Voltairine's emotional and intellectual development, and in later years she used her convent experience to dramatize the conflict between oppression and freedom, authority and anarchy. She came to believe that the convent's repressive Catholicism had turned her into a rebellious spirit; other anarchists went further, claiming that Voltairine heroically refused to accede to her father's demand for her to become a nun, thus earning numerous beatings that broke her health and hardened her hatred of repressive institutions. Presented in this manner, de Cleyre's years in the convent allowed comparisons to the privations suffered by women revolutionaries in other countries. The United States did not provide the equivalent of Russia's Peter and Paul Fortress or Siberian exile, nor did it have penal colonies like the French prison camp in which the Communard Louise Michel earned her reputation as an anarchist saint. Lacking these, the anarchists found de Cleyre's convent "imprisonment" an acceptable if considerably tamer substitute.[6]

Magnified in this way, de Cleyre's convent years became an important symbol of repressive authoritarianism both for de Cleyre as an individual who needed to rationalize her own rebellion and for the American anarchists as a group. But the reality of de Cleyre's youthful period in the convent school was somewhat different. In the first place, Hector de Claire never tried to coerce his daughter to become a nun. Rather, he sent her to Our Lady of the Lake for two reasons: she possessed superior intellectual gifts, and she resisted discipline. De Claire might have entrusted the development of her mind to any good private school—surely, the thousand dollars spent on her education would have sent her to a reputable female academy—but convent schools also had a reputation for enforcing discipline. De Claire chose Our Lady of the Lake despite the vehement opposition of his estranged wife, a devout Protestant with an aversion to Catholicism.[7]

Both de Claires were concerned about Voltairine's intractability, and Hector finally obtained Harriet's agreement to his decision by emphasizing the need to make their younger daughter more amenable to discipline. He told his wife that Voltairine would not only receive an excellent academic education but also learn to be a lady, which would prevent her from wanting to spend her adult life "in barrooms, as you are so very sure she will." Her convent schooling would "refine her, so she knows how to behave herself and cure her of laziness and a love of idleness." Further, he expected that the nuns would "show her she has to meet many things she does not like and also [that] there are duties to be performed as she goes whether she likes them or not; in short, give her ideas of proprieties, of order, rule, regulation, time and industry, as I doubt not you know she needs." Finally, and not least, he promised Harriet that discipline "will break up her impudence, and impertinence so very prominent in her."[8]

Voltairine herself, notwithstanding her retrospective view of convent life in which she pictured herself martyred under the yoke of Catholic monasticism, was ambivalent about her experience. For a time, affected by heroine worship, she actually thought about taking the veil. Later her stubbornness resurfaced. She distinguished herself by disagreeing with her teachers, by running away, and by refusing to apologize for her infractions. Such behavior did not seem to affect her academic work, in which she had such pride that even as an anarchist she mentioned her scholastic achievements at the academy, wearing for several years after she left the convent the medal she won for her graduation essay.[9]

The convent's most profound effect on de Cleyre's later life and work was that it developed in her a love of order and a powerful belief in the necessity of self-control. For the rest of her life these aspects of her emotional make-up conflicted strongly with the passionate, nearly irrational urge for untrammeled liberty that her undisciplined childhood had generated. Her simultaneous embrace of opposite qualities created severe mental anguish for her; yet, perhaps not surprisingly, the resultant tension helped to produce her most insightful work. Her convent stay also freed her from the demands of her family at an important stage of her life, and that freedom prepared her to become more fully independent as a young adult. Although she made an attempt to return to St. Johns after her graduation in December of 1883, she stayed less than three years. Having refused outright to remain with her father, whom she denominated a "petty tyrant," she went home to her guilt-inducing mother and Adelaide, who believed that the family had unduly favored her younger sister with an education while leaving her to shift for herself. After the years of relative relief from family tensions, de Cleyre found it hard to remain at home. Besides, she encountered difficulty in trying to earn a living as a private teacher. The people of St. Johns felt little need for lessons in music, French, and penmanship.[10]

It was her inability to establish a career that provided her with an opportunity to leave home. In 1886 she moved to Greenville, Michigan, boarding with an aunt. In 1887 she left the family circle for good by moving to Grand Rapids and becoming active in the small radical circle there. During her brief stay in Grand Rapids she became a free-thought lecturer and wrote for the *Progressive Age* under the pseudonym "Fannie Fern" (a variant spelling of the nom de plume of a controversial novelist known for her tough-minded independence from men in both her writings and her life). Her travels on lecture tours shortly thereafter brought her into contact with radicals and reformers throughout the East and Midwest. Having decided to rebel against the status quo, she used this period of travel to explore the various radical and reform movements. The organized women's rights movement was too conventional for her, although she considered herself a feminist and expressed admiration for the suffragists. The free-thought movement began to seem increasingly narrow, and she never felt tempted by the moral reform groups. This left socialism (in its many manifestations) and anarchism.[11]

As early as 1887 she declared herself in opposition to the existing norms of political and social behavior, complaining to her mother that "it is a fact that people are wedded to form and custom." She added: "It is so strange to me that you are so afraid of anarchy and socialism. I am neither one nor the other and the methods of the former are abhorrent to one—but why, why does the whole world point to anarchy as the great evil" when the evils of contemporary society were far greater?[12] Two years after she wrote that letter she had embraced, then abandoned, socialism and chosen anarchism as her political creed. Anarchism met de Cleyre's intellectual and temperamental needs far better than socialism. With the socialists she had felt constricted not only by political collectivism but also by their conventional standards of behavior. In contrast, the anarchists seemed to have room for her iconoclastic temperament as well as her political nonconformity.

De Cleyre's development as an anarchist intellectual was heavily influenced by Dyer D. Lum (1839–1893), whom she met in 1888. Lum, an intimate associate of Albert Parsons (one of the men hanged in connection with the Haymarket bombing), was a mutualist-anarchist. Lum's ideas were close to the anarcho-syndicalists of the early twentieth century in that he stressed the importance of worker organization into unions, viewed industrial associations as the natural core groups within the future anarchist society, and considered strikes the most potent form of direct action. Lum did not oppose violence. He considered himself a revolutionary and was willing to accept the deaths of the Haymarket victims as inevitable casualties in the war against capitalism. It was he who smuggled into prison the dynamite capsule with which Louis Lingg committed suicide.[13] In the late eighties he edited Parsons's paper, the *Alarm*. Long active in the Knights of Labor in Chicago, as late as 1892 he worked as a union organizer among southern coal miners. Had he been born a generation later he probably would have found a congenial home within the Industrial Workers of the World. As it was, he remained precariously balanced between anarchism and unionism, growing increasingly pessimistic about the possibilities of unifying the two in any practical sense.[14]

Lum found in de Cleyre a willing pupil. She shared his frustration with the factional disputes that split the anarchist movement and—they both believed—alienated working-class converts. Like Lum, she committed herself to the development of a theoretical position that would unite all anarchist factions; she, too, would find such a task impossible. De Cleyre shared psychological as well as intellectual characteristics with Lum; both were subject to severe periodic emotional depressions that produced suicidal tendencies. (Lum finally succeeded, after several failed attempts, in committing suicide in 1893; both of de Cleyre's attempts were unsuccessful.) Undoubtedly, the discovery of a kindred intellectual and temperamental spirit facilitated her acceptance of anarchism. For a time Lum and de Cleyre were lovers, but their affair was hampered by her ambivalence and his unwillingness or inability to divorce his wife or to commit himself to a settled relationship. His alcoholism and her simultaneous involvement with another man (who fathered her only child) contributed to the instability of their liaison. Nevertheless, they remained close friends and intellectual collaborators until his death.[15]

Just as the ideas and the personality of Dyer Lum influenced the direction of de Cleyre's development as an anarchist theorist and activist, so her relationship with James Elliott (1849–1935) significantly affected the development of her views on marriage, motherhood, and childrearing. Elliott was a Philadelphia carpenter active in the free-thought movement and an ardent disciple of Thomas Paine. Intellectually inferior to de Cleyre and increasingly eccentric as he grew older, his appeal to an intelligent and ambitious young woman like de Cleyre remains a mystery. Nevertheless, the attraction was sufficiently strong for her to agree to live with him. When de Cleyre became pregnant in the fall of 1889 she apparently intended to have an abortion, then rejected the idea on the advice of a doctor who believed her health was too precarious. Her decision to have the child was perhaps the only sensible choice under the circumstances, but motherhood embittered her. Although de Cleyre lived in the same house as Elliott until 1894—after spending the year following her son's birth in Kansas—her disaffection with the relationship dated from the pregnancy, for which she held Elliott completely responsible. De Cleyre's self-concept did not include motherhood, and she refused to accept parental responsibility. The only located letter to Elliott from the period that the two lived in Elliott's mother's house is a long chatty missive that does not once mention their son. In fact, her extant correspondence before 1906 does not refer to him. Harry de Cleyre remembered that he was unaware of his mother's existence until he was fifteen years old.[16]

De Cleyre's obvious neglect of her son, in light of her widespread reputation for kindness and self-sacrifice, is somewhat puzzling. After her death her comrades often claimed inaccurately that Elliott deliberately kept the child from her. When de Cleyre's sister had asked Voltairine for permission to care for Harry, the response was callous: "It's nothing to me, what Elliott does with his boy."[17] De Cleyre and Elliott lived only a streetcar ride apart for years after their separation. Elliott, having moved from eccentricity to mental imbalance, left Harry to shift for himself when the boy was ten years old. The radical circle in Philadelphia was small enough so that de Cleyre must have known of these conditions, yet she chose to ignore them.[18]

De Cleyre was able to shut her son out of her life without discernible regret or serious reflection. Perhaps she had decided that her contribution to the anarchist cause was far too important for her to be hampered by parental responsibility. She did attempt to establish a relationship with Harry when he was in his teens, for which he seemed pathetically grateful. Perhaps the bitterness of her dealings with Elliott made it impossible for her to feel affection for their son. More significantly, her behavior as a mother reflected the anarchists' belief that the freedom of the adult took primacy over the well-being of the child. That this theoretical position might easily result in child-neglect was well-illustrated by de Cleyre's treatment of her son.

It is neither possible nor desirable to analyze de Cleyre's development as an anarchist or a feminist without an understanding of her personal life, because to a degree her choices in the more intimate sphere of her life helped to shape her political decisions. Her contradictory impulses toward freedom and authority—created in her childhood and refined during her years in the convent—helped to form her understanding of human psychology; the discovery of a kindred intellectual spirit in Dyer Lum eased her entry into the anarchist ranks; and her experience as a reluctant (and unmarried) mother sharpened her feminist consciousness.

Although Dyer Lum directed and to a large extent shaped de Cleyre's early education as an anarchist, on the Woman Question he had little of substance to offer her. Perhaps in part in reaction to his passive reliance on the unconscious evolution of the "race" to generate sexual egalitarianism, she produced a systematic examination of the nature of female oppression. De Cleyre's active exploration of the Woman Question, manifested both in her published work and private correspondence, dated from 1891, a year after the birth of her son. Prior to that time, although she had demanded the freedom to make her choices as a human being without the hindrance of feminine constraints, she was less aware of the costs of such an assertion; motherhood forced her to confront the consequences of her stance. Having realized first-hand that free love did not by itself assure equality, she drew on the work of the anarchist-feminists of the 1880s and, to a lesser degree, of Moses Harman as well in order to begin to develop the most complete articulation of the anarchist-feminist position to appear in the nineteenth century.[19]

Two essays in particular, "The Gates of Freedom," published in 1891, and "The Case of Woman vs. Orthodoxy," published in 1896, illuminated de Cleyre's feminist theory and also demonstrated the maturation of her feminist philosophy. From the beginning she insisted that the questions of marriage and economic independence were inextricably connected. Opening "The Gates of Freedom" with an unequivocal denunciation of marriage, she declared: "Young girls! if any one of you is contemplating marriage remember . . . what the contract means. The sale and control of your person in return for 'protection' and support." Yet opposition to marriage was insufficient; women needed also to declare their emotional independence from men. "I say right here, candidly, *that as a class* I have nothing to hope from men. . . . [My] hope lies in creating rebellion in the breasts of women." Despite her disappointment in the legalistic and political emphases of the organized women's rights movement, de Cleyre praised mainstream feminists for articulating some feminine discontents, so that "Woman, through a dimly roused consciousness, is beginning to feel her servitude." Nevertheless, feminists had yet to wrest from men the most important precondition for equality, individual autonomy—"*the freedom to control her own person*." And how were women to bring themselves to this threshold of freedom? Not by the grace of men. "I never expect men to *give* us liberty. No, women we are not *worth* it, until we *take* it."[20]

De Cleyre's ultimate solution for the problem of sexual equality was the standard anarchist remedy of "the liberation of land and capital," with which most anarchists—particularly women who realized that economic independence was crucial to their liberty—believed that there would come into being "a society so organized that two hours labor per day would be more than sufficient for the needs of the day." Women need not wait for anarchism in order to force men to recognize their demands, however. Rather, de Cleyre argued, they must act "by making rebels wherever we can. By ourselves *living our beliefs*. 'Propaganda by the deed' is the favorite expression of a revolutionist. We are revolutionists. And we shall use propaganda by speech, deed, and most of all life—*being* what we teach." Her imagery is suggestive; this is warlike speech, for women must be prepared to engage in war. Significantly, however, she did not invoke the image of an Amazonian sisterhood, nor did she, at a more prosaic level, urge a united front on the part of women against oppressive conditions. Rather, the single warrior captured her attention:

> In my dreams, I see . . . a lonely figure out in the desolate prairie with nothing over her but the gray sky. And I see her looking . . . and whispering: "How broad it is! It is cold and dark and frowning, but it is broad—and high!" Such will be your figure, O Woman, such your words on the day of your emancipation. In the day when you break from your cell, this warmed, round cell, whose horizon is your children's eyes, whose light is your husband's smile. . . . Better the pitiless gray of the clouds than the white ceiling of a prison. . . . Better the war of freedom than the peace of slavery.[21]

Two ideas, in addition to her arguments about the interconnectedness of marriage and economic dependence, were central to de Cleyre's feminism in 1891: first, that women should expect nothing from men; second, that women should not invest their hopes in an organized movement because independence can best be achieved by individual acts of rebellion. Turning aside from the notion of sisterhood, de Cleyre wanted women—in countless singular defiant acts—to challenge traditional feminine expectations, to refuse to marry, to bear children, or to fulfill wifely and maternal duties. In effect, she advocated a leaderless general strike against marriage and motherhood. Her goal in this essay was to find an anarchist solution to the problem of female subordination, and she exhibited therein both the strengths and the weaknesses of the anarchist-feminist position. One of the chief difficulties was to find a means of liberation that would place the isolated act of rebellion in a social context, since she realized that a spontaneous general strike of women against men was unlikely in at least the forseeable future.

By the time she produced her second major statement on the

Woman Question, she had added a measure of Marxian materialism to her analysis, declaring that "material conditions determine the social relations of men and women; and if material conditions are such as to make these relations impossible of maintenance, they will be compelled to assume others."[22] Although such a facile application of Marxian rhetoric might not satisfy a serious student of dialectical materialism, for de Cleyre it served an important dual purpose. It explained contemporary female subordination, and it promised the ultimate elimination of inequality through changes in the economic system. Just as for the socialists industrial capitalism was a necessary precursor to the proletarian revolution, so for de Cleyre it became an essential (if evil) means through which liberation would eventually be achieved. De Cleyre was certainly not insensitive to the problems caused by industrialization; nevertheless, the unsafe, unfair, and unhealthful conditions under which women worked would in the long run be less important, she believed, than the crucial fact that women were earning their own incomes. "I know all of the evils resultant to woman from the factory system; I would not prolong them. But I am glad that by these very horrors . . . women have learned to be socially useful and economically independent—as much so as men are."[23]

By ignoring the inescapable fact that women workers universally earned far less than men, de Cleyre exaggerated the degree of female economic independence. She was more optimistic than realistic because economic autonomy had become relatively more important to her as a means of achieving total equality. In 1891 she had urged women to repudiate domesticity without being able to provide a method for doing so beyond the fantastic counsel of a general female strike against women's traditional roles. But by 1896 she believed that a change in the economic functions of women could lead to a rejection of conventional feminine behavior and eventually to a restructuring of the entire system of relationships between men and women and between adults and children. She argued that "the basis of independence and individuality is bread. As long as wives take bread from their husbands because they are not capable of getting it any other way, so long will the decree obtain: 'Thy desire shall be to thy husband, and he shall rule over thee.'" De Cleyre still advised women to assert themselves through acts of individual defiance, but she set the notion of singular rebellion within a socioeconomic context.[24] She did not encourage feminist organization explicitly since, as an anarchist, she shunned rigid structures. Her hopes for a sexually egalitarian society therefore rested still on the individual, but now acting in concert with impersonal economic forces.

During the period in which de Cleyre developed her feminist theory she also struggled as a woman radical within an inegalitarian society to create a personal space within which she was both liberated from economic and emotional dependence on men yet free to enjoy sexual relationships. Anarchist philosophy was more congenial to the notion of singular defiance than to group protest, and it was the act of individual rebellion that stood at the core of nineteenth-century anarchism. Applying these ideological constructs to her own existence, de Cleyre chose to live frankly outside the boundaries of conventional society. It was not a decision she found thoroughly satisfying, particularly in her mid-twenties.[25] At that time, while contending with questions of self-definition, de Cleyre revealed in her correspondence that grinding poverty drove her to contemplate marriage for economic security, that she suffered periods of acute despondency because she considered her personal life a failure, and that on one occasion her depression nearly resulted in suicide. On the other hand, she did emerge from this period of profound mental and emotional turmoil with a heightened commitment to the intellectual decisions she had made when she became an anarchist. By 1893 she had reaffirmed her belief in a program that combined individual rebellion against traditional canons of feminine behavior (in practice, a rejection of domesticity) with participation in the larger radical community as the most assured means of bringing about the social revolution.[26]

De Cleyre's only important theoretical contribution during the 1890s was her analysis of the Woman Question. In other areas, reflecting her decision to commit herself to a combination of individual direct action and participation in the larger radical community, she engaged heavily in action and less so in speculation. In the early part of the decade most of her public activity reflected her conception of herself as an emissary of anarchism to the nonanarchist world. During these years she eschewed direct espousal of revolutionary tactics, preferring instead to emphasize the congruence of anarchism with America's decentralist heritage. One of her principal tactics, as a result, was to join or organize groups where anarchist views could be debated in a context of open discussion with other radicals or reformers. To this end she was a founding member in 1890 of the Women's National Liberal Union, and in 1893 she was a principal organizer of the Philadelphia Ladies Liberal League, which served as a forum for the discussion of public questions from various political viewpoints. She also spoke frequently to anarchist audiences in Philadelphia and occasionally in New York, and she inaugurated the Radical Library, an organization made up of her own small anarchist circle together with a number of her young Russian Jewish students whom she had converted to anarchism.[27]

De Cleyre abandoned her attempts to convert reform-minded men and women to anarchism through organizations like the Women's National Liberal Union or the Ladies Liberal League toward the end of the nineties for at least two reasons. First, after Alexander Berkman's abortive assassination attempt against Carnegie Steel Company executive Henry Clay Frick, anarchists— whether revolutionaries or nonviolent activists— found themselves distinctly less welcome in larger reform circles. Second, de Cleyre herself tired of her attempts at cloaking revolutionary principles in nonrevolutionary phrases. As she became more aware of how difficult it was to demonstrate the superiority of anarchism to nonbelievers, she turned more frequently to anarchist-sponsored platforms to express her views.

Perhaps a third force was also at work. She might have begun to view the open forums, which she had advocated so ardently in the early nineties, as a threat to her own anarchist faith. Although her speeches, poems, and sketches during the second half of the decade still indicate a firm belief in the ultimate triumph of anarchist principles, they also betray a new ambivalence about its immediate future. Some of her less overtly polemical works suggest that while the struggles of individual rebels would contribute to the eventual success of the social revolution, anarchists ought not to expect to witness concrete achievements in their own lifetimes.[28]

Such ambivalence was not reflected in her expressly political works nor in her increased activity. Activism may have served to shield her from growing doubts; from the mid-nineties until shortly after the turn of the century she increased the tempo and the range of her work of an explicitly anarchist nature. A lecture tour of England and Scotland in 1897 enhanced her international reputation and brought her the acquaintance of leading anarchists in Britain such as Peter Kropotkin and John Turner.[29] Back home in Philadelphia she organized a group of local anarchists as open-air orators in the City Hall courtyard and continued to work closely with the Russian Jewish anarchists. During these activist years her theoretical contribution was minimal, although she remained convinced that she had chosen a political creed appropriate both for the modern industrial world and her own intellectual and emotional needs. She refused to admit that her choice might have brought her hardship, declaring in 1897: "I never made any sacrifices, in the true sense of the word. Whenever I give up one thing it is to gratify a stronger wish for something else; and I am not sorry for anything I have done. . . . I am satisfied that *I bent things to my will.*"[30]

During the last fifteen years of her life she was never again so completely sure of herself. Following the McKinley assassination she witnessed the murderous hysteria on the part of Americans against anarchists. She herself was the target of an assassination attempt that left her critically wounded. After she began to recover from her wounds she developed a chronically painful ear and throat infection that sometimes left her unable to speak or concentrate for weeks on end. Her emotional depressions, which during the nineties had on occasion incapacitated her, became blacker and more intractable as ill-health aggravated them. She began to take on, albeit in a somewhat gentler aspect, the bleak pessimism of Lum. She alternated between periods of intense activism and unreasoning despair. Yet although in a personal sense her life often seemed in ruins about her, it was during these last years that she produced her most valuable contributions to anarchism. Though she seemed to consider her ambiguity a weakness, it allowed her to become a more dispassionate analyst, stripping her essays of rhetoric and sentimentality and presenting the anarchist case far more lucidly. On the other hand, she also saw more clearly its contradictions, and understood that anarchists had brought themselves to an intolerable position. Outside the movement, however, there was nowhere that she could fit in, with her odd personality composite of hedonism and moral rectitude.

Three of de Cleyre's essays that lucidly express her intellectual growth and the maturation of her thought during the last fifteen years of her life are "The Making of an Anarchist" (first published in 1903), "Anarchism and American Traditions" (published in 1908), and "The Dominant Idea" (published in 1910).[31] "The Making of an Anarchist" is not typical of de Cleyre's essays because it is deliberately personalized, specifically presenting her own conversion to anarchism as a model of behavior. Significantly, she revealed somewhat less of herself than in other essays in which she was less conscious of self. This stylized self-revelation was the closest de Cleyre came to autobiography, and to a certain degree "The Making of an Anarchist" follows the convention of autobiography, as de Cleyre engaged in public self-assessment. Why, she asked, do people hold to particular philosophies? "At bottom," she argued, "convictions are mostly temperamental. And if I sought to explain myself on other grounds I should be a bewildering error in logic; for by early influences and education I should have been a nun, and spent my life glorying in Authority in its most concentrated form."[32] The description of convent life that followed presented it as a torment that forced her to display her rebelliousness, and as a crucible (she would not have been adverse to that word) in which her anarchism was created. She had transformed the convent school into a battleground:

> How I pity myself now, when I remember it, poor lonesome little soul, battling solitary in the murk of religious superstition, unable to believe and yet in hourly fear of damnation, hot, savage, and eternal, if I do not instantly confess and profess! . . . . I struggled my way out at last, and was a freethinker when I left the institution three years later, though I had never seen a book or heard a word to help me in my loneliness. It had been like the Valley of the Shadow of Death, and there are white scars on my soul yet, where ignorance and superstition burnt me with their hell-fire in those stifling days. . . . Beside that battle of my young days all others have been easy, for whatever was without, within my own Will was supreme.[33]

This was a public version of her earlier assertion that she had used the force of her will to dominate events. It was an attempt as well to demonstrate that rational conviction can grow from temperamental predilections. And it served as an affirmation of her continued belief that she controlled the circumstances of her existence, a theme that recurred throughout the essays written during the last decade of her life. The anarchist creed as such received scant attention. She simply indicated that for the anarchist, "all forms of external authority must disappear to be replaced by self-control only." The differences between Individualism and communism were not of fundamental importance:

> My personal conviction is that both forms of society, as well as many intermediations, would, in the absence of government, be tried in various localities, according to the instincts and material condition of the people, but that well founded objections may be offered to both. Liberty and experiment alone can determine the best form of society.[34]

Her chief difficulty came, as it did for most anarchists, in describing how society would move from its current repressive, authoritarian mode to one which would result from "the whole unchaining of life after two thousand years of Christian asceticism and hyprocrisy."[35] Her vague pronouncements indicated that while she still had faith, she did not have definite suggestions to offer, nor did she fall back on the idea of the unconscious movement of the "race" toward progress, which had been one of her major themes during the nineties. Rather, it seemed that she hoped for education and propaganda to move the people to revolt against capitalism:

> While it would be idle to say that anarchists in general believe that any of the great industrial problems will be solved without the use of force, it would be equally idle to suppose that they consider force a desirable thing, or that it furnishes a final solution to any problem. From peaceful experiment alone can come final solution. . . . I can see no end of retaliations unless someone ceases to retaliate. But let no one mistake this for servile submission or meek abnegation; my right shall be asserted no matter at what cost to me, and none shall trench upon it without my protest.[36]

This is unclear enough, but at the end she was left with something still more ephemeral, a chimerical hope.

> I earnestly hope that as so far it has been my lot to work, and work hard, and for no fortune, so I may continue to the end; for let me keep the integrity of my soul, with all the limitations of my material conditions, rather than become the spineless and idealless creation of material needs. My reward is that I live with the young; I keep step with my comrades; I shall die in harness with my face to the east—The East and the Light.[37]

This essay is important for several reasons. First, de Cleyre had lost her confidence in unconscious revolutionary intellectual progress, but she had yet to find a substitute for it. Nevertheless, she remained convinced that anarchism was attainable. Second, she had begun to move toward an antimaterialist ethos, antimaterialist primarily in arguing for the importance of ideas, but also, in the popular sense, in abhorring the striving after things. Third, although there are contradictory pieces of evidence in the essay, her closing lines suggest that it may not be important whether anarchism succeeds or fails as a movement; the important thing for de Cleyre was the personal intellectual, spiritual, and emotional reward derived from having an ideal and pursuing it.

By the time she published "Anarchism and American Traditions" and "The Dominant Idea," her two strongest essays on American industrial society and its future, she had become profoundly pessimistic about the future of anarchism. The former was aimed at analyzing the changes in American society that had occurred since the Revolution. Although she idealized the American colonists, finding anarchist tendencies in their small communities and ignoring the rigid social control practiced in the New England towns, she accurately perceived that the liberties taken for granted in an agrarian nation where power was decentralized were harder to maintain in an industrialized and nationalized economy. Unlike the members of all other reform and radical groups in the country—including socialists and Progressives—de Cleyre for the anarchists warned against the threat of the overweening bureaucracy needed to conduct a complex centralized economy and political system.

Yet despite her insights into the nature of the problem, she realized that she lacked the weapons to fight the problems of the age. If, as she argued, "the love of material ease has been, in the mass of men and permanently speaking, always greater than the love of liberty," how does a radical group effect a revolution which is opposed to materialism?[38]

> Nine hundred and ninety-nine women out of a thousand are more interested in the cut of a dress than in the independence of their sex; nine hundred and ninety-nine men out of a thousand are more interested in drinking a glass of beer than in questioning the tax that is laid on it. . . . This it is which begets the complicated mechanism of society; this it is which, by multiplying the concerns of government, multiplies the strength of government and the corresponding weakness of the people; this it is which begets indifference to public concern, thus making the corruption of government easy.[39]

This was the core of the problem with which anarchists or any reformers had to contend if they wanted to restore liberty. "The problem then becomes, Is it possible to stir men from their indifference?" While she argued strenuously that bigness, complexity, and national and international economic interdependence were among the great enemies of liberty, against them she could only argue for decentralization, for a small-scale economy, and for a return to the land.[40]

Yet affirmation of those goals did not suffice. There must be a plan of action. Here de Cleyre candidly admitted that she trod uncertain ground:

> I am so well satisfied that the mass of mankind prefer material possessions to liberty, that I have no hope that they will ever, by means of intellectual or moral stirrings merely, throw off the yoke of oppression fastened on them by the present economic system.[41]

This was an argument for historical necessity. If people are oppressed, she argued, perhaps they will eventually resist oppression; they might then overcome their "reverence and fear of property," which in turn would rouse the spirit of liberty.[42] Several processes would encourage such changes:

> If . . . the tendency of invention to simplify, enabling the advantages of machinery to be combined with smaller aggregations of workers, shall follow its own logic, the great manufacturing plants will break up, population will go after the fragments, and there will be seen . . . thousands of small communities stretching along the lines of transportation, each producing very largely for its own needs. . . . The same rule holds good for societies as for individuals—those may be free who are able to make their own living.

Secondly, in order to eliminate the threat of military domination, she argued:

> The logic of Anarchism is that the least objectionable form of armed force is that which springs up voluntarily . . . and disbands as soon as the occasion which called it into existence is past: that the really desirable thing is that all men—not Americans only—should be at peace; and that to reach this, all peaceful persons should withdraw their support from the army; that neither pay nor pensions are to be provided for those who choose to make man-killing a trade.

Finally, anarchism safeguarded the rights of individuals, "demanding no jealous barrier or isolation," because "it knows that such isolation is undesirable and impossible. . . . It teaches that by all men's strictly minding their own business, a fluid society, freely adapting itself to mutual needs, wherein all the world shall belong to all men, as much as each shall need or desire, will result."[43]

In this essay de Cleyre appositely criticized the loss of liberty inherent in a society dependent on great centralized institutions, and lucidly explained the anarchist alternative. Although she still believed that world-wide revolution was not only desirable but possible, she was forced to admit that the possibility was a remote one. As a result, in "The Dominant Idea" (1910) she emphasized more strongly the impact of anarchist philosophy on the individual and its ability to restructure the lives of its adherents, even if the rest of society refused its offer of regeneration. "The Dominant Idea" contained her most explicit attack on the materialist conception of history:

> Our modern teaching is that ideas are but attendant phenomena, impotent to determine the actions or relations of life. . . . It is thus that the

so-called Materialist Conception of History, the Modern Socialists, and a positive majority of Anarchists would have us look upon the world of ideas,—shifting, unreal . . . , having naught to do in the determination of Man's life, but so many mirror appearances of certain material relations, wholly powerless to act upon the course of material things. . . . I think this unqualified determinism of the material is a great and lamentable error in our modern progressive movement.[44]

Materialism, she argued, had destroyed the idea that individuals can make choices. "The doctrine of Materialistic Determinism has produced shifting, self-excusing, worthless, parasitical characters, who are *this* now and *that* at some other time, and anything and nothing upon principle."[45] De Cleyre believed in ideas, in will, and in a measured degree of freedom in that will: "My conception of mind . . . is not that it is a powerless reflection of momentary conditions of stuff and form, but an active modifying agent, reacting on its environment and transforming circumstances, sometimes greatly, sometimes, though not often, entirely."[46]

Against the idea of an economic foundation as the substructure of all society, de Cleyre proposed the Dominant Idea. The dominant idea of modern industrial society she called "The Much Making of Things" and defined as "the shameless, merciless driving and over driving, wasting and draining of the last bit of energy, only to produce heaps of . . . things ugly, things harmful, things useless, and at the best largely unnecessary." Deploring the "desire for the possession of things, the exaltation of the possession of things,"[47] which she claimed was the center of the lives of most Americans, she still believed that individuals could break free from the dominant ethos. "The dominant idea of the age and land does not necessarily mean the dominant idea of any single life."[48]

Although de Cleyre could not promise a revolution, she did offer an ideological alternative for those men and women who would "invest themselves with the dignity of an aim higher than the chase for wealth; choose a thing to do in life outside the making of things, and keep it in mind—not for a day, nor a year, but for a lifetime." The reward may not be a better world, but it will be a more satisfied self, one who has "proved by a lifetime that there is that in man which saves him from the absolute tyranny, which in the end conquers and remolds circumstance—the immortal fire of individual will which is the salvation of the future."[49]

In these three essays de Cleyre moved from an attempt through autobiography to make sense of her own role within the movement and to define both herself and anarchism in the light of her incipient rejection of unconscious progress and her growing realization that the ideal to which she had given her life would not be realized in the foreseeable future, to an assertion that success or failure could not be measured by widespread social change but by the changes in a multitude of individual lives. None of the three essays carried an explicitly feminist message. Nor did de Cleyre during this entire period add much to her feminist philosophy as she had articulated it in the 1890s. Nevertheless, she had not abandoned feminism. A careful reading of her work as a whole suggests that she tried to anticipate an anarchist future in which gender would not serve as a defining characteristic for social roles, in which neither men nor women would feel restricted by sex. For the most part the connections between anarchism and feminism were indirect, perhaps even indistinct; but in her expressly feminist writings she retained her deep antagonism toward the constraints placed on women, and continued to find the source of those constraints within the domestic relationship. In 1908 she denounced it with as much vehemence as she had in 1891 as an institution "which stales love, brings respect into contempt, outrages the privacies and limits the growth of all parties." It was not the legal form of marriage, but the notion of men and women living together in a nuclear family, whether formalized or not, which she found intolerable. The abolition of marriage, construed in this fashion, was necessary to her ultimate goal, that is, the development of "the free individual, implying all the conditions necessary to that freedom." De Cleyre's feminism had in fact sharpened, rather than abated, since her early essays on the subject, although its major outlines remained the same.[50]

In every area de Cleyre's thought had become increasingly sophisticated during the last fifteen years of her life. But as she appreciated the complexities of human relationships in both their intimate and social contexts, it became more difficult for her to cling to a belief in an essentially simple faith. She did not abandon anarchism;

after her recovery from the gunshot wounds she received when a former student attempted to assassinate her, she resumed her heavy schedule of speaking engagements and writing assignments. In 1908 she faced the only arrest of her career—for inciting to riot—and was acquitted. But during this time doubts assailed her, and she considered retirement from active work. In 1910, plagued by recurrent illness and by bleak depressions, she left Philadelphia for Chicago. One of her letters to Alexander Berkman during her period of despair expressed her loss of faith:

> I cannot preach anarchism now, because I do not believe it with any great force or strength. I have not "backslid." I believe in government no more than I ever did for twenty-one years. But I can't make a fervent gospel of anarchism now. I can't honestly tell anyone it's worth trying for. And I am rather displeased with the whole appearance of our work since 1887. I see we have steered the thing into such a theoretical channel, that if a direct struggle between capitalist and worker takes place, we must *keep out of it* because of our sympathy with the strikers. What a charming result! Our name is such a prejudice that we must save our friends from its contamination![51]

Her disappointment lasted until 1911, when she discerned in the Mexican Revolution a renewed possibility of the creation of an anarchist society. Before she could either become disillusioned or undertake active participation she died as a result of complications following an ear operation.

Henry May has said of the groups he called "scoffers," in which he included anarchists, that they left a more important legacy to the twentieth century than political radicals like the socialists:

> Social revolution in America has so far proved a dream; cultural revolution has been an important reality. Indirectly and directly, the cultural changes of the twentieth century owe a large debt to the bold iconoclasts of the left, the Wobblies and anarchists and others, hard-boiled and yet romantic, outspoken, and unwilling to compromise.[52]

Such an assessment emphasizes the cultural connections between radicals and the mainstream. De Cleyre's unconventionality notwithstanding, neither she nor the anarchists in general can be understood outside the framework of the society against which they reacted. And quite apart from questions of cultural integration is the issue of defining, however imprecisely, the impact of a single individual.

De Cleyre's importance as a feminist rests primarily on her willingness to confront issues that the organized women's rights movement sidestepped or avoided, such as the emotional and psychological (in addition to the economic) dependence on men within the nuclear family structure, and female sexuality. She also lived in conformity with her feminist principles, which forced those who came in contact with her to confront her philosophy in the particular as well as in the abstract. Within her own movement, anarchist men in theory embraced the belief in an economic self-sufficiency combined with sexual liberation embodied in a humanistic erotic ethos. Nevertheless, for the most part they also accepted the notion that women were inherent nurturers and hearth-keepers, and that after the revolution, when women would be freed from the depredations of capitalism, these "natural" predilections would flower in a new environment. De Cleyre fought against this view not only rhetorically but through her own life, retaining not only the respect but often the reverence of her comrades, and leaving the historian with an understanding of the immense personal costs paid by women who refused to accept normative behavioral standards. Her legacy to late-twentieth-century feminists, therefore, is her articulation on several levels of the need for an examination of the society's most intimate institutions as well as its legal and political ones.

The significance of de Cleyre's life as a thoughtful and unconventional woman attempting to transcend the limitations of traditional femininity has escaped notice in part because of the way her comrades and succeeding generations of anarchists have dealt with her. The anarchists evolved a myth of Voltairine de Cleyre, begun while she was still alive but embellished and enlarged after her death, a myth in which the woman who sometimes doubted her ability to sustain her commitment to independence, who understood the nature of the price she paid for her iconoclasm yet often resented that cost, who suffered from deep depressions, who considered herself a passionate yet also aloof woman, became a "revolutionary vestal," a "priestess of pity and vengeance." For the anarchists in the United States she became the American version of Louise Michel, the French anarchist teacher who had engaged in terrorist activity during the Paris Commune, had endured several prison sentences, and was the recognized saint of international anarchism.

Louise Michel had lived in deep privation, gave all her possessions to fellow revolutionaries, and spent a life of devoted self-sacrifice in the cause of anarchism. Her one self-indulgence was a passionate devotion to her mother. Anarchists emphasized the similarities between Michel and de Cleyre. Both were teachers; both nearly had been assassinated by former followers and had refused to prosecute their attackers; both tended toward extreme generosity toward the movement, although at least for de Cleyre that generosity stemmed in part from her fear of ever taking anything from another human being because she did not wish to be obligated to or dependent upon that person. The extent to which anarchists went in finding parallels between the two women is evident in the way they dealt with de Cleyre's relationship to her mother. Emma Goldman said that de Cleyre "fairly worshipped" her mother,[53] when in reality de Cleyre felt more pity than love. She helped her mother financially and emotionally, but more out of a sense of responsibility than devotion. In one letter to her sister, which repeatedly expressed bitterness against her mother's defense of her lover against herself (in an incident which had occurred some ten years previous to the letter), de Cleyre noted, "I no more than you have any inclination to be affectionate with mother. In fact, it's sometimes rather repulsive to me."[54] Perhaps more revealing than comparisons to Michel were the attitudes of the anarchists toward de Cleyre's refusal to take parental responsibility for her son Harry. Whenever possible, the very fact of her motherhood was ignored, as it failed to enhance the image of a revolutionary vestal who had reserved all passion for her cause. When this was impossible, the anarchists placed all the blame for Harry's neglect on Elliott, who allegedly "deprived [de Cleyre] of opportunity to see her child, kept [her] in ignorance even of its whereabouts." An anarchist paper that memorialized de Cleyre in 1950 claimed that Elliott "took the child with him. Voltairine did not see her son again until 1905, when he was fifteen."[55] This was not strictly true, but it preserved an unsullied image.

Emma Goldman's biography of de Cleyre, published in 1932 and until recently almost the sole source of readily available information about her, contributed to the myth. This biography is especially interesting because, although it was set almost in the form of a eulogy, Goldman used both subtle and overt comments to belittle her old rival. Goldman noted with a martyred air:

> I had often been censured by Voltairine for my "waste" of effort to reach the American Intellegentzia [sic] rather than to consecrate all my efforts to the workers, as she did so ardently. But, knowing her deep sincerity; the religious zeal which stamped everything she did, no one minded her censorship; we went on loving and admiring her just the same.[56]

On the subject of de Cleyre's attitude and appearance, Goldman was unkind and inaccurate:

> Her whole nature was that of the old-time saints who flagellated their bodies and tortured their souls for the glory of God. Figuratively speaking, Voltairine also flagellated herself, as if in penance for our Social Sins; her poor body was covered with ungainly clothes and she denied herself even the simplest joys, not only because of lack of means, but because to do otherwise would have been against her principles.[57]

Yet de Cleyre described herself, even during the last decade of her life, after she had nearly died from an assassination attempt and her ill-health sometimes incapacitated her, as capable of "wild gaity." She expressed her exhilaration after a mountain excursion in Norway as "one of my great, great days, . . . one of the days when I lived clean to my fingers and toe-tips."[58]

One suspects that either Goldman was never favored with the lively side of de Cleyre's personality or that the old rivalry would not abate. Goldman was unkind about de Cleyre's appearance. "But physical beauty and feminine attraction were withheld from her, their lack made more apparent by ill-health and her abhorrence of artifice."[59] Yet her numerous lovers and admirers found her strikingly handsome and appealing despite Goldman's implication that de Cleyre's unattractiveness was the reason why her life (unlike Goldman's?) "courted emotional defeat." Of Dyer D. Lum, who was passionately and hopelessly in love with de Cleyre, Goldman said only that he "was one man in Voltairine's life who cherished her for the beauty of her spirit and the quality of her mind."[60]

Despite the fact that Goldman's depiction contained a sharp edge of unkindness, it nevertheless solidified the image of de Cleyre as a revolutionary ascetic—grim, humorless, totally devoted to the revolution, self-sacrificing to a fault. Goldman at the same time managed to suggest that de Cleyre, unlike herself, had never managed to put any fun into the revolution. Most of the points that Goldman raised had already become part of the de Cleyre legend. A year after de Cleyre's death, the *Syndicalist* called her a radical of "the type that always hews to the line, that is never lured from the straight direct road to freedom."[61] And Jay Fox, editor of the *Demonstrator*, eulogized her in these words:

> Nature has the habit now and then of producing a type of human being far in advance of the times; an ideal for us to emulate; a being devoid of sham, uncompromising, and to whom the truth is sacred; a being whose selfishness is so large that it takes in the whole human race and treats self only as one of the great mass; a being keen to sense all forms of wrong, and powerful in denunciation of it; one who can reach into the future and draw it nearer. Such a being was Voltairine de Cleyre.

Hippolyte Havel used this tribute to open his introduction to de Cleyre's selected works.[62] De Cleyre's friend Harry Kelly saw her life as one of "austerity that has hardly a parallel even in revolutionary ranks." Only Leonard Abbott seemed willing to allow her humanness, saying that "she fought without illusions, but she fought to the end." But the anarchists, in decline and disarray, were unable to face de Cleyre without illusions, so they canonized her.[63]

It is difficult to sift through the legend in order to understand clearly the extent of her influence within the anarchist movement. The anarchists themselves could not agree. When they evaluated her importance, it was always in comparison to Emma Goldman. Carl Nold, a friend of both women, said that de Cleyre not only "stood mentally above Emma Goldman," but that the former often gave unacknowledged assistance to the latter; in fact, "a good deal of what Emma Goldman and Alexander Berkman wrote . . . first went through the hands of Voltairine de Cleyre for approval and correction before it went into print." In the same letter he noted that de

Cleyre "did not make as much noise as Emma Goldman did, but what she did do was done more thoroughly as a private teacher, in private schools, in writing and speeches." He then touched on the essential distinction between the two women. "Emma Goldman tried to attract her hearers with a bass-drum. Voltairine de Cleyre has done it with a violin."[64]

On the other hand, both Emma Goldman herself and Joseph Ishill were privately less impressed with de Cleyre's importance. Goldman told Ishill that "Voltairine was hardly known to anyone in Europe except to the Comrades in England whom she got to know through her visit there and through *Mother Earth*. The fact is that Voltairine had little influence in America, which of course did not speak against her. It was due to her personality, as it was hard for her to get out of her shell."[65] Ishill concurred with Goldman:

> Much of the writing of Voltairine has been decidedly over-rated and does not approach literature at all. It is perhaps her active life as a revolutionist in which her spirit so beautifully dedicated itself to the downtrodden, that is most significant and enduring. But even so you have contributed much more during all the years of your own active life.[66]

In the final analysis, neither woman was successful in her most cherished goal: to bring about a revolution that would crush capitalism, topple male supremacy, and usher in new freedoms for men, women, and children. In another sense, however, both were great successes. Goldman felt that despite her defeats, her life was indeed worth living. De Cleyre, a more introspective and questioning person, sometimes felt doubt about her choices. Yet she lived her life as a free and independent woman, and participated in a work that she believed had the potential to liberate humankind economically, politically, socially, and sexually. Because of de Cleyre, and the other anarchist-feminists, we can understand far better what it meant to choose to live in contradiction to the larger society, and to be aware of the costs and consequences of such a choice.

7
Neither Heroines nor Heroes: Radicals and Feminist Politics

One must write not only for oneself. But for others. For those far-away, unknown women who will live then. Let them see that we were not heroines or heroes at all. But we believed passionately and ardently.

Aleksandra Kollontai

Most women who considered themselves both radicals and feminists in the late nineteenth and early twentieth centuries bypassed anarchism and embraced one or another of the varieties of socialism. In the 1870s and early 1880s neither socialists nor anarchists regarded the two movements as fundamentally dichotomous or antagonistic— the Communist-anarchists especially viewed themselves as participants in the international socialist movement, while the Individualists often referred to themselves as voluntary socialists. Radical groups cooperated during these years, reflecting an ideological fluidity and a shared conviction that the most important aspect of their politics was opposition to the status quo, which implied an absolute determination to abolish industrial capitalism.

But such coexistence was not without discord, and by the mid-1880s the socialists and anarchists had ceased to cooperate in any meaningful sense. The socialist belief that the state would necessarily act as the instrument of liberation from capitalism took on increasing significance as socialists placed a greater emphasis on gaining power within the system through participation in electoral politics. The anarchists utterly disdained this approach. Also the socialists became eager to disassociate themselves from the anarchists after the Haymarket bombing and its aftermath had provided the public with a frightening image of the typical anarchist. The socialists were comparatively successful. Their ideas influenced professionals and intellectuals, appealing to an organizational age that admired scientific and technological solutions to social problems (including the Woman Question). The credibility of anarchism declined, on the other hand, as the larger society inaccurately but effectively characterized it as a haven for fanatics and eccentrics.

The strains, cracks, then open rupture between the anarchists and the socialists reflected profound ideological differences. Robert Nisbet exaggerated, but not greatly, when he claimed that anarchism and socialism offered fundamentally different world views:

> Revolutionary in most respects the anarchists were; but their transcending significance seems to me to lie, not so much in a stress upon revolution—with its implications of violence, centralization of power, myth in the form of philosophy of history, and other elements we have located in [Marxism]—as in *renewal*. I mean the kind of renewal of human life proclaimed in anarchist doctrines of mutualism, non-violence, cooperation, free association, and the close relation of man to nature and in the whole spirit of voluntarism that characterizes the great majority of anarchist writings.[1]

Anarchists, in other words, searched for natural forms of social organization, while the Marxists wanted to destroy old patterns of thought and create a completely new society based on a rational philosophy. Although Nisbet seriously underplayed the revolutionary nature of anarchism, his argument has merit. For example, contrast the socialist whole-hearted acceptance of technology with anarchist ambivalence; the former's reliance on a centralized, bureaucratic state with the latter's belief in small, self-sustaining, and freely cooperating communities; and the socialist emphasis on economic equality with the anarchist stress on personal liberation.

By the last decade of the nineteenth century potential radicals realized that by choosing socialism or anarchism they made a statement about their vision of a new social order. That feminist radicals preferred socialism is therefore significant; what, then, did socialism offer? Perhaps one of the more important things was serious theoretical attention, if not in the United States, at least on an international level. While the principal male anarchist theorists were at best indifferent and at worst hostile to the Woman Question, two major figures of the European socialist movement addressed the problem sympathetically. Frederick Engels's *The Origin of the Family, Private Property, and the State* examined the issue of female subordination using the research of anthropologist Edward Morgan. The Engels treatise and August Bebel's *Woman Under Socialism,* a more detailed and extended treatment, constituted the principal sources from which later socialist-feminists elaborated their ideology and drew their examples.[2] Engels had tied the subordination of women to the development of private property, contending that women would always suffer oppression under capitalism or any social system dependent upon private property. Engels assumed that before the development of property, women and men had enjoyed commensurate status. Their functions differed, but their positions were equal. Such equality, he claimed, derived from the practice of matrilineal descent in certain primitive societies. In these societies, according to Morgan, "marriages" were ephemeral and nonexclusive. But, as society evolved, the "group marriage" of the earliest societies was replaced by "pairing marriage" (serial monogamy), then by monogamy. Concomitantly the position of women declined; the abandonment of matrilineal descent symbolized the deterioration of their status. Engels argued:

> Thus on the one hand, in proportion as wealth increased it made the man's position in the family more important than the woman's, and on the other hand created an impulse to exploit this strengthened position in order to overthrow, in favor of his children, the traditional order of inheritance. This, however, was impossible so long as descent was reckoned according to mother right. Mother right, therefore, had to be overthrown, and overthrown it was. This was by no means so difficult as it looks to us today. For this revolution—one of the most decisive ever experienced by humanity—could take place without disturbing a single one of the living members of a gens. . . . The overthrow of mother right was the *world historical defeat of the female sex.* The man took command

in the home also; the woman was degraded and reduced to servitude; she became the slave of his lust and a mere instrument for the production of children.[3]

The modern family, founded on property rather than love (except among proletarians who had no property), served the needs of men. As for women, "The modern individual family is founded on the open or concealed domestic slavery of the wife, and modern society is a mass composed of these individual families as its molecules." The solution to the problem of inequality for Engels depended on removing women from domestic isolation and making them productive units in the larger society. Therefore, "The first condition for the liberation of the wife is to bring the whole female sex back into public industry, and . . . this in turn demands that the characteristic of the monogamous family as the economic unit of society be abolished."[4] Engels carefully abolished the family only "as the economic unit of society," being unprepared to eliminate the monogamous relationship as a social unit. "Having arisen from economic causes," he asked, "will monogamy then disappear when these causes disappear?" He answered in the negative, suggesting that perhaps:

> It will on the contrary begin to be realized completely. For with the transformation of the means of production into social property there will disappear also wage labor, the proletariat, and therefore the necessity for a certain—statistically calculable—number of women to surrender themselves for money. Prostitution disappears; monogamy, instead of collapsing, at last becomes a reality—also for men.[5]

The abolition of private property would insure that men and women could marry for love, "and as sexual love is by its nature exclusive—although at present this exclusiveness is fully realized only in the women—then marriage based on sexual love is by its nature individual marriage."[6] His assertion of the exclusivity of sexual love seems a little disingenuous; one senses that it offered a comparatively noncontroversial means for Engels to resolve the problem of the future relation of the sexes under socialism. His advocacy of the abolition of the "supremacy of the man and . . . the indissolubility of marriage" was as far as he could bring himself.[7] Those two things, he felt sure, would no longer exist in the socialist state. Unwilling to predict categorically the nature of the family in the future, he closed his analysis of monagamy with a quote from Morgan, who argued that it was "at least supposable that [the monogamous family] is capable of still further improvement until the equality of the sexes is attained."[8]

Engels's analysis has faced criticism in the twentieth century, both for its anthropological inaccuracy and for its theoretical confusion. Simone de Beauvoir found the materialist position inadequate to describe the nature of female subordination. "Historical materialism takes for granted facts that call for explanations. . . . It cannot provide solutions for the problems we have raised, because these concern the whole man and not that abstraction: *Homo oeconomicus*." De Beauvoir argued that woman's oppression is at bottom not based on economic factors, for "if the human consciousness had not included the original category of the Other and an original aspiration to dominate the Other, the invention of the bronze tool could not have caused the oppression of woman." More recently Ann Lane has attacked not materialism but Engels's inconsistency in applying it. She has argued that Engels mistakenly believed "that the responsibilities of home and family, and the economic ties that bind them together, are not an important part of what establishes their cohesion, that society can remove a vital function of an institution in order to perfect it. Socialist society will strip the family of most of its traditional jobs, but the family itself, in its pristine state, untouched by history or reality, shall remain."[9]

In the nineteenth century no socialist theorist questioned the validity of the materialist analysis of sexual inequality, and only a few confessed to doubts about the ability of monogamous marriage to survive the transition to socialism. August Bebel was one of those few. Bebel agreed with Engels that only socialism could promise sexual equality, and in the later editions of his book he strengthened his ties to Engels's analysis by incorporating the latter's anthropological insights about the origin and early development of sexual inequality. But he departed from Engels in his willingness to admit that sex-based oppression transcended class differences. Women in the nineteenth century, argued Bebel, suffered in two ways: first, "from economic and social dependence upon man";

second, "from the economic dependence that women in general, the working woman in particular, finds herself in along with the working man."[10] All women, therefore, not just those of the proletariat, suffered from male domination. And although Bebel argued that the working-class male, to his credit, "mostly strives to enlighten woman . . . , and to educate her into a fellow combatant in the struggle for the emancipation of the proletariat from capitalism," his honesty compelled him to admit that male workers also oppressed women. He deplored the common masculine tendency—shared by the bourgeoisie and the proletariat—to treat women as "the sexual, never the social being."[11]

Bebel conscientiously strove to provide a dispassionate analysis of woman's condition and her potential for growth. Although he reluctantly accepted prevalent "scientific" evidence of woman's intellectual inferiority and her greater propensity to fall victim to emotional disorders, he nevertheless refused to believe them irreversible. He argued that woman's intellectual capacity had become stunted by centuries of masculine repression; freedom under socialism would reverse the process. Woman would grow in intellectual ability and her "biological" predisposition to certain mental illnesses would disappear. Only by discontinuing oppression would society be able to discover the true extent of woman's capabilities. Bebel's argument from justice remains unanswerable: "Woman has the same right as man to unfold her faculties and to the free exercise of the same: she is human as well as he: like him, she should be free to dispose of herself as her own master."[12]

The socialization of the economy and the integration of women into the labor force as productive members of society were for Bebel, as they had been for Engels, the keys to the liberation of women. But in other ways Bebel went further than Engels had dared. Engels had concluded that the economic functions of the family would disappear under socialism, leaving its social and psychological functions unaltered, or perhaps enhanced. Bebel, on the other hand, was not convinced of the desirability of monogamy. Refusing to forecast the future of the family, he argued only that society must not place restraints on relationships of the heart, that marriages ought to be freely entered into, and just as freely dissolved.[13] On issues related to marriage, such as eroticism and contraception, Bebel expressed rather more conventional views. Foreshadowing arguments by the American socialist Charlotte Perkins Gilman, he declared that women as well as men were overly concerned with sexuality and suggested that both sexual desire and fertility would decline as civilization advanced. While not specifically disallowing birth control, he was unwilling to separate sexuality from reproduction. His hopes as well as his suppressed doubts appeared in the statement that "in the last analysis, the number of population is regulated without harmful abstinence and without unnatural preventatives in a society that lives according to the laws of nature."[14]

Because eroticism remained connected to childbearing, it was important for Bebel to place the rearing of children in a socialist context, and that context was a female one; childrearing fell to the lot of women, although not necessarily to the mother. Bebel did not view maternity as a possible hindrance to woman's emancipation, however, since children, "where she has any, do not impair her freedom: they can only fill all the fuller the cup of her enjoyments and her pleasures in life. Nurses, teachers, female friends, the rising female generations—all these are readily at hand to help the mother when she needs help."[15] Bebel's conventional views on birth control and childrearing should not blind the reader to his essential commitment to an egalitarian society. After all, many feminists, particularly within the organized women's rights movement but not exclusive to it, agreed with such sentiments.

Daniel De Leon, the head of the Socialist Labor Party in the United States, translated *Woman Under Socialism* into English, and felt compelled in his introduction to disassociate himself from Bebel's more unconventional views of women. In a statement that echoed Engels in its sentiments (but was far more rigid), De Leon argued:

> For one, I hold there is as little ground for rejecting monogamy, by reason of the taint that clings to its inception, as there would be ground for rejecting co-operation, by reason of the like taint that accompanied its rise, and also clings to its development. . . . For one, I hold that the monogamous family—bruised and wounded in the cruel rough-and-tumble of modern society . . . will have its wounds staunched, its bruises

healed, and, enabled by the slowly acquired moral forces of conjugal, paternal, and filial affection, bloom under socialism into a lever of mighty power for the moral and physical elevation of the races.[16]

When De Leon repeatedly admonished women that feminism must be subordinated to the (masculine) needs of the working-class revolution, he spoke for the typical American male socialist. He informed women that "the history of Class Rule throws its light before the feet of the Woman's movement; it explains the errors, accounts for them, that the movement slips into; the emotional vagaries with which the movement is often marred; its futile tears; its frequently barren efforts"; and he ridiculed the assumption of feminists "that woman was smitten down because of her sex. She was not." At great pains to point out that women had no special problem related to their femaleness, he constantly reminded them that their true mission lay in assisting working-class men to create the socialist revolution.[17]

The response of socialist women to the attitudes of male supremacy displayed by De Leon, of chivalry shown by Engels, and of the well-intentioned but still occasionally ambivalent support by Bebel depended to a large extent on their own political and ideological orientation within the socialist movement. At least four distinct viewpoints existed: (1) the non-Marxist, decidedly feminist, almost Bellamyite socialism of Charlotte Perkins Gilman; (2) the native-American, agrarian socialism represented by Kate Richards O'Hare; (3) the De Leonite urban-oriented version of socialism demonstrated most effectively in a pamphlet by Olive Johnson; and (4) the socialism of the Greenwich Village feminists of the second decade of the twentieth century, akin in several ways to the anarchist-feminists and drawing some inspiration from them.

Charlotte Perkins Gilman—brilliant, outspoken, and iconoclastic—was both a socialist and a leader of the organized women's rights movement. Undoubtedly the most radical of the second generation of suffrage leaders, she attacked the home and domesticity because of its deadening influence on the female mind and spirit, and she announced her willingness—even eagerness—to abandon the conventional social structure to which most of her sisters in the mainstream feminist movement were committed. Gilman's socialism was non-Marxist; Edward Bellamy, the author of *Looking Backward* and a sequel, *Equality*, had influenced her profoundly. Both of Bellamy's utopian visions, but particularly the latter, advocated participation of women in the work force in traditionally masculine occupations such as engineering and the skilled crafts as well as in more conventionally feminine pursuits; economic equality; and the removal of domestic tasks, including child care, to the public realm.[18]

Gilman concurred that equality would never be possible without full participation in economic life. And such participation required the socialization of childrearing and domestic tasks. Men and children, as well as women, would benefit under the new arrangement. An economically independent woman would marry for love, and children would grow to maturity in an environment that consisted not merely of an untrained mother's efforts, but of the attention of specialists in child care and education. Although she attacked conventional domestic arrangements, Gilman was not against the family. She argued:

> Like all natural institutions the family has a purpose; and is to be measured primarily as it serves that purpose; which is, the care and nurture of the young. To protect the helpless little ones, to feed and shelter them, to ensure them the benefits of an even longer period of immaturity, and so to improve the race—this is the original purpose of the family.[19]

Men, she determined, had subverted that purpose: "What man has done to the family, speaking broadly, is to change it from an institution for the best service of the child, to one modified to his own service, the vehicle of his comfort, power and pride."[20] In order to create a mutually rewarding family life—a family "based on love and . . . maintained because of its happiness and use"—society must destroy the old notion of home.[21] People trained for the tasks of cooking, cleaning, and child care could better perform housekeeping duties than the isolated wife. Women would become free to develop their special talents, and Gilman believed that a free womanhood was necessary to full social development. Gilman, like Bebel and Engels, integrated the causes of labor and feminism; but she altered the priorities: "The great woman's movement and labor movement of today are parts of the same pressure, the same world-progress. An economic democracy must rest on a free womanhood; and a free womanhood inevitably leads to an economic democracy."[22] Gilman's practical device for freeing women before the victory of socialism was the cooperative apartment house, containing common kitchens, laundry facilities, and nurseries, thus liberating the individual couple from the unshared burden of those responsibilities. Her idea never came to fruition, and William O'Neill has suggested that her scheme was inadequate:

> Her solution to the problem was largely mechanical, a matter of revised domestic arrangements, which would free women for outside work. The alternative would seem to have been some kind of socialist order that would provide the institutions—public nurseries, paid maternity leaves, and the like—necessary to fulfill the promise of feminine emancipation. Surprisingly enough, the key writings of this professed socialist neglected the point. She believed that feminism would have to socialize the home, but she apparently believed it possible to have socialized homes in a capitalist society. . . . Mrs. Gilman was a socialist and a feminist, yet in her mind the two remained separate and distinct causes. In the end, her failure to integrate them prevented her from fully utilizing the insights she had gained from each.[23]

Charlotte Perkins Gilman put her feminism before her socialism; Kate Richards O'Hare, who served on the National Committee of the Socialist Party of America and worked closely with Eugene Debs, reversed that pattern. Although O'Hare supported women's suffrage, her feminist argument nevertheless differed in important respects from Gilman's. For example, O'Hare was not convinced that an emancipated, economically productive womanhood was an essential precondition for a socialist society. Not opposed to working women per se (no good socialist could be), O'Hare nevertheless emphasized the importance of female domesticity. Although she expected that a socialist society both would alter the conditions of work and provide support systems such as communal kitchens and laundries, she was far less radical then Gilman in her conception of woman's place. For example, she suggested that the care of children under socialism would rest primarily with the mother, who during the period when her children were growing up would not engage in outside work.[24]

The emphasis that O'Hare placed on woman's role as nurturer ought to have endeared her to those suffragists who idealized domesticity and who used it in their struggle to gain the vote. She forcefully expressed her domestic predilections in her lament that young women had lost the art of homemaking because "we insist that our girls be educated. . . . We provide teachers for them in art and science . . . but entirely ignore the greatest art known to man, that of making a house a home, and giving life to well-born children." While she claimed that she was not denigrating intellectual or artistic education for women, she still insisted that girls had "an inalienable right" to a "domestic" education as well. One suspects that her priorities would not have changed drastically after the revolution. O'Hare did argue that men should participate more actively in the process of raising children, that they should be educated "for the duties of fatherhood" and must learn "to be helpers and sustainers" within the domestic circle. Given the overall character of her argument, it seems probable that O'Hare's conception of fatherhood was simply an extension of Catharine Beecher's view that the home should serve as the focal point of human activity for both sexes. O'Hare was not anticipating the argument of some late-twentieth-century feminists that since women have the right to participate completely in what used to be called "man's world," men ought similarly to enter fully into the joys and responsibilities of childrearing.[25]

Despite O'Hare's prominent position in the Socialist Party, on the whole the party itself paid little attention to developing a feminist stance. Its leaders actively discouraged specific women's activities until 1907, when the International Congress of Socialists formally endorsed woman suffrage. After that the American Socialist Party's neglect of women's needs became a point of controversy. The *Socialist Woman* (later the *Progressive Woman*) resulted from the awakened interest. Nevertheless, despite the success of the new journal, party leaders disapproved and ultimately retracted support from the venture. Mari Jo Buhle has argued that the actions of the Socialist Party were shortsighted in the extreme, and has suggested that feminists "would continue to search for an appreciation of woman's struggle among Socialists and would become discouraged by its absence."[26] The Socialist Party of America, during its peak years from 1908 through 1912, was the closest the American left has come to creating a mass movement; that the women who participated in it were ignored or, perhaps more insultingly, patronized shows the severity of the difficulties women faced when they tried to act as both feminists and radicals within the organized left.

The enthusiastic reception of *Socialist Woman* suggests that the women of the Socialist Party of America struggled against the attitudes of their male comrades. The Socialist Labor Party, however, provided a contrasting picture of women who emphasized their hositlity toward the feminists. Olive M. Johnson, in a pamphlet written in 1907 for the express purpose of attracting women to the party, seemed bent on putting potential converts in their proper (subordinate) place. Specifically denying the feminist claim of sisterhood (the belief that women by virtue of their sex share a common bond regardless of social class), Johnson proclaimed that "as the concern of this pamphlet is to find . . . women who are or should be directly interested in the Socialist Movement, we have . . . nothing to do with the women of the upper classes. It is the working women that concern us."[27] Her antifeminism at times reflects disdain for women themselves, as in the following claim: "There is not a woman alive, unless she is utterly blinded by prejudices, who will not admit that woman's best friend is man and that her worst enemy is woman herself." Feminists, she contended, were inspired simply "by a desire to rule and domineer" rather than by a justifiable anger because of sex-based discrimination. As a consequence, women's rights advocates "were bound to make themselves ridiculous [and] overbearing."[28] The socialist woman differed from such unnatural creatures: A tenacious fighter for the cause of proletarian revolution, she nonetheless gloried in stereotypical feminine and maternal qualities. After all, "nothing is more repugnant than the unsexed, boldfaced, rude, masculine girl, unless it be the weazened, physically deteriorated, effeminate man." Unlike the rest of the socialist movement, Johnson, in speaking for the Socialist Labor Party, subscribed to the view that women ought not to participate in the labor market. Although Kate Richards O'Hare opposed work outside the home for mothers, she did not extend her proscription to other women. Johnson, on the other hand, argued specifically that industrial labor "unsexes [woman] and makes her unfit to become a wife and mother."[29]

The Socialist Labor Party published and endorsed Johnson's pamphlet, indicating that woman's role in the creation of the new order would be that of helpmeet, and refusing to extend a promise of equality after the revolution. Under socialism women would continue to behave in traditional ways, Johnson affirmed, since socialist women "are modest and quiet and proud of being womanly and ready for the work they can do, whatever it may be. They do not try to imitate man. Why should they? Their usefulness consists of being women! They do not aspire to the place of man. Why should they? They have . . . made a place for themselves."[30]

The Victorian gallantry of Engels, the genuine if troubled egalitarianism of Bebel, the implacable feminism of Gilman, the ambivalence of O'Hare, and the strident antifeminism of Johnson and the Socialist Labor Party—all represented socialist answers to the Woman Question. Yet some socialist women remained unsatisfied. Prominent among them were the Greenwich Village socialists, a diverse group of writers, artists, and teachers who came to the Village during the first and second decades of the twentieth century. June Sochen, in her study of Greenwich Village feminism, singled out Crystal Eastman, Neith Boyce, Susan Glaspell, and Henrietta Rodman as representative of those newly liberated socialist women. As professional women, they identified with mainstream feminism by working for suffrage, while at the same time they attempted to prod organized feminists toward socialism. Crystal Eastman possessed a broad vision of a future egalitarian society which included civic and legal equality for women, an end to job discrimination, the right of access to birth-control information, and economic independence for all women based on the socialist principle of the responsibility of the society as a whole to provide for its individual members. Henrietta Rodman, a teacher and the mainstay of the Village's Feminist Alliance, confined her activities more closely to the New York area, waging an unsuccessful battle with the New York Board of Education over the right of women with children to acquire or retain teaching jobs in the public schools. Susan Glaspell and Neith Boyce were novelists whose work centered on the difficulties faced by women struggling to survive intellectually and emotionally in contemporary society.[31]

The antidomesticity of Charlotte Perkins Gilman influenced their views on social organization; both Rodman and Eastman tried to encourage the construction of apartment houses based on the Gilmanesque model. Nevertheless, they did not share Gilman's pronounced antierotic biases. Their views of sexuality more closely resembled the attitudes of the anarchist-feminists, and the Greenwich Village socialist-feminists possessed the additional advantage of living in a social environment supportive of those views. Perhaps the most important aspect of that supportive community was the active participation of Greenwich Village men in the feminist cause. Two editors of the *Masses*, Crystal Eastman's brother Max and Floyd Dell, used that journal for vigorous advocacy of feminist issues. In it Eastman attacked American socialist men for their indifference to women's rights. "The members of the Socialist Party in America, on the whole, have been like every other group of sexually selfish men. None of them got up and actively went into the suffrage propaganda until after they saw that suffrage was coming and they would soon have to be asking for women's votes." He demanded of the socialists: "Sex Equality is a question by itself. Answer it."[32]

The *Masses* was the only male-edited socialist journal that consistently affirmed the importance of equality as essential for the full development of the lives of both men and women. In a satiric piece, Floyd Dell took up the arguments of the antifeminists. "I thought, you see, that [women] were persons like myself. Well, they aren't. I know better now." Regarding the argument of the antisuffragists that woman's biological difference from man offered convincing proof of her inability to participate in civic life, Dell conceded that "of course I knew about these things—quite intimately, indeed. I knew that women had babies, and that every twenty eight—in short, I knew. But I did not know the dreadful significance of these things. I did not know that they cut woman off forever from political and intellectual life." Now that he knew, "Give her the vote? Give her nothing." He concluded:

Neither Heroines nor Heroes 165

The [antisuffrage] pamphlets puzzle me. Having established these dark facts about woman, they tell you to cherish her, worship her, make her the queen of the kitchen and nursery and the bedroom, the consolation and delight of your life. Why, I should like to know? I can't get any consolation or delight out of that kind of creature. . . . I don't want to cherish her, I don't want to protect her. I don't want anything to do with her.[33]

Eastman took the same line. Under an egalitarian political and social system, girls

will grow up to be interested and living individuals, and satisfy their ambitions only with the highest prizes of adventure and achievement that life offers. And the benefit of that will fall upon us all—but chiefly upon the children of these women when they are mothers. . . . Only a developed and fully constituted individual is fit to be the mother of a child. Only one who has herself made the most of the present, is fit to hold in her arms the hope of the future.[34]

Because of the cooperation between men and women in feminist causes, and perhaps even more so because of the position of these Village feminists as independent professionals living in a self-consciously avant garde community, the Village feminists, to a greater extent than women in other segments of American society, succeeded in living as free and independent women in a supportive subculture without relinquishing their freedom to choose sexually active lives (with or without marriage) or to bear children. But these women, and their male allies, also recognized that behavior that was possible in Greenwich Village might be impossible in Peoria.[35] In their unique environment was the secret of their success and of their inability to transplant that success to the rest of the nation. Sochen argued that in the long run:

Their failures . . . were greater than their successes. As they became more unique, so they became more unsuccessful. . . . Their uniqueness took them further away from majority interests and concerns. As they devised bold new feminist schemes, they lost touch with most women and men around them.[36]

Although each of the four versions of socialist womanhood illustrated here possessed distinct features, they might be placed into two categories, Mavericks and Conformists. The Mavericks—the Gilmanesque and Greenwich Village socialists—placed feminism at the heart of their visions of the future, their socialism in large measure deriving from a belief that only a socialist society could create the material conditions necessary to bring about sexual equality. On the other hand, Conformist socialist women—if Kate O'Hare and Olive Johnson represented the dominant views of the women of the Socialist Party of America and the Socialist Labor Party—believed that the Woman Question was not a central issue. For Johnson it was less important than for O'Hare, and while both endorsed woman suffrage, they also believed that the problems of class demanded far greater attention than those of sex. In placing class at the center of their analysis, the Conformists followed the advice of Engels and Bebel, who despite their keen and sympathetic analysis of sex-based oppression did not countenance special programs or separate organizations for women. The Mavericks, on the other hand, more closely resembled the anarchist-feminists in their willingness to take the theoretical analyses of Bebel and Engels far beyond the intentions of the two men.

In the final analysis, neither socialism nor anarchism, emerging as they did from an intellectual world dominated by men, considered sexual equality to be of the first importance. Among the anarchists, none of the principal theoreticians gave much attention to the Woman Question, and the men of the rank-and-file followed suit. Proudhon himself believed that the future society without laws required the patriarchal family structure in order to preserve social control. And Kropotkin argued that feminists should not intrude such parochial issues as female subordination into the primary question of (male) working-class liberation. Nevertheless, despite a lack of specific theoretical consideration from male theorists, anarchist-feminists could rely on the simple proposition, which lay at the center of all anarchist thought, that every individual possessed the right to complete liberty, limited only by a moral obligation not to encroach on the freedom of others. As a result, although anarchism was by no means an expressly feminist ideology, it had the capacity to become so.

Because the principal ideologues of anarchism had little to say on the Woman Question, the anarchist-feminists faced a theoretical vacuum and thus had the opportunity to analyze the doctrine of absolute liberty as it applied to women without having to reinterpret established anarchist sacred texts. Their ideological fluidity enabled them to move quickly beyond the issues of legal and economic inequality, both in the larger society and inside the family circle, to the question of the role of the nuclear family in maintaining women's intellectual and psychological dependence on men. Such a focus led them to place fundamental importance on the economic independence of women less for financial reasons than because it would allow women to function as fully developed human beings—intellectually, emotionally, and not least erotically—outside the confines of the nuclear family. Because of this the long-range implications of anarchist-feminism included the eventual destruction of institutions cherished by many radicals as well as non-radicals. The nuclear family as the dominant form of household arrangement would cease to exist, and its function as the principal institution for the socialization of children would come to an end. The abolition of the traditional role of woman as homemaker in the psychological and spiritual sense would follow from the dissolution of the family. Women would no longer bear the primary responsibility for nurturing children, or for providing emotional sustenance within domestic relationships, or for acting as the dispenser of the physical comforts of domesticity.

Whether or not the anarchist-feminists themselves fully realized the implications of their ideology, they did believe that their proposals would restructure relationships at all levels between the sexes and between adults and children. In their insistence on placing the domestic relationship at the heart of their analysis of female subordination, the anarchist-feminists offered the greatest sexual challenge to the nineteenth century. The century refused to take it up, although in the hysteria that greeted anarchism one senses at least a subliminal recognition of the profundity of its threat to the established patterns. At the level of rational discourse, however, the anarchist-feminists found it difficult to gain a foothold, even among radical women. This was not only because the anarchist-feminists failed to develop a sustained feminist analysis which would encompass the problems of class conflict, poverty, and violence in the society as a whole, but also because they, unlike the socialists, were unable to provide an organizational framework for their feminism.

As the strength of anarchist-feminism rested in its recognition of the primacy of the domestic relationship in the perpetuation of sexual inequality, so the great strength of socialist-feminism lay in its ability to provide a coherent integrated analysis of social problems and a suitable institutional framework for dealing with them. If the anarchist description of the problem was more profound, the socialist solution seemed not only less frightening but also more readily achievable. Socialist-feminists argued that socialism promised tangible benefits to women: it would free them from domestic drudgery by allowing them to participate equally in productive and rewarding labor; recognize childbearing as a service to society; compensate financially those women who wished to remain at home to rear their children and provide child care for those who did not; and remove the economic dependence of women on their spouses. Further, until socialism arrived, socialist-feminists could feel comfortable in supporting those bourgeois reform movements aimed at removing some of the burdens women carried in a world both class-dominated and ruled by men. Consequently, socialist-feminists actively supported woman suffrage, and many of them worked for protective legislation for children and women workers. Often they cooperated with mainstream feminists. In short, socialist-feminism could offer both attainable short-term goals and long-range promises. It relied on organized society to solve the problems of inequalities of the work place. What the socialist-feminists lacked, at least in the United States, was an ability to look beyond economic changes, to confront the emotional and spiritual issues adressed by the anarchist-feminists.

No American socialist-feminist successfully integrated the anarchist-feminist analysis of domestic oppression into a socialist framework; even the Greenwich Village socialists, who combined Gilman's antidomesticity with a demand for sexual liberation, did not come to terms with the implications of such a combination. Nevertheless, a socialist framework existed, in the work of Aleksandra Kollontai. Kollontai, a Russian Marxist revolutionary who participated in the birth of the Bolshevik state, wrote her most extensive analysis of the Woman Question while in exile in Western Europe in the years immediately preceding World War I.[37] Following Bebel and Engels, Kollontai argued that the first requisite for women's emancipation was productive work outside the confines of the domestic circle. However, participation in the work force would not free women unless there were also changes in the industrial system. Ultimately, of course, the workers must overthrow capitalism, Kollontai declared. But, more immediately, socialists should work for shorter hours, less dangerous working conditions, paid maternity leaves, nursery facilities in all factories, and scheduled breaks from work so that mothers could breast feed their babies.[38]

Not all socialists agreed with Kollontai on the above issues. Most men and some women refused to countenance the urging of special reforms for women because they believed it undermined the solidarity of the proletariat. But Kollontai further extended her analysis of female oppression to include an attack on the emotional dependence of women upon men. Barbara Clements has shown that for Kollontai "woman's inferiority was imbedded in the pattern of erotic love, the most private of human relationships." Socialism for her, therefore, was more than the overthrow of capitalism as an economic system. It promised the creation of a new order in which men and women could live together and love in harmony and in community.[39] Clements has demonstrated Kollontai's unique place within Marxism:

> Other contemporaries, most eloquently Virginia Woolf but also feminists such as the Pankhursts, knew the price of female emancipation, but of the Marxists, only Kollontai gave it a place within the ideology. Into a socioeconomic theory that valued rationality as the road to social liberation, Kollontai introduced an emotional understanding of woman alone in an isolating world.[40]

Kollontai's emphasis on psychological and emotional liberation was remarkably similar to American anarchist-feminism, but she differed in her insistence on integrating these issues into an uncompromising materialist analysis. She believed that "solitude and women's struggle for independence [were] economically determined and therefore . . . soluble. She remained resolutely an ideologue and an optimist."[41] Kollontai's analysis in the pre-World War I years did not find its way into the work of American socialist-feminists, and it is not clear that they would have accepted her views had they been exposed to them. Nevertheless, her integration of the most important aspects of anarchist-feminism into socialist ideology offered a tantalizing possibility for the creation of a truly feminist radicalism. That the promise remains to be fulfilled does not detract from her accomplishment.

Conclusion

Enough! or Too much.

William Blake

The anarchist women who appear in these pages represent but a handful of the numerous feminists who challenged, in various ways, traditional notions about woman's place in late-nineteenth- and early-twentieth-century America. Their significance rests not on the smallness of their numbers nor their relatively limited impact on feminist contemporaries but on the way in which they shed light on two larger issues. The first of these is historical and has to do with the ways in which women responded to and helped to shape some of the forces which changed the patterns and processes of American society: the alterations in habits of work and leisure that accompanied industrialization; the erosion of women's traditional functions that occurred with factory production; and the changes in family life that emerged with an urbanizing culture. The goal of this text has been to examine the responses of women who advocated positions widely regarded as extreme, with the hope of coming to grips with the question of the degree to which an individual might repudiate conventional attitudes and habits of behavior in order to find solutions to social problems without totally severing the bonds that connected her to the larger community. The second issue concerns a question of perhaps greater importance to twentieth-century feminists: What are the institutions that need to be changed, and in what direction, in order to create a sexually egalitarian society?

The anarchist-feminists of the late nineteenth century articulated and practiced an ideology that set them at odds with contemporaries on the questions of the sanctity of marriage, the inviolability of the maternal instinct, and the idea of the family as a refuge from a hostile and chaotic outside world. Their attacks on marriage and the family, set in the context of a liberated female sexuality, alienated them not only from most feminists but also from many of their male comrades. Yet they persisted in their refusal to be bound by convention, pushing vigorously against the constraints that defined the limits of acceptable nonconformity. Occasionally they received the support of younger men and women, who in the years preceding World War I began to feel stifled by the strictures of their elders. But more often they struggled at great personal cost against both external circumstances and inner conflict, illustrating the extent to which their liberation was limited by the culture they shared with their less iconoclastic sisters.

Anarchist women faced their most intense external opposition—from nonanarchists and from certain segments of the anarchist community—when they argued for absolute economic independence from men; for sexual varietism with its implicit denial of emotional possession; and for the proposition that men and women were essentially the same psychologically and intellectually, a premise that negated the belief in a female nurturing instinct. Their most serious inner conflicts arose from their rejection of the domestic relationship. Voltairine de Cleyre, for example, in anguish over what she viewed as a propensity toward jealousy, ended an important relationship because she felt unable to conquer her possessiveness. And Helena Born anxiously weighed a decision to acknowledge her liaison with a married comrade, both because of her inner conflict and out of a fear of criticism. At a more general level, there was the positive reception accorded William Morris's *News from Nowhere*, an anarchist utopian novel in which women possess both equality and a natural predilection for the tasks of domesticity. The lack of anarchist-feminist criticism of Morris's novel may be puzzling

Conclusion 173

until one realizes that these women, often isolated in their struggle against the norms of society and the strictures of their own upbringing, must have yearned, at least occasionally, for the simplicity of a definition of social roles based on "nature." These examples illustrate the ways in which the common culture continued to influence the anarchist-feminists. In the final analysis, it seems that it is not possible to pioneer in violating the norms of the society without having feelings of ambivalence, perhaps even of guilt. What is important is that despite these feelings the anarchist-feminists transcended those norms to a significant extent in order to create a vision of a new society that would provide satisfying, meaningful, and fundamentally different social roles for women.

At the center of anarchist-feminist ideology—and a reason for its hostile reception—was its insistence that the roots of sexual inequality were embedded in the nuclear family. Only by abolishing it, they argued, could the society demonstrate its commitment to eradicating female subordination. This analysis takes on particular significance for late-twentieth-century feminists, who have witnessed the triumph of the suffrage amendment, the extraordinary growth of women in the work force (albeit with serious inequality in wages), and the inclusion of women in federal and some state antidiscrimination laws, but yet have not seen an end to sexual inequality. The mainstream feminists of the late nineteenth and early twentieth centuries reasoned that without political clout equality was impossible; the mainstream feminists of the mid-twentieth century contended that without equal economic opportunity women would remain subordinate. Political power, legal rights, and access to economic opportunity, it might be argued, are essential preconditions to equality, but they do not constitute the thing itself. As long as women, because they are women, are principally responsible for the nurturing functions within the family and are the primary caretakers of children, their choices as human beings will remain more circumscribed than those of men. The anarchist-feminists made their most radical contribution by declaring that if gender distinctions ought not to inhibit women from participating in the economic and political life of the society, neither were they valid in determining roles within our most intimate institutions. They maintained that if we are ever to build an egalitarian society, differences in roles—whether in sexual relationships, childrearing, political life, or work—must be based on capacity and preference, not on gender.

Appendix: Women as Activists

It has been the concern of this study not only to identify characteristics common to anarchist women but also, insofar as possible, to find out what distinguished anarchist women from other activists. This analysis does not pretend to be scientific. Rather, qualitative evidence has been organized in a quantitative manner. First, ten anarchist women were chosen, not on a random basis but because they were women about whom sufficient biographical information was available. Next, using *Notable American Women*[1] as a reference source, a random sample of ten women was selected from each of the following categories: socialist, mainstream suffragists, and labor organizer/reformer. These women were categorized by class, ethnicity, family size, father's occupation, mother's occupation, their own occupations, marital status, and number of children, as well as by certain attitudinal variables and by their own social mobility. The generalizations that appear in Chapter 2 are derived from the information provided by this sample of forty. Although it was a small sample, statistical analysis was done by computer, relying most heavily on chi-square and discriminant function analysis.[2]

The tables at the end of this appendix summarize the major findings. Following immediately is a list of the women in each category. Within each group, some of the names are very familiar, others less so.

Appendix

Anarchists

Margaret Anderson
Helena Born
Voltairine de Cleyre
Marie Ganz
Emma Goldman
Florence Finch Kelly
Marie L.
Mollie Steimer
Lois Waisbrooker
Victoria Woodhull

Mainstream Suffragists

Susan B. Anthony
Ada M. C. Bittenbender
Lillie Devereaux Blake
Laura Clay
Clara Colby
Phoebe Couzins
Ida A. H. Harper
Marilla Marks Ricker
Nettie Rogers Shuler
Lila Valentine

Socialists

Martha Gallison Moore Avery
Elizabeth Glendower Evans
Charlotte Perkins Gilman
Elizabeth Gilman
Carrie Herron
Florence Kelley
Helen Marst
Caroline Amanda Sherfy Rand
Ellen Starr
Rose Pastor Stokes

Labor Activists

Leonora M. K. Barry
Jennie Collins
"Mother" Jones
Kate Kennedy
Agnes Nestor
Lenora O'Reilly
Mary K. O'Sullivan
Elizabeth Flynn Rodgers
Alzena Stevens
Maud O'Farrell Swartz

TABLE 1. Women Activists by Place of Birth

Type	Born in U.S.		Born in Northern or Western Europe		Born in Southern or Eastern Europe		Total
	No.	%	No.	%	No.	%	
Anarchist	6	60	1	10	3	30	10
Socialist	9	90	0	0	1	10	10
Mainstream feminist	9	90	1	10	0	0	10
Labor activist	5	50	5	50	0	0	10

Total in sample: 40.
Total in Table: 40.
Chi-square significant at 0.01.
Note: Due to rounding, not all percentages equal 100.

TABLE 2. Women Activists by Ethnic Background of Father

Type	Father born in U.S.		Father born in Northern or Western Europe		Father born in Southern or Eastern Europe		Total
	No.	%	No.	%	No.	%	
Anarchist	4	44.4	2	22.3	3	33.3	9
Socialist	9	90.0	0	0	1	10.0	10
Mainstream feminist	7	70.0	3	30.0	0	0	10
Labor activist	1	11.1	8	88.9	0	0	9

Total in sample: 40.
Total in Table: 38.
Chi-square significant at 0.005.
Note: Due to rounding, not all percentages equal 100.

TABLE 3. Women Activists by Ethnic Background of Mother

Type	Mother born in U.S.		Mother born in Northern or Western Europe		Mother born in Southern or Eastern Europe		Total
	No.	%	No.	%	No.	%	
Anarchist	4	44.4	2	22.2	3	33.3	9
Socialist	8	88.9	0	0	1	11.1	9
Mainstream feminist	8	80.0	2	20.0	0	0	10
Labor activist	2	22.2	7	77.8	0	0	9

Total in sample: 40.
Total in Table: 37.
Chi-square significant at 0.005.
Note: Due to rounding, not all percentages equal 100.

Appendix

TABLE 4. Comparative Educational Levels for Women Activists

Type	Elementary education or lower		Female seminary or equivalent		College or professional school		Total
	No.	%	No.	%	No.	%	
Anarchist	6	60.0	2	20.0	2	20.0	10
Socialist	1	11.1	3	33.3	5	55.6	9
Mainstream feminist	0	0	6	60.0	4	40.0	10
Labor activist	4	44.4	5	55.5	0	0	9

Total in sample: 40.
Total in Table: 38.
Chi-square significant at 0.01.
Due to rounding, not all percentages equal 100.

TABLE 5. Women Activists by Social Class

Type	Lower class		Skilled working and lower middle class		Middle class		Upper middle		Upper class		Total
	No.	%	No.	%	No.	%	No.	%	No.	%	
Anarchist	5	50	1	10	2	20	2	20	0	0	10
Socialist	2	20	0	0	1	10	5	50	2	20	10
Mainstream feminist	0	0	0	0	7	70	0	0	3	30	10
Labor activist	2	20	7	70	1	10	0	0	0	0	10

Total in sample: 40.
Total in Table: 40.
Chi-square significant at 0.0000.
Due to rounding, not all percentages equal 100.

TABLE 6. Women Activists According to Earliest Known Occupation

Type	Semilegitimate		Unskilled, semiskilled, or service		Skilled		Lower nonmanual or semiprofessional		Volunteer social service		Professional		Total
	No.	%	No.	%	No.	%	No.	%	No.	%	No.	%	
Anarchist	1	10.0	4	40.0	0	0	0	0	1	10.0	4	40.0	10
Socialist	0	0	1	11.1	0	0	1	11.1	2	22.2	5	55.6	9
Mainstream feminist	0	0	0	0	0	0	0	0	3	30.0	7	70.0	10
Labor activist	0	0	6	60.0	2	20.0	1	10.0	0	0	1	10.0	10

Total in sample: 40.
Total in Table: 39.
Chi-square significant at 0.03.
Due to rounding, not all percentages equal 100.

TABLE 7. Women Activists According to Last Known Occupation

Type	Unskilled, semiskilled, or service		Skilled		Lower nonmanual or semiprofessional		Volunteer social service		Professional		Total
	No.	%	No.	%	No.	%	No.	%	No.	%	
Anarchist	3	33.3	1	11.1	1	11.1	0	0	4	44.4	9
Socialist	0	0	0	0	0	0	5	50.0	5	50.0	10
Mainstream feminist	0	0	0	0	0	0	3	30.0	7	70.0	10
Labor activist	0	0	4	40.0	0	0	0	0	6	60.0	10

Total in sample: 40.
Total in Table: 39.
Chi-square significant at 0.005.
Due to rounding, not all percentages equal 100.

TABLE 8. Attitudes Toward Violence

Type	Unqualified approval		Approval of retaliatory violence		Nonviolent		Total
	No.	%	No.	%	No.	%	
Anarchists	3	30	3	30	4	40	10
Socialists	0	0	1	10	9	90	10
Mainstream feminists	0	0	0	0	10	100	10
Labor activists	0	0	1	10	9	90	10

Total in sample: 40.
Total in Table: 40.
Chi-square significant at 0.016.
Due to rounding, not all percentages equal 100.

TABLE 9. Marital and Sexual Behavior

Type	No identifiable sexual liaisons with men or women		Conventional marriage		Unconventional patterns		Total
	No.	%	No.	%	No.	%	
Anarchist	0	0	0	0	10	100	10
Socialist	3	30	3	30	4	40	10
Mainstream feminist	3	30	5	50	2	20	10
Labor activist	4	40	4	40	2	20	10

Total in sample: 40.
Total in Table: 40.
Chi-square significant at 0.0067.
Due to rounding, not all percentages equal 100.

Notes

Introduction

1. George Woodcock, *Anarchism: A History of Libertarian Ideas and Movements* (New York: World Publishing Co., 1962), p. 17.
2. David de Leon, *The American as Anarchist* (Baltimore: Johns Hopkins University Press, 1978), esp. pp. 9–10, 18–21, 24–25, 37–39.
3. Shulamith Firestone, *The Dialectic of Sex: The Case for Feminist Revolution* (New York: Bantam Books, 1971).

Chapter 1

1. *Red Ruin; or the Romance of Anarchy* (New York: Richard K. Fox, 1888), pp. 55–56.
2. Dyer D. Lum to Voltairine de Cleyre, May 4, 1892, Houghton Library, Harvard University, Cambridge, Mass.
3. The quote is from Philip Foner, *The Haymarket Autobiographies* (New York: Humanities Press, 1969), p. 8. The most extensive treatment of Haymarket remains Henry David, *The History of the Haymarket Affair* (New York: Russell and Russell, 1936).

4. Richard Ely, "Socialism in America," *North American Review* 355 (June 1886): 523.

5. On Berkman's and Czolgosz's assassination attempts, see Richard Drinnon, *Rebel in Paradise* (Boston: Beacon Press, 1961), pp. 49–54, 68, 76; on the Lexington Avenue bombing, see *New York Times*, July 5, 1914, sec. II, p. 2; and Will Durant, *Transition* (New York: Simon and Schuster, 1927), pp. 206–13, which offers an account of the bombing thinly disguised as fiction. (Paul Avrich's forthcoming book on the Modern School Movement [Princeton: Princeton University Press, 1980] will deal with the Lexington Avenue bombing.)

6. George Woodcock, *Anarchism: A History of Libertarian Ideas and Movements* (New York: World Publishing Company, 1962), p. 17; *Public Opinion*, May 15, 1888, pp. 81–87, reprinted editorial reaction to the Haymarket bombing. The quotes are from the *Chicago Tribune*, p. 82, and the *New York Tribune*, p. 83. Their views were representative of the newspapers whose editorials were reprinted here.

7. Estimates of anarchist strength by nonanarchist contemporaries ranged from a conservative 15,000 to upwards of 200,000; see Richard Ely, "Socialism," p. 523; Herbert Osgood, "Scientific Anarchism," *Political Science Quarterly* 4 (March 1889): 18, 31.

8. Woodcock, *Anarchism*, pp. 165–71, 178–81. The Communist-anarchists descended intellectually from the Collectivists.

9. James J. Martin, *Men Against the State* (Colorado Springs: Ralph Myles, 1970), pp. 213–15. Martin's is still the best treatment of the Individualists although William O. Reichert, *Partisans of Freedom* (Bowling Green, Ohio: Popular Press, 1978), also deals with Tucker and the others.

10. Martin, *Men Against the State*, pp. 15–19, 43, 51. The anarchist William Bailie wrote a biography of Warren entitled *Josiah Warren, the First American Anarchist* (Boston: Small, Maynard and Co., 1906); for Warren's communitarianism, see Michael Fellman, *The Unbounded Frame* (Westport, Conn.: Greenwood Press, 1973), pp. 9–19; on Proudhon, see Woodcock, *Anarchism*, pp. 106–45.

11. Martin, *Men Against the State*; David de Leon, *The American as Anarchist* (Baltimore: Johns Hopkins Press, 1978), p. 61 ff.; De Leon's dissertation, also entitled "The American as Anarchist" (Ph.D. diss., University of Iowa, 1972), esp. pp. 238–39; Billie Jean Stephenson, "The Ideology of American Anarchism" (Ph.D. diss., University of Iowa, 1972), pp. 139–41. Benjamin F. Tucker, *Instead of a Book* (New York: Haskell House, 1969; reprint of 1897 edition), is a compilation of *Liberty* columns covering most aspects of Individualism. The Individualists themselves did not publish very systematically.

12. These women are discussed fully in Chapter 2.
13. The Collectivists developed a differential distribution of goods, while the Communist-anarchists expected that one's support by the community would not be tied to one's labor. The difference is well explained in Martin A. Miller, *Kropotkin* (Chicago: University of Chicago Press, 1976), pp. 194–95; D. Novak, "The Place of Anarchism in the History of Political Thought," *Patterns of Anarchy,* ed. L. I. Krimmerman and Lewis Perry (New York: Doubleday, 1966), p. 10.
14. Woodcock, *Anarchism,* p. 461.
15. *Liberty* 1 (Oct. 15, 1881): 1; *Liberty* 1 (Nov. 26, 1881); Martin, *Men Against the State,* pp. 213–14.
16. Chester M. Destler, *American Radicalism, 1865–1901* (New York: Octagon Books, 1963), pp. 78–104; Martin, *Men Against the State,* p. 216. Sometimes anarchists called themselves "Voluntary Socialists," as distinct from Marxian "State Socialists." The imprecision of terms before the late eighties reflects a certain ideological fluidity.
17. Miller, *Kropotkin,* esp. pp. 183–98; Terry M. Perlin, "Anarchist-Communism in America, 1890–1914" (Ph.D. diss., Brandeis University, 1970), discusses the maturation of Communist-anarchism.
18. Chapter 2 contains a more elaborate discussion of class and ethnicity, based on some statistical as well as impressionistic evidence. Several contemporary essays assessed the class, ethnic, and geographical patterns of anarchism; see especially R. Warren Conant, "Anarchism at Close Quarters," *Arena* 28 (Oct. 1902): 338-45; R. Heber-Newton, "Political, Economic, and Religious Causes of Anarchism," *Arena* 27 (Feb. 1902): 113-15; Washington Gladden, "The Philosophy of Anarchism," *Outlook* 69 (Oct. 1901): 449–54.
19. Drinnon, *Rebel in Paradise,* p. 314. Drinnon's work on Goldman, including not only *Rebel* but also his introduction to Goldman's own *Anarchism and Other Essays* (New York: Dover reprint, 1969), and his *Nowhere at Home* (New York: Schocken Books, 1975), which he edited with Maria Drinnon, is excellent. Goldman wrote her autobiography, *Living My Life* (New York: Dover Press, 1970; first published 1931).
20. There is no biography of Berkman; for information about him, see Drinnon, *Rebel in Paradise,* esp. pp. 39–42, 232–39, 291–300; Drinnon and Drinnon, eds., *Nowhere at Home;* Goldman, *Living My Life,* esp. pp. 5, 26, 96, 292–94, 323, 615-22; and Berkman's own *Prison Memoirs of an Anarchist* (New York: Mother Earth, 1912).
21. On the Populists as radicals, see Norman Pollock, *The Populist Response to Industrial America* (New York: Norton, 1966); Edward Bellamy, *Looking Backward* (New York: New American Library, 1969).

22. Michael Shatz, ed., *The Essential Works of Anarchism* (New York: Quadrangle, 1972), p. xx; Woodcock, *Anarchism,* pp. 25–26; Richard King, *The Party of Eros* (New York: Dell, 1973), p. 35.

23. Miller, *Kropotkin,* p. 194; Henry David Thoreau, *Walden and Civil Disobedience, the Variorem Editions* (New York: Washington Square Press, 1968), especially "Sounds," pp. 83–96; Henry Adams, *The Education of Henry Adams* (New York: The Modern Library, 1931), particularly, but not only, the famous "The Dynamo and the Virgin," pp. 379–90. In Barry Commoner's recent treatise, *The Politics of Energy* (New York: Alfred A. Knopf, 1979), decentralist arguments similar to those of the anarchists appear in a context reminiscent of some of Kropotkin's technological views.

24. Martin, *Men Against the State,* pp. 113–17, 133–34; Woodcock, *Anarchism,* p. 460.

25. Woodcock, *Anarchism,* p. 121. Marx added insult to his critique of Proudhon's *System of Economic Contradictions, or the Philosophy of Poverty* by entitling his attack on it *The Poverty of Philosophy*.

26. An interesting analysis of the differences between Marxism and anarchism from a structural approach is in Robert Nisbet, *The Social Philosophers* (New York: T. Y. Crowell, 1973), pp. 280–92, 319–20, 354–82. David Shannon, *The Socialist Party of America* (New York: MacMillan, 1955), remains a very good survey of American socialism. A good compilation of arguments from different viewpoints is John H. M. Laslett and Seymour Martin Lipset, eds., *Failure of a Dream? Essays in the History of American Socialism* (New York: Doubleday, 1974).

27. Floyd Dell, *Homecoming* (Port Washington, N.Y.: Kennikat Press, 1969; first published in 1933), pp. 182–83. For Sanger and the anarchists, see Emma Goldman's letters to Sanger, March 9, 1914, March 21, 1914, and Dec. 7, 1915, Library of Congress; James Reed, *From Private Vice to Public Virtue* (New York: Basic Books, 1978), pp. 48–52.

Chapter 2

1. Robert Nisbet, *The Social Philosophers* (New York: T. Y. Crowell, 1973), pp. 367–68; *Alarm,* Aug. 18, 1888.

2. *New York Times,* July 19, 1888, p. 4; *Public Opinion,* May 14, 1888, p. 82.

3. See Appendix.

4. The Appendix lists the women in other movements used for comparison with the anarchist women.

Notes

5. Florence Finch Kelly's autobiography, *Flowing Stream* (New York: E. P. Dutton, 1939), discusses her involvement with the anarchists (pp. 190–97) and offers a somewhat different view of her anarchist phase than either *Frances: A Story for Men and Women* (New York: Sanfred and Company, 1889) or *On the Inside* (New York: Sanfred and Company, 1890). For representative articles, see *Liberty* 2 (Aug. 23, 1884): 4; *Liberty* 5 (Feb. 15, 1888): 4; and *Liberty* 5 (March 31, 1888): 5.
6. Kelly, *Flowing Stream*, p. 195.
7. This aspect of anarchist-feminism is explored fully in Chapter 3.
8. See especially Kelly, *On the Inside*, pp. 61, 176–78, 181.
9. *Liberty* 5 (May 12, 1888): 6–7; *Liberty* 8 (Nov. 29, 1891): 1; *Liberty* 8 (Oct. 31, 1891): 1.
10. Kelly, *Flowing Stream*, p. 196.
11. Helena Born's papers, including letters and scrapbooks, are in New York University's Tamiment Collection. Helen Tufts (Bailie) wrote a short biography of her as a preface to Born's *Whitman's Ideal Democracy* (Boston: Everett Press, 1902). See also letters from Bertha Johnson to Agnes Inglis, September 1933, Labadie Collection, University of Michigan.
12. Born's scrapbooks, Tamiment.
13. Born, *Whitman's Ideal Democracy*, p. xviii.
14. Ibid., p. xxxv.
15. Ibid., p. xxxi.
16. The career of Voltairine de Cleyre is analyzed in Chapter 6.
17. Born, *Whitman's Ideal Democracy*, p. xvx.
18. Ibid., p. xxxiv.
19. Helena Born to William Bailie, June 20, 1898, and Sept. 28, 1898; Born, *Whitman's Ideal Democracy*, p. 9.
20. Marie Ganz's autobiography is *Rebels—Into Anarchy and Out Again* (New York: Dodd, Mead and Co., 1920); see also Nat Ferber, *I Found Out: A Confidential Chronicle of the Twenties* (New York: Dial Press, 1939), pp. 49–59, 90–97; *New York Times*, May 1–9, 1914, July 5, 1914, p. 2; Richard and Maria Drinnon, eds., *Nowhere at Home* (New York: Schocken Books, 1975), pp. 148–49, 153, 159.
21. Irving Howe, *World of Our Fathers* (New York: Simon and Schuster, 1976), pp. 124–25.
22. Ganz, *Rebels*, pp. 88–89.
23. In her autobiography, Ganz mentioned nothing of the years 1906–1914.
24. Ganz, *Rebels*, p. 119.
25. Ibid., pp. 183–89; *New York Times*, May 1, 1914, p. 4.

imes, May 3, 1914, sec. 3, p. 3; Ganz, *Rebels*, pp. ̰ information for Mollie Steimer's life comes from per-̰dence, 1978–79; also Zoza Szajkowski, "Double Jeopardy—̰s Case of 1919," *American Jewish Archives*, Apr. 1971, pp. 6–32; ̰al Relief Committee, *Sentenced to Twenty Years Prison* (New York: ̰olitical Relief Committee, n.d.) (pamphlet).

28. Mollie Steimer to Margaret Marsh, Jan. 15, 1978.
29. *Twenty Years Prison*, p. 9.
30. Szajkowski, "Double Jeopardy," p. 25.
31. Steimer to Marsh, Jan. 15, 1978.
32. Szajkowski, "Double Jeopardy," p. 15.
33. Steimer to Marsh, Jan. 15, 1978.
34. Hutchins Hapgood, *An Anarchist Woman* (New York: Duffield, 1909), and Hapgood, *Spirit of Labor* (New York: Duffield, 1907), are both important for an understanding of Hapgood's relationship with the anarchists. His autobiography, *A Victorian in the Modern World* (New York: Harcourt, Brace, and World, 1939), pp. 199–201, discusses the writing of *An Anarchist Woman*.
35. Hapgood, *An Anarchist Woman*, p. 101.
36. Ibid., pp. 106–07.
37. Ibid., p. 304.
38. Biographical information on Margaret Anderson is in her autobiographies, *My Thirty Years War* (London: Alfred A. Knopf, 1930); *The Fiery Fountains* (New York: Horizon, 1970); *The Strange Necessity* (New York: Horizon, 1970); and in Albert Parry, *Garrets and Pretenders* (New York: Dover, 1969; reprint of 1933 edition), pp. 197–99. See reviews of *Thirty Years War* in *Road to Freedom* 1 (Sept. 1930): 5; *Bookman* 2 (Aug. 1930): 566; and *Nation* 130 (June 18, 1930): 707; and a review of all her works in *New York Times Book Review*, Aug. 16, 1970, p. 1 ff.
39. Anderson, *Thirty Years War*, pp. 126–28, 133–35, 188–90, 195–96.
40. Ibid., p. 74.
41. Ibid., pp. 133–35; *Road to Freedom* 1 (Sept. 1930).
42. Anderson, *Thirty Years War*, p. 231.
43. Ibid., p. 138.
44. These observations on anarchist women are impressionistic conclusions drawn from reading the following anarchist periodicals, especially during the years listed: *Lucifer*, 1894–1906; *Liberty*, 1883–1889; *The Alarm*, 1886–1887; and *Mother Earth*, 1906–1916; *Road to Freedom* 3 (Sept. 1, 1926) on Lizzie Holmes and *Tomorrow* (Oct. 1906) on Lois Waisbrooker.

Chapter 3

1. On anarchism, James J. Martin, *Men Against the State* (Colorado Springs: Ralph Myles, 1970); Eunice Minette Schuster, *Native American Anarchists: Smith College Studies in History* 17 (Oct. 1931–July 1932); Terry M. Perlin, "Anarchist-Communism in America, 1890–1914" (Ph.D. diss., Brandeis University, 1970).

2. Kathryn Kish Sklar, *Catharine Beecher: A Study in American Domesticity* (New Haven: Yale University Press, 1973), p. 137; Robin Miller Jacoby, "Feminism and Class Consciousness in the British and American Trade Union Leagues, 1890–1925," in *Liberating Women's History*, ed. by Bernice Carroll (Chicago: University of Illinois Press, 1976), pp. 137–38.

3. Blanche Glassman Hersh, *The Slavery of Sex* (Chicago: University of Illinois Press, 1978), is a very good analysis of the relationship between feminism and abolitionism.

4. Ellen du Bois, *Feminism and Suffrage* (Ithaca, N.Y.: Cornell University Press, 1978), p. 46.

5. Ibid., pp. 197, 184; on p. 197 du Bois mentions Thomas Wentworth Higginson's denial that suffrage would cause social disruptions, which he proclaimed at the first convention of the American Woman Suffrage Association, but du Bois's position seems to be that suffrage remained a radical demand.

6. Susan B. Anthony, "Social Purity," in *The American Sisterhood*, ed. by Wendy Martin (New York: Harper and Row, 1972), p. 91; Elizabeth Cady Stanton et al., eds., *History of Woman Suffrage*, vol. 3, 1876–1885 (New York: Arno Press, 1969; reprint of 1886 edition), p. 78.

7. William O'Neill, *Everyone Was Brave* (New York: Quadrangle, 1969), pp. 5–7, 31–38; Aileen Kraditor, *Ideas of the Woman Suffrage Movement* (New York: Columbia University Press, 1965), pp. 56–74.

8. Wendy Martin, ed., *The American Sisterhood* (New York: Harper and Row), pp. 91, 208; Charlotte Perkins Gilman, *Woman and Social Service* (Warren, Ohio: NAWSA, 1912), p. 9 (pamphlet); Sklar, *Beecher*, esp. pp. 171–82.

9. *Liberty* 9 (Jan. 24, 1891): 3; *Liberty* 5 (May 12, 1888): 7; *Alarm*, Aug. 25, 1888. Representative selections of the work of the Grimkés and Fuller are reprinted in Aileen Kraditor, ed., *Up from the Pedestal* (Chicago: Quadrangle, 1968), pp. 53-71. The quote from Sarah Grimké is from Miriam Schnier, ed., *Feminism: The Essential Historical Writings* (New York: Vintage Books, 1972), p. 38.

10. *Liberty* 4 (March 12, 1887): 8; *Liberty* 3 (Jan. 23, 1886): 7.

11. *Alarm* (June 23, 1888); letter from Voltairine de Cleyre to her mother, Jan. 13, 1893, Labadie Collection, University of Michigan; *Mother Earth* 7 (Oct. 1912): 266, 264.

12. *Liberty* 5 (May 26, 1888): 6–7; *Liberty* 6 (Sept. 15, 1888): 7–8; *Liberty* 5 (June 23, 1888): 5–6.

13. *Liberty* 5 (March 31, 1888): 5.

14. The analysis of anarchist women is in Chapter 2.

15. *Liberty* 5 (Feb. 25, 1888): 4.

16. Voltairine de Cleyre, "Sex Slavery," in her *Selected Works* (New York: Mother Earth, 1914), pp. 348–49; Lois Waisbrooker, *Nothing Like It* (Boston: Colby and Rich, 1875), pp. 178–79; *Liberty* 3 (Jan. 9, 1886): 7; see also *Alarm*, March 10, 1888, and Aug. 25, 1888.

17. "Sex Slavery," p. 349; *Liberty* 3 (Jan. 23, 1886): 7; *Liberty* 5 (Feb. 25, 1888): 4.

18. *Liberty* 5 (May 12, 1888): 6, the emphasis is added; *Alarm*, Aug. 18, 1888.

19. *Liberty* 5 (May 12, 1888): 6–7; *Liberty* 5 (Sept. 15, 1888): 7; Linda Gordon, "Voluntary Motherhood: The Beginnings of Feminist Birth Control Ideas in the United States," in Mary Hartman and Lois Banner, eds., *Clio's Consciousness Raised* (New York: Harper and Row, 1974), p. 67. Gordon expands this argument in her book, *Woman's Body, Woman's Right* (New York: Grossman, 1976).

20. *Liberty* 8 (Nov. 21, 1891): 1. In *Liberty* 8 (Oct. 31, 1891): 1, Tucker urged women, if they wished to find employment at all, to bargain with employers to work for lower wages than men were commanding.

21. Emma Goldman, *Living My Life* (New York: Dover Publications, 1970), esp. pp. 34–35; see also Joseph Labadie's letter in *Liberty* 5 (Feb. 23, 1889); see Hutchins Hapgood, *A Victorian in the Modern World* (New York: Harcourt, Brace and World, 1939), pp. 330–31, as well as his *An Anarchist Woman* (New York: Duffield, 1909), for explorations into the relationships between men and women among the Communist-anarchists.

22. *Twentieth Century*, May 8, 1890.

23. Moses Harman is discussed more thoroughly in Chapter 4; letter from Dyer D. Lum to Voltairine de Cleyre, Jan. 9, 1891, Houghton Library, Harvard University.

24. *Liberty* 7 (Jan. 24, 1891): 3; *Liberty* 10 (April 25, 1895): 5.

25. *Liberty* 3 (Sept. 12, 1885): 6; Emma Goldman, "The Traffic in Women," in *Anarchism and Other Essays* (New York: Dover Publications, 1969), p. 179.

26. *Liberty* 5 (May 26, 1888): 7.

27. Voltairine de Cleyre, "The Gates of Freedom," *Lucifer*, 1891. This

essay is located in a clipping file in the Joseph Ishill Collection at Houghton Library, Harvard University. The dates are not on the clipping. De Cleyre, "The Case of Woman vs. Orthodoxy," *Boston Investigator*, Sept. 18, 1896, pp. 1–3; *Mother Earth* 9 (Feb. 1915): 392–94; Emma Goldman, "Suffrage for Women," in *Anarchism*, p. 197.

28. *Liberty* 10 (April 6, 1895): 7; *Liberty* 10 (May 4, 1895): 7; Lois Waisbrooker, *Suffrage for Women* (St. Louis, Mo.: Clayton and Babington), pp. 2, 4.

29. Ezra Heywood, *Uncivil Liberty* (Princeton, Mass.: Cooperative Publishing Company, 1877), p. 7; *Liberty* 8 (Aug. 25, 1894): 2; see *Liberty* 10 (Oct. 6, 1894): 2, 3, for other arguments for and against woman suffrage.

30. Matilda Joslyn Gage, ed., *Women's National Liberal Union: Report of the Convention for Organization* (Syracuse, N.Y.: Mason and Stone, 1890), esp. pp. 2, 6, 4, 17–18, 46–49, 87–89.

31. *Rebel* 1, no. 2 (Oct. 20, 1895): 18; 1, no. 3 (Nov. 20, 1895): 31–32; 1, no. 4 (Jan. 1896): 43–44.

32. Martin, *Men Against the State*, pp. 115–17, 203; O'Neill, *Everyone Was Brave*, pp. 34, 29. Newspapers devoted considerable space to the anarchists in the late nineteenth and early twentieth centuries, particularly after the Haymarket tragedy; for a sampling of opinion, see *New York Times*, July 19, 1888, p. 4; *New York Times*, April 20, 1892, p. 4; *Public Opinion* 17 (May 15, 1886): 81–87.

33. Richard Sennett, *Families Against the City* (New York: Random House, 1974), esp. pp. 116–19. For the working-class family, see Daniel Walkowitz, "Working Class Women in the Gilded Age: Factory, Community, and Family Life among Cohoes, New York, Cotton Workers," *Journal of Social History* 5 (Summer 1972): 464–90; on women and socialism, see Olive M. Johnson, *Woman and the Socialist Movement* (New York: Socialist Labor Party, 1919; first published in 1907) (pamphlet). Also see Jeanneth D. Pearl, "Women in Society," *Unity* 1 (Jan. 1911): 6–8; R. B. Tobias and Mary Marcy, *Women as Sex Vendors* (Chicago: Chas. H. Kerr, 1918).

Chapter 4

1. The view of sexuality described here differs from the argument of Billie Jean Stephenson, "The Ideology of American Anarchism" (Ph.D. diss., University of Iowa, 1972), pp. 252–53. Stephenson contends that the anarchists did not view their attacks on marriage as attacks on the family structure itself.

2. Kathryn Kish Sklar, *Catharine Beecher: A Study in American Domesticity* (New York: Norton and Company, 1976); William O'Neill, *Everyone Was Brave: A History of Feminism in America* (New York: Quadrangle, 1969), pp. 351–57; Ann Douglas, *The Feminization of American Culture* (New York: Alfred A. Knopf, 1977), pp. 48, 71–76.

3. Blanche Glassman Hersh has demonstrated convincingly the continuities of antebellum and post-Civil War suffragism, without losing sight of its increasingly conservative nature, in *The Slavery of Sex* (Chicago: University of Illinois Press, 1978), esp. pp. 50–51, 58–59, 67, 103–04, 170, 202, 207–08, 253–54. The quote is on p. 208.

4. Richard Sennett, *Families Against the City* (New York: Random House, 1974), esp. p. 116, but also pp. 98–119.

5. Linda Gordon, *Woman's Body, Woman's Right* (New York: Grossman Press, 1976), p. 73.

6. Emanie S. Sachs, *The Terrible Siren: Victoria Woodhull, 1838–1927* (New York: Harper, 1928), pp. 117, 132–35, 186–89; Hal D. Sears, *The Sex Radicals: Free Love in High Victorian America* (Laurence, Kan.: Regents Press, 1977), p. 23.

7. Ezra Heywood, *Cupid's Yokes* (Princeton, Mass.: Cooperative Publishing Company, 1876), p. 5.

8. Ibid., p. 4.

9. Ibid., p. 16.

10. Ibid., p. 20.

11. Ibid., p. 21.

12. For published material on Waisbrooker, see Sears, *Sex Radicals*, pp. 229–45; Charles Pierce Le Warne, *Utopias on Puget Sound* (Seattle: University of Washington Press, 1975), pp. 183–89; *Tomorrow*, Oct. 1906.

13. Lois Waisbrooker, *Nothing Like It* (Boston: Colby and Rich, 1879), pp. 235–36.

14. Ibid., p. 180.

15. Lois Waisbrooker, *The Plain Guide to Naturalism* (Los Angeles: Lois Waisbrooker, 1879), passim.

16. *Lucifer*, April 13, 1901.

17. For a thorough account of *Lucifer* and its editor, see Sears, *The Sex Radicals*, pp. 58–63, 74–80, 125–35, and passim. Harman found it difficult to change with the times; his article on marriage in *Lucifer*, Sept. 28, 1905, is a good example of his failure to be affected by the twentieth-century emphasis on sexual pleasure.

18. Voltairine de Cleyre, "Sex Slavery," in *The Selected Works of Voltairine de Cleyre* (New York: Mother Earth, 1914), p. 344.

19. *Liberty* 5 (May 26, 1888): 6.

20. *Liberty* 5 (May 26, 1888): 6.
21. *Liberty* 5 (Feb. 15, 1888): 4.
22. *Liberty* 5 (March 31, 1888): 5.
23. Florence Finch Kelly, *Frances: A Story for Men and Women* (New York: Sanfred and Co., 1889), p. 251.
24. Florence Finch Kelly, *On the Inside* (New York: Sanfred and Co., 1890), p. 20.
25. Ibid., pp. 61, 181.
26. *Liberty* 6 (Aug. 21, 1888): 5.
27. *Liberty* 5 (April 28, 1888): 6; on the Drs. Foote, see Sears, *Sex Radicals*, pp. 195–203.
28. *Liberty* 5 (April 28, 1888): 6; John S. and Robin M. Haller, *The Physician and Sexuality in Victorian America* (New York: Norton, 1977), pp. 195–200.
29. *Liberty* 5 (April 28, 1888): 6.
30. Ibid., p. 5.
31. *Liberty* 5 (May 12, 1888): 6.
32. Ibid. (emphasis added).
33. Ibid.
34. Ibid., p. 7.
35. *Liberty* 6 (Sept. 15, 1888): 7.
36. *Liberty* 4 (Dec. 11, 1886): 4; *Liberty* 1 (May 27, 1882): 1, 4; *Liberty* 2 (April 14, 1883): 1; *Liberty* 4 (July 17, 1886): 4.
37. *Liberty* 6 (Feb. 23, 1889): 2.
38. *Liberty* 6 (July 20, 1889): 6–7.
39. *Liberty* 10 (May 19, 1894): 4.
40. Both the article and the rejoinder are in *Liberty* 11 (Nov. 16, 1895).
41. *Liberty* 9 (Sept. 24, 1892): 3.
42. For example, see *Liberty* 10 (April 25, 1895).
43. *Liberty* 11 (June 1, 1895): 6–8.
44. James Reed, *From Private Vice to Public Virtue: The Birth Control Movement and American Society since 1830* (New York: Basic Books, 1978), p. 54; William O'Neill, *Divorce in the Progressive Era* (New Haven: Yale University Press, 1967), p. 124.
45. Voltairine de Cleyre, "They Who Marry Do Ill," *Mother Earth* 2 (Jan. 1908); see also Emma Goldman, "Marriage and Love," in *Anarchism and Other Essays* (New York: Dover, 1969), pp. 227–39.
46. Hutchins Hapgood, *An Anarchist Woman* (New York: Duffield, 1909), pp. 153–54.
47. Reed, *Private Vice*, pp. 46–53, discusses the birth-control agitation of Emma Goldman and Ben Reitman.

48. The letters of Emma Goldman to Margaret Sanger indicate the context in which anarchists placed sex-related questions: Goldman to Sanger, April 9, 1914, and Dec. 7, 1915; William Sanger to Emma Goldman, March 14, 1916 (Library of Congress), suggests that nonanarchists could misunderstand that context; see also Ada-May Krecker, "The Passing of the Family," *Mother Earth* 7 (Oct. 1912): 258–65.
49. *Mother Earth* 11 (Apr. 1916): 472; *Mother Earth* 11 (Jan. 1917): 738–39.
50. *Little Review* 2 (March 1915): 16–18; J. William Lloyd, *Dawn Thought on the Reconciliation* (Westfield, N.J.: The Lloyd Group, 1904), pp. 78–81, is an earlier and considerably more oblique affirmation of homosexuality.
51. O'Neill, *Everyone Was Brave*, p. 312; Reed, *Private Vice*, p. 53, discusses why the severance of birth control from radicalism was necessary for the public acceptance of contraception.
52. *Liberty* 9 (March 18, 1893): 4–5.
53. Benjamin F. Tucker, *Instead of a Book* (New York: Haskell House, 1969; reprint of 1897 edition), pp. 134–36.
54. *Liberty* 11 (Aug. 10, 1895): 7.
55. *Liberty* 9 (Sept. 3, 1892): 2–4.
56. *Liberty* 6 (Sept. 1, 1888): 6–7.
57. *Liberty* 5 (Aug. 4, 1888): 3; *Liberty* 5 (June 23, 1888): 5–6; *Liberty* 6 (Nov. 10, 1888): 7.
58. Dyer D. Lum to Voltairine de Cleyre, Dec. 20, 1890, Houghton Library, Harvard University.
59. Although a Mutualist-anarchist, Dyer Lum's position on children and family life was closer to the communists in "A Consideration of Family Life Under Anarchy," *Alarm*, June 23, 1888; Henry Addis, "Essays on the Social Problem," *Free Society Library* 6 (June 1898): 20; *Why?* 1 (March 1913): 9–10; Emma Goldman believed children were better off away from parental influence, "Francisco Ferrer: The Modern School," in *Anarchism and Other Essays*, pp. 149–53.

Chapter 5

1. Juliet Mitchell, *Woman's Estate* (New York: Random House, 1971), esp. p. 68.
2. This was not a problem peculiar to the anarchists. William O'Neill has argued that Charlotte Perkins Gilman faced similar problems in attempting to unify socialism and feminism; see O'Neill, *Everyone Was Brave* (New York: Quadrangle, 1971), pp. 132–33.

3. Emma Goldman, "Francisco Ferrer and the Modern School," in *Anarchism and Other Essays* (New York: Dover, 1969), p. 165; Richard King, *The Party of Eros* (New York: Dell, 1973), p. 35.

4. Voltairine de Cleyre, "Anarchism," in *The Selected Works of Voltairine de Cleyre*, ed. by Hippolyte Havel (New York: Mother Earth, 1914), pp. 113–15.

5. Voltairine de Cleyre, "Anarchism and American Traditions," in *American Radical Thought: The Libertarian Tradition*, ed. by Henry J. Silverman (Lexington, Mass.: D. C. Heath, 1970), p. 163.

6. The nature of de Cleyre's feminism is dealt with extensively in Chapter 6. Mitchell, *Woman's Estate*, p. 68 and passim.

7. *Liberty* 4 (Feb. 12, 1887): 6; see also *Liberty* 4 (July 7, 1886): 7–8, and *Liberty* 5 (Aug. 13, 1887): 7.

8. *Liberty* 3 (Nov. 8, 1884): 3.

9. *Little Review* 2, no. 4 (Summer 1915): 36–37.

10. For the controversy between de Cleyre and Goldman over the type of audiences to whom anarchists ought to appeal, see *Mother Earth* 5 (Dec. 1910): 320–24; and *Mother Earth* 5 (Jan. 1911): 360–63; also Margaret Anderson, *My Thirty Years War* (London: Alfred A. Knopf, 1930), p. 71.

11. *Mother Earth* 11 (Sept. 1916): 622; *Little Review* 2 (Sept. 1915): 25–26.

12. *Mother Earth* 10 (March 1915): 435–36.

13. Voltairine de Cleyre, "Direct Action," in *Selected Works*, p. 223.

14. Emma Goldman, "Anarchism: What It Really Stands For," in *Anarchism*, pp. 56–57.

15. De Cleyre, "Direct Action," in *Selected Works*, p. 223.

16. For various views on violence by anarchist women, see Gertrude Kelly in *Liberty* 4 (May 22, 1886): 6; Florence Finch Kelly in *Liberty* 5 (Dec. 3, 1887): 4; Voltairine de Cleyre, "McKinley's Assassination from an Anarchist Standpoint," *Mother Earth* 2 (Sept. 1907): 303–06; "Rebecca Edelsohn's Speech" (on the Lexington Avenue explosion in 1914), *Mother Earth* 9 (July 1914): 144–46; Emma Goldman, "The Psychology of Political Violence," in *Anarchism*, pp. 79–108.

17. *Red Ruin; or the Romance of Anarchy* (New York: Richard K. Fox, 1888), pp. 56, 60.

18. *Brooklyn Eagle*, Mar. 15, 1908 (clipping file, New York Public Library).

19. The most complete account of the Haymarket disaster and its aftermath is still Henry David, *The History of the Haymarket Affair* (New York: Russell and Russell, 1936). Lingg's bombs were fashioned in a different manner.

20. Emma Goldman, *Living My Life* (New York: Dover Publications,

1970), pp. 87–89, 296–317; Alexander Berkman, *Prison Memoirs of an Anarchist* (New York: Mother Earth, 1912), pp. 1–43; Drinnon, *Rebel in Paradise* (Boston: Beacon Press, 1961), pp. 49–54. Will Durant, in *Transition* (New York: Simon and Schuster, 1927), pp. 206–13, offered a fictionalized account of the Lexington Avenue explosions; Marie Ganz's account, in *Rebels: Into Anarchy and Out Again* (New York: Dodd, Mead, 1920), pp. 228–45, was highly colored by her recent disaffection from the anarchists; see also *New York Times*, July 5, 1914, sec. II, p. 2; Paul Avrich provided me with information on the bombing from his forthcoming book, *The Modern School Movement* (Princeton: Princeton University Press, 1980).

21. Frank Harris, *The Bomb* (Chicago: University of Chicago Press, 1969; first published in 1909), pp. 110, 162.

22. Drinnon, *Rebel*, pp. 57–59; Voltairine de Cleyre, *In Defense of Emma Goldman and the Right of Expropriation* (Philadelphia: Voltairine de Cleyre, 1894), p. 3.

23. Drinnon, *Rebel*, pp. 140–41; Voltairine de Cleyre to Harriet de Claire (her mother), Sept. 22, 1901, Houghton Library, Harvard University.

24. Voltairine de Cleyre to Harriet de Claire, Sept. 22, 1901 (Houghton); James Reed, *From Private Vice to Public Virtue* (New York: Basic Books, 1978), pp. 87–88; Drinnon, *Rebel*, pp. 167, 168–70.

25. *Mother Earth* 11 (April 1916): 450, 479.

26. Ibid., pp. 468–75; also William Sanger to Emma Goldman, March 14, 1916, and Emma Goldman to Margaret Sanger, Dec. 7, 1915, Library of Congress.

27. De Cleyre, *In Defense of Emma Goldman*, p. 9.

28. *Philadelphia Public Ledger*, Feb. 21, 1908, p. 1; *Philadelphia Inquirer*, Feb. 21, 1908, p. 1. Paul Avrich, *An American Anarchist: The Life of Voltairine de Cleyre* (Princeton: Princeton University Press, 1978), pp. 200–203, discusses the Broad Street Riot in detail.

29. "The True History of the Broad Street Riot" (Philadelphia, 1908), broadside; *Mother Earth* 3 (May 1908): 156–57; *Mother Earth* 3 (July 1908): 217–23; Harry de Cleyre to Agnes Inglis, Feb. 15, 1948, Labadie Collection, University of Michigan.

30. The arrests of Mollie Steimer and Marie Ganz are discussed in Chapter 2. See *Liberty* 4 (Sept. 18, 1886): 5; *Liberty* 4 (May 22, 1886): 6; *Mother Earth* 2 (Sept. 1907): 303–06; *Mother Earth* 9 (June 1914): 99; *Little Review* 2 (Dec. 1915): 5.

31. Michael Fellman, *The Unbounded Frame: Freedom and Community in Nineteenth Century American Utopianism* (Westport, Conn.: Greenwood Press, 1973), is a very good introduction to Utopian thought; see also

Rosabeth Moss Kanter, *Commitment and Community* (Cambridge: Harvard University Press, 1972). For a contemporary unfriendly account of Josiah Warren's "Modern Times," see John B. Ellis, *Free Love and Its Votaries; or American Socialism Unmasked* (New York: AMS, 1971; reprint of 1870 edition).

32. Edward Bellamy, *Looking Backward* (New York: New American Library, 1960); Kenneth Roemer, *The Obsolete Necessity* (Kent, Ohio: Kent State University Press, 1976), p. 91.

33. William Morris, *News from Nowhere* (London: Longmans, Green, and Company, 1936), pp. 69–70.

34. For an excellent account of the Home colony, see Charles Pierce Le Warne, *Utopias on Puget Sound* (Seattle: University of Washington Press, 1975), chap. 6. The best account of Stelton is in Laurence Veysey, *The Communal Experience* (New York: Harper and Row, 1973), chap. 2.

35. E. A. Slosson, "An Experiment in Anarchy," *Independent* 55 (April 2, 1903): 779–85; Le Warne, *Utopias on Puget Sound*, p. 224.

36. Slosson, "An Experiment in Anarchy," p. 783.

37. Le Warne, *Utopias on Puget Sound*, pp. 184, 195.

38. Alexis Ferm and Joseph J. Cohen, *The Modern School of Stelton* (Stelton, N.J.: Modern School Association of New Jersey, 1925), p. 44; Veysey, *Communal Experience*, p. 126, noted that "to middle-class eyes, Stelton became a scene of ugliness and squalor."

39. *Twentieth Century* 8 (May 23, 1892).

40. Veysey, *Communal Experience*, p. 87.

41. Emma Goldman, "The Child and Its Enemies," in *Red Emma Speaks*, ed. by Alix Kates Shulman (New York: Random House, 1972), p. 115; Goldman, "The Social Importance of the Modern School," in *Red Emma*, pp. 120–21.

42. Voltairine de Cleyre, "Modern Educational Reform," in *Selected Works*, p. 339 and pp. 321–41, passim; Emma Goldman, "La Ruche," in *Mother Earth* 2 (Nov. 1907): 388–94.

43. Veysey, *Communal Experience*, pp. 168–69; Ferm and Cohen, *The Modern School*, p. 34; *Stelton Gossiper* 1 (Aug. 15, 1920).

Chapter 6

1. The best biography of Emma Goldman is Richard Drinnon, *Rebel in Paradise* (Beacon Press, 1970; first published in 1961). Less comprehensive, but representative of Goldman's appeal to modern feminists, is Alix Kates Schulman, *To the Barricades: The Anarchist Life of Emma Goldman*

(New York: T. Y. Crowell, 1971). Goldman's autobiography is *Living My Life* (New York: Dover Publications, 1970; first published in 1931).

2. Emma Goldman, *Voltairine de Cleyre* (Berkeley Heights, N.J.: Oriole Press, 1932), perpetuated the myth of de Cleyre as a grim ascetic and was until 1978 the only full-length treatment of her life.

3. Paul Avrich, *An American Anarchist: The Life of Voltairine de Cleyre* (Princeton, N.J.: Princeton University Press, 1978).

4. The principal exception to these generalizations among the women studied here was Helena Born, whose background was privileged.

5. Agnes Inglis, "Notes for a Biography of Voltairine de Cleyre" (typewritten, [1934]). Most of Inglis's information came from Adelaide Thayer (de Cleyre's sister), some from Harry de Cleyre (Voltairine's son). See also Adelaide Thayer to Agnes Inglis, Nov. 5, 1934, Labadie Collection, University of Michigan.

6. Hector Auguste de Claire to Harriet de Claire, Sept. 17, 1880; Inglis, "Notes." Only Voltairine and Harry spelled their name "de Cleyre."

7. Inglis, "Notes."

8. Hector Auguste de Claire to Harriet de Claire, Sept. 17, 1880 (Labadie).

9. Inglis, "Notes."

10. Harry de Cleyre to Agnes Inglis, Oct. 12, 1947 (Labadie); Inglis, "Notes"; Adelaide Thayer to Joseph Ishill, Nov. 17, 1934, Houghton Library, Harvard University.

11. Inglis, "Notes"; Voltairine de Cleyre to Adelaide de Claire (later Berry, Thayer), Jan. 16, 1888, and Feb. 7, 1888 (Houghton).

12. Voltairine de Cleyre to Harriet de Claire, Dec. 18, 1887 (Houghton).

13. Harry de Cleyre to Agnes Inglis, Nov. 21, 1947; see also Dyer D. Lum to Joseph Labadie (1887), and Dyer D. Lum to [Joseph Labadie], Dec. 26, 1888, for other information on Lum and Haymarket (Labadie).

14. There is no biography of Lum, but a brief analysis of his ideas is provided in Voltairine de Cleyre, "Dyer D. Lum," *The Selected Works of Voltairine de Cleyre* (New York: Mother Earth, 1914), pp. 284–96; see also de Cleyre, "The Economics of Dyer D. Lum," *Twentieth Century* 11 (Dec. 7, 1897).

15. For example, Dyer D. Lum, "You and I" (poem), manuscripts in the Labadie Collection and Houghton Library; "A Valentine" (poem), and "Ma Cherie, mon suel faisceau!" (poem), manuscripts of both at Houghton; Dyer D. Lum to Voltairine de Cleyre, Oct. 7, 1889; Dyer D. Lum to Voltairine de Cleyre, Oct. 1, 1889, late November or early December 1889, and Nov. 22, 1890 (Houghton).

Notes   199

16. Harry de Cleyre to Agnes Inglis, Feb. 15, 1948, and March 4, 1950; Alice Graystone Baker Furst to Agnes Inglis, June 5, 1934; Voltairine de Cleyre to James Elliott, Oct. 8, 1894; Voltairine de Cleyre to Harriet de Claire, June 25, 1895 (Labadie); Voltairine de Cleyre to Adelaide de Claire Berry, Sept. 14, 1900 (Houghton).
17. Adelaide de Claire Thayer to Joseph Ishill, Feb. 3, 1935 (Houghton).
18. Harry de Cleyre to Agnes Inglis, March 4, 1950. Harry's daughter, Renée, has a less rose-colored view of the relationship between her father and grandmother than Harry had (Renée Buckwalter to Margaret Marsh, Aug. 7, 1976).
19. For example, Voltairine de Cleyre to Harriet de Claire, Dec. 18, 1887 (Houghton).
20. Voltairine de Cleyre, "The Gates of Freedom," speech delivered before the Liberal Convention at Topeka, Kansas, March 15, 1891, and reprinted in *Lucifer* that same year. Copy in clipping file at the Labadie Collection. Neither dates nor page numbers are on the clipping.
21. De Cleyre, "Gates of Freedom."
22. Voltairine de Cleyre, "The Case of Woman vs. Orthodoxy," *Boston Investigator*, Sept. 19, 1896, p. 1.
23. Ibid., p. 3.
24. Ibid., p. 3.
25. Voltairine de Cleyre to Harriet de Claire, Jan. 13, 1893 (Labadie); Dyer D. Lum to Voltairine de Cleyre, July 7, 1892, and July 16, 1892 (Houghton).
26. Voltairine de Cleyre to Harriet de Claire, Jan. 13, 1893 (Labadie).
27. Voltairine de Cleyre, "The Past and Future of the Ladies Liberal League," *Rebel* 1, no. 2 (Oct. 20, 1895): 18; 1, no. 3 (Nov. 20, 1895): 31–32; and 1, no. 4 (Jan. 1896): 43–44; Nathan Navro, "Voltairine de Cleyre" (manuscript, n.d.), pp. 2–3 (Houghton). For a discussion of the organizations in which she participated and the kinds of activity in which she engaged, see Avrich, *An American Anarchist*, esp. pp. 94–101.
28. Especially "She Died for Me," *Open Court* 9 (Dec. 26, 1895); "I Am," *Open Court* 6 (Jan. 21, 1892); and "Ave et Vale," in *Selected Works*, pp. 70–73.
29. Voltairine de Cleyre to the Duff family, Sept. 27, 1897 (Houghton).
30. Voltairine de Cleyre to Harriet de Claire, June 18, 1897 (Labadie).
31. Voltairine de Cleyre, "The Making of an Anarchist," in *Selected Works*, pp. 154–63, originally published in the *Independent*, Sept. 24, 1903; "Anarchism and American Traditions" is readily available in Henry Silverman, ed., *American Radical Thought: The Libertarian Tradition*

(Lexington, Mass.: D.C. Heath, 1970), pp. 154–65; "The Dominant Idea" is in *Selected Works*, pp. 79–95, and was first published in *Mother Earth* 5 (May 1910) and 5 (June 1910).
32. De Cleyre, "The Making of an Anarchist," p. 155.
33. Ibid., pp. 155–56.
34. Ibid., p. 158.
35. Ibid., p. 162.
36. Ibid., p. 163.
37. Ibid., p. 163.
38. De Cleyre, "Anarchism and American Traditions," p. 160.
39. Ibid., p. 160.
40. Ibid., pp. 162–63.
41. Ibid., p. 163.
42. Ibid., p. 163.
43. Ibid., p. 165.
44. De Cleyre, "The Dominant Idea," pp. 80–81.
45. Ibid., p. 82.
46. Ibid., p. 83.
47. Ibid., pp. 87–88.
48. Ibid., p. 89.
49. Ibid., pp. 93–94.
50. Voltairine de Cleyre, "They Who Marry Do Ill," *Mother Earth* 2 (Jan. 1908): 501, 511.
51. Voltairine de Cleyre to Alexander Berkman, Feb. 17, 1910, and Feb. 7, 1911 (International Institute of Social History, Amsterdam, Holland).
52. Henry F. May, *The End of American Innocence* (New York: Alfred A. Knopf, 1959), p. 174.
53. Emma Goldman to Joseph Ishill, Sept. 8, 1932 (Houghton).
54. Voltairine de Cleyre to Adelaide Thayer, Aug. 14, 1911 (Houghton).
55. Goldman, *De Cleyre*, p. 35; *Freedom*, April 29, 1950 (clipping file at Labadie).
56. Goldman, *De Cleyre*, p. 25 and passim; for an earlier public demonstration of the Goldman-de Cleyre rivalry, see Goldman's "Rejoiner" to de Cleyre's "Tour Impressions," in *Mother Earth* 5 (Dec. 1910): 323.
57. Goldman, *De Cleyre*, p. 29.
58. Voltairine de Cleyre to Harriet de Claire, Sept. 2, 1903 (Labadie).
59. Goldman, *De Cleyre*, p. 29.
60. Ibid., pp. 32–33.
61. *Syndicalist* 3 (July 1, 1913) (clipping file, Labadie).

62. Hippolyte Havel's "Introduction" to de Cleyre, *Selected Works*, p. 5.
63. *Mother Earth* 7 (July 1912); *Mother Earth* 7 (Sept. 1912); *Mother Earth* 8 (June 1913); see also *Why?* 1 (Aug. 1913): 10-12. For later elaboration of the de Cleyre image, see *Road to Freedom* 4 (June-July 1928): 5, and 6, 3 (Nov. 1929): 4.
64. Carl Nold to Agnes Inglis, Jan. 18, 1931 (Labadie).
65. Emma Goldman to Joseph Ishill, Feb. 13, 1931 (Houghton).
66. Joseph Ishill to Emma Goldman, June 3, 1930 (Houghton).

Chapter 7

1. Robert Nisbet, *The Social Philosophers: Community and Conflict in Western Thought* (New York: T. Y. Crowell and Co., 1973), pp. 281, 272–73. Nisbet's insights on some of the important differences between anarchists and socialists are very useful, although he tends to underplay the importance of violence within anarchism and correspondingly to overstress Marxian belief in violent revolution.
2. August Bebel, *Woman Under Socialism*, trans. and intro. by Daniel De Leon (New York: Labor News Press, 1904); Frederick Engels, *The Origin of the Family, Private Property, and the State*, with an intro. by Eleanor Burke Leacock (New York: International Publishers, 1972).
3. Engels, *Origin of the Family*, pp. 119–21.
4. Ibid., pp. 137, 138.
5. Ibid., p. 139.
6. Ibid., p. 144.
7. Ibid., p. 145.
8. Ibid., p. 146.
9. Ann J. Lane, "Woman in Society: A Critique of Frederick Engels," in *Liberating Woman's History*, ed. by Bernice Carroll (Chicago: University of Illinois Press, 1976), p. 23; Simone de Beauvoir, *The Second Sex*, trans. by H. M. Parshley (New York: Alfred A. Knopf, 1975), pp. 56, 58.
10. Bebel, *Woman Under Socialism*, p. 4.
11. Ibid., pp. 126, 89, 90; Ann Lane argues that Engels was aware of the oppression of working-class women by working-class men, but that in *The Family* he ignored the implications of his evidence (Lane, "Woman in Society," esp. p. 16).
12. Bebel, *Woman Under Socialism*, pp. 114, 195, 192.
13. Ibid., p. 343.

14. Ibid., pp. 126–30, 368–69, 361.
15. Ibid., p. 343.
16. Daniel De Leon, "Introduction," in Bebel, *Woman Under Socialism*, p. vi.
17. Mary P. Ryan, *Womanhood in America* (New York: Franklin Watts, 1975), pp. 244–45; Daniel De Leon, *Woman's Suffrage* (New York: Labor News Co., 1914), pp. 4–5, 18–19.
18. Edward Bellamy, *Equality* (Westport, Conn.: Greenwood Press, 1969; originally published in 1897), esp. pp. 43, 140–43.
19. Charlotte Perkins Gilman, *The Man-Made World* (New York: The Charlton Company, 1911), p. 27.
20. Ibid.
21. Ibid., p. 43.
22. Ibid., p. 26.
23. William O'Neill, *Everyone Was Brave* (New York: Quadrangle, 1969), pp. 132–33.
24. Kate Richards O'Hare, *The Sorrows of Cupid* (St. Louis, Mo.: National Rip-Saw Publishing Company, 1912), pp. 17, 59–69, 203–08.
25. Ibid., pp. 49–50, 52.
26. Mari Jo Buhle, "Socialist Woman, Progressive Woman, Coming Nation," in *The American Radical Press, 1880–1960*, 2, ed. by Joseph R. Conlin (Westport, Conn.: Greenwood Press, 1974): 444, 448–49.
27. Olive M. Johnson, *Woman and the Socialist Movement* (New York: Socialist Labor Party, 1919; originally published 1907), p. 6.
28. Ibid., pp. 34–35.
29. Ibid., p. 23.
30. Ibid., p. 46. See also R.B. Tobias and Mary E. Marcy, *Women as Sex Vendors* (Chicago: Charles H. Kerr, 1918).
31. June Sochen, *The New Woman* (New York: Quadrangle, 1972), esp. pp. 8–10, 28–29, 60–61, 115–16 (Sochen also places Ida Rauh in this group with I think less justification); Blanche Weisen Cook, ed., *Crystal Eastman on Women and Revolution* (New York: Oxford University Press, 1978), esp. pp. 41–52.
32. William O'Neill has collected some of the best of *The Masses* in *Echoes of Revolt: The Masses, 1912–1917*. The quote given here is on p. 132.
33. Ibid., pp. 199–201.
34. Ibid., p. 204.
35. Sochen, *The New Woman*, pp. 131, 137.
36. Ibid., p. 144.
37. An excellent new biography of Kollontai is Barbara Evans Clem-

ments, *Bolshevik Feminist: The Life of Aleksandra Kollontai* (Bloomington Ind.: Indiana University Press, 1979).
 38. Ibid., pp. 58–59.
 39. Ibid., p. 69; Aleksandra Kollontai, *The Autobiography of a Sexually Emancipated Woman and "The New Woman"* (London: Orbach and Chambers, 1972), esp. pp. 95, 99–100.
 40. Clements, *Bolshevik Feminist*, p. 75.
 41. Ibid., p. 75.

Appendix

 1. Edward T. James, ed., *Notable American Women*, 3 vols. (Cambridge, Mass.: Harvard University Press, 1971). The women in these volumes, like the anarchist women, ranged from nationally known activists to minor figures in the various movements.
 2. Norman Nie et al., *Statistical Package for the Social Sciences* (New York: McGraw Hill, 1975), pp. 218–22, 434–46.

A Note on Sources

The study of American anarchism should begin at the Labadie Collection at the University of Michigan or the Joseph Ishill Papers at Houghton Library, Harvard University. The International Institute of Social History in Amsterdam also contains valuable American sources. Other extremely useful manuscript collections are the Tamiment Collection, New York University, the papers of the Modern School Association (for the Stelton Colony) at Rutgers University, the Emma Goldman Papers at the New York Public Library, and the Margaret Sanger Collection at the Library of Congress.

Numerous anarchist journals were published during the late nineteenth and early twentieth centuries. Among the most important for this study are *Liberty* (1881–1908), the Individualist journal; *Lucifer* (1883–1907); and *Mother Earth* (1906–1917), Emma Goldman's journal, for a long time edited by Alexander Berkman. Other important journals are Albert Parsons's (later Dyer D. Lum's) *Alarm* (1884–1889); *Free Society* (1897–1904); *Rebel* (1895–1896); *Road to Freedom* (1924–1932); and *Freedom* (1933–1934). Margaret Anderson's *Little Review* is also important during her anarchist phase (1915–1917). Nonanarchist periodicals that took an interest (often hostile but sometimes more objective) in anarchism included *Outlook*, *North American Review*, *Arena*, and *Open Court*.

Some of the most helpful books are the autobiographies of anarchists, near-anarchists, former anarchists, and their friends and sympathizers. These included Margaret Anderson, *My Thirty Years War* (London: Alfred A. Knopf, 1930), which contains a revealing account of her three-year involvement with the anarchists. Marie Ganz's autobiography, *Rebels—Into Anarchy and Out Again* (New York: Dodd, Mead, and Co., 1920), sheds important light on some of the ephemeral attractions of the anarchists. Ganz's husband, Nat Ferber, wrote a memoir that included insights on his wife's radical career: *I Found Out: A Confidential Chronicle of the Twenties* (New York: Dial Press, 1939). Emma Goldman's autobiography, *Living My Life* (New York: AMS, 1970; reprint of 1934 edition), is a classic. Hutchins Hapgood, a friend of many anarchists, talked about them in his autobiography, *A Victorian in the Modern World* (New York: Harcourt, Brace, and World, 1939). Other important autobiographical works are Florence Finch Kelly, *Flowing Stream* (New York: E. P. Dutton, 1939); Margaret Sanger, *My Fight for Birth Control* (New York: Maxwell Reprint Co., 1969; reprint of 1931 edition); and Floyd Dell, *Homecoming* (Port Washington, N.Y.: Kennikat Press, 1969; reprint of 1933 edition). There are also two major biographies of anarchist women that deserve mention here: Paul Avrich, *An American Anarchist: A Life of Voltairine de Cleyre* (Princeton, N.J.: Princeton University Press, 1978); and Richard Drinnon, *Rebel in Paradise: A Biography of Emma Goldman* (Boston: Beacon Press, 1961).

There are several studies of American anarchism, varying in accuracy and in depth and breadth of analysis. Henry David, *The History of the Haymarket Affair* (New York: Russell and Russell, 1936), remains the best account of that event and its aftermath. David de Leon, *The American as Anarchist* (Baltimore: Johns Hopkins Press, 1978), is especially interesting for its controversial argument that anarchism is America's most important radical tradition. William O. Reichert, *Partisans of Freedom* (Bowling Green, Ohio: Popular Press, 1976), is an uncritical survey of anarchists active in the United States. James J. Martin, *Men Against the State* (Colorado Springs, Col.: Ralph Myles Publishers, 1970), is a good survey of the men (but very few of the women) who were important Individualists. Eunice Minette Schuster, "Native American Anarchism," Smith College *Studies in History* (Oct. 1931–July 1932), is still useful. Finally, George Woodcock, *Anarchism* (New York: World Publishing Company, 1962), while it does not focus on the United States, covers some of the important highlights of the movement here.

Most of the information on women and anarchism is scattered throughout the manuscript collections, the anarchist and nonanarchist journals, and the autobiographies noted above and cited more completely in the notes.

Voltairine de Cleyre's collected works are in her *Selected Works* (New York: Mother Earth, 1914), and Emma Goldman published an important book of essays, *Anarchism and Other Essays* (New York: Dover Reprints, 1969, first published 1911).

Index

Abbott, Leonard, 149
Abolitionists, 56
Abortion, 69, 76, 93
Adams, Henry, 16
Age of Consent Symposium (1895), 90
Aiken, Mary Herma, 60
American Civil Liberties Union, 111
American Federation of Labor, 15
American Labor Reform League, 16
"Anarchism" (de Cleyre), 103
"Anarchism and American Traditions" (de Cleyre), 103, 140–42
Anarchist-communism. *See* Communist-anarchism
Anarchist Woman, An (Hapgood), 22, 39
Anderson, Margaret, 41–43; on anarchism, 105; and Emma Goldman, 94, 105–06; on homosexuality, 41–42, 94; and violence, 114
Andrews, Stephen Pearl, 11, 73; and Victoria Woodhull, 70
Anthony, Susan B., 48, 70
Antifeminism, 164–65; and anarchism, 53–55; and socialism, 158, 162
Antislavery movement, 47
Avrich, Paul, 124

Bailie, Helen (Tufts), 27
Bailie, William, 28
Bebel, August, 166; and *Woman Under Socialism*, 155–57
Beecher, Catharine, 47, 49; and the ideology of domesticity, 66–67
Beecher, Henry Ward, 70
Bellamy, Edward, 116, 158–59
Berg, Charles, 109
Berger, Louise, 109
Berkman, Alexander, 8, 109; and Voltairine de Cleyre, 145; and Marie Ganz, 30; and Emma Goldman, 14–15, 114
Birth control, 92–93; anarchism and, 75; and direct action, 111–12, 114; Emma Goldman on, 93; Moses Harman on, 76; Ezra Heywood on, 72; socialism and, 156–57; and voluntary motherhood, 69; Zelm on, 78–79
Black International, 12
Blackwell, Alice Stone, 24
Blackwell, Antoinette Brown, 67
Blackwell, Elizabeth, 49
Bolshevik Revolution, 121
Bolsheviks, 32

Bomb, The (Harris), 110
Born, Helena, 11, 20, 25–29
Boston anarchists, the, 11, 21; women among, 25–26
Boyce, Neith, 163–64
Bristol Gas Workers and General Laborers Union, 26
Bristol Women's Liberal Association, 25–26
Bryant, Louise, 106
Buhle, Mari Jo, 161

Capitalism: and anarchism, 13, 22, 139–40; and feminism, 134; and prostitution, 72; and socialism, 151–52
Carlin, Terry, 40
Caron, Arthur, 109
Carpenter, Edward, 91
"Case of Woman vs. Orthodoxy, The" (de Cleyre), 134–35
Celibacy, 72, 79, 89
Chavez, Marie, 109
Child-abuse, 95–98
Child-labor, 58
Children, 52; and anarchist households, 83–85; and anarchist philosophy, 94–99; socialist views of, 157–58, 160–61, 168
Class, and women activists, 178
Clements, Barbara, 169
Clothed with the Sun, 118
Communist-anarchism, 12–14; and children, 98–99; and the family, 51–52; and feminism, 54–55; and social class, 12, 20–21, 43
Communitarianism, 115–16; in literature, 116–17. *See also* Societies, communal
Comstock Law (1873), 69, 93
Conquest of Bread (Kropotkin), 32
Contraception. *See* Birth control
Cupid's Yokes (Heywood), 71–73
Czolgosz, Leon, 8

Daniell, Miriam, 26–27, 89–90
Davidson, Clara Dixon, 96–97
De Beauvoir, Simone, 155
Debs, Eugene, 160
Decentralization, 15–17, 141–43
De Claire, Adelaide, 125–27

De Claire, Harriet, 125–28
De Claire, Hector Auguste, 125–27
"Declaration of Sentiments" (Seneca Falls, N.Y., 1848), 48
De Cleyre, Harry, 130–31, 147
De Cleyre, Voltairine, 122–50; as activist, 136–37; on anarchism, 102–04, 137–44; arrest of, 113, 145; childhood, 125–27; early career of, 128–30; education of, 125–27; on education, 119–20; and James Elliott, 130–31; and feminism, 51, 103, 131–35, 144–46; and Emma Goldman, 111, 148–50; and Moses Harman, 77; and Ladies Liberal League, 61, 136; and Dyer D. Lum, 129–30, 148–49; on marriage, 92; and Mexican Revolution, 145; and Modern School Movement, 119–20; on violence, 112–14; on woman suffrage, 58; and Women's National Liberal Union, 60–61, 136
De Leon, Daniel, 157–58
De Leon, David, 4
Dell, Floyd, 18, 164–65
Dietrick, Ellen Batelle, 57, 59
Direct action, 18, 107–14
Divorce, 60, 91
Domesticity, 65, 68; and anarchism, 84–86, 132–34, 166–68; ideology of, 66–67, 124; in *News from Nowhere*, 116–17; and socialism, 160–63
Domestic reformers, 67. *See also* Beecher, Catharine
"Dominant Idea, The" (de Cleyre), 142–44
Drinnon, Richard, 110
Durant, Will, 120

Eastman, Crystal, 163–64
Eastman, Max, 164–65
Education: anarchist ideas of, 118–22; of women activists, 178
Elliott, James, 130–31
Ellis, Havelock, 75, 91
Ely, Richard, 8–9
Engel, George, 7
Engels, Frederick, 166; and *The Origin of the Family, Private Property and the State*, 153–55
Equality (Bellamy), 159

Equal Rights Amendment, 5
Ethnicity, of women activists, 176–77

Family, 63, 65, 68–69; and anarchism, 78, 84–86, 167–68; and anarchist-feminism, 5, 45–46, 89–92, 173–74; inequality and, 5; and socialism, 153–55, 157–61
Fatherhood: and anarchism, 52, 98; and socialism, 161
Feminism, 4–5, 64, 172–74; and anarchist theory, 100–04, 107; and anarchist women, 4–5, 56–64, 171–74; and Voltairine de Cleyre, 103, 131–35, 144, 146; and the ideology of domesticity, 66–68; in the nineteenth century, 47–50. *See also* Woman Question, Woman suffrage
Feminist alliance, 163
Ferber, Nat, 31
Ferrer, Francisco, 119
Fielden, Samuel, 7
Finch, Florence. *See* Kelly, Florence Finch
Firestone, Shulamith, 5
Fischer, Adolph, 7
Fleshin, Senya, 38
Foote, E.B., Jr., 82
Fox, Jay, 149
Frances: A Story for Men and Women (Kelly), 80
Freedom (anarchist group, New York City), 32
Free love, 46, 69–94. *See also* Sexuality
Free thought, 128
Frick, Henry Clay, 8, 14, 109
Friendship Liberal League, 61
Fuller, Margaret, 50

Gage, Matilda Joslyn, 60, 62
Ganz, Marie, 29–32; and Alexander Berkman, 30; and violence, 114
Garrison, William Lloyd, 107
"Gates of Freedom, The" (de Cleyre), 132–33
Gender, and sex-roles, 3–4, 19, 27, 46, 124
George, Henry, 8
Gilman, Charlotte Perkins, 49, 83, 158–60

Glaspell, Susan, 163–64
Goldman, Emma, 14–15, 20, 123–24; and Margaret Anderson, 41–42; and Alexander Berkman, 14–15; on birth control, 93, 111–12; and Voltairine de Cleyre, 111, 148–50; and direct action, 111–12; and education, 119–20; and free speech, 111; and Marie Ganz, 29; as leader, 101–02; and Margaret Sanger, 111; and violence, 109, 110–11; on woman suffrage, 59; and youth, 22, 41–42, 105–07
Greene, William B., 11, 16
Greenwich Village, and feminism, 158, 163–65, 168–69
Grimké, Sarah, 50
Gurdjieff, G.I., 42

Hanson, Carl, 109
Hapgood, Hutchins, 39, 41, 92
Harman, Lillian, 76, 86–87, 90
Harman, Moses, 55–56; on marriage, 76–77
Harris, Frank, 110
Havel, Hippolyte, 149
Haymarket bombing, 6–7, 9, 107–10
Henri, Robert, 120
Heywood, Angela, 11
Heywood, Ezra, 11; on free love, 71–73; on woman suffrage, 59–60
Holmes, Lizzie May, 109–10, 118–19
Holmes, Justice Oliver Wendell, 39
Holmes, Sarah Elizabeth (pseud. Zelm), 78–79, 86, 97–98
Home, Washington (anarchist colony), 117–18
Homestead Strike, 115
Homosexuality, 22, 75–76, 94

Independent, 117–18
Individualism, 10–13; and children, 95–98; and the family, 52–53, 54–55; and feminism, 54–55; and social class, 11, 20–21, 43
Industrialization, 8–9, 24, 134, 139–43, 171
Industrial Workers of the World, 30
International Congress of Socialists (Second International), 161

Ishill, Joseph (anarchist publisher), 149–50
Jews as anarchists, 14, 29–32, 38–39, 136
Johnson, Olive, 158, 162–63
Kelly, Allen, 25
Kelly, Florence Finch, 22–25, 125; on anarchist ideology, 104–05; and feminism, 52–53; and free love, 80; on marriage, 79; early novels, 80–81
Kelly, Gertrude B., 50–51, 53–54, 57–58, 104
Kelly, Harry, 149
Key, Ellen, 75
Knights of Labor, 129
Kollontai, Aleksandra, 169–70
Krecker, Ada May, 52
Kropotkin, Peter, 13–14, 137; on the family, 19–20; on technology, 16; on women, 54, 166

L., Marie. *See* Marie L.
Labadie, Joseph, 87
Labor activists, 21, 176–81
Ladies Liberal League, 61
Lane, Ann, 155
La Ruche, 120
Lexington Avenue bomb explosion (New York City), 8, 109
Liberty, 10–11; on sexuality and domesticity, 76–78; on women and work, 55; on women's rights, 24–25
Lingg, Louis, 7, 109, 110
Little Review, The, 22, 41, 105, 114
Lloyd, J. William, 81–84, 98
Looking Backward (Bellamy), 116
Louise, Marie, 50, 58
Lucifer, 55–56, 60; on sexuality and domesticity, 76–77
Ludlow Massacre (Colorado), 30–31
Lum, Dyer D.: and Voltairine de Cleyre, 129–30, 148–49; and domestic arrangements, 51; on factionalism, 13, 129; on fatherhood, 98; and Moses Harman, 77; and Haymarket, 7

Mc Kinley, William, 109
"Making of an Anarchist, The" (de Cleyre), 138–40
"Male continence," 72

Marie L., 39–41, 92
Marie Louise. *See* Louise, Marie
Marriage, 65; and anarchism, 22, 28, 72, 76–92, 172; and socialism, 153–58; among women activists, 181
Marx, Karl, 17
Marxism, 12–13, 17–18, 152; and anarchist theory, 133–34; and women, 153–57, 169
Masses, The, 17, 164–65
Materialism, 142–43, 155
Maternal instinct, 85–86, 97–98
Maternal mystique, 48
May, Henry, 145
Men: as antifeminists, 53–55, 157–58; as feminists, 55, 164–66; and woman suffrage, 59–60, 164
Mental impregnation, 82–83
Mexican Revolution, 103, 145
Michel, Louise, 126, 147
Militarism, 142
Mitchell, Juliet, 100, 103–04
Modernization, 66
Modern School: movement, 119–21; in New York City, 119–20; at Stelton, N.J., 120–22
Modern Times (anarchist community), 70, 115
Morgan, Edward, 153, 155
Morris, William, 26, 116–17
Most, Johann, 12–13, 55
Mother Earth, 60, 63, 112
Motherhood: and anarchism, 52, 95–98; and socialism, 157–62; Voltairine de Cleyre, 130–31

National Civil Liberties Bureau, 111
Neebe, Oscar, 7
New England Free Love League, 71
New England Labor Reform League, 16
News from Nowhere (Morris), 26, 116–17
New York Times, 20, 25, 29
Nicol, Robert, 26
Nisbet, Robert, 152
Nold, Carl, 149
Nothing Like It (Waisbrooker), 73–74

Occupations, of women activists, 179–80
O'Hare, Kate Richards, 158, 160–61

Index 213

O'Neill, William, 48, 94
On the Inside (Kelly), 80–81
Origin of the Family, Private Property, and the State, The (Engels), 153–55
Owen, Robert, 115

Parenthood, 52, 72, 82, 95–98
Parsons, Albert, 7, 108
Parsons, Lucy, 108, 110
Pentecost, Hugh, 55
Pittsburgh Congress (1883), 12–13, 17
Plain Guide to Naturalism, The (Waisbrooker), 73–75
Populism, 15, 116
Progressive Age, 128
Progressive Woman, 161
Promiscuity, 22
Prostitution, 57–58
Proudhon, Pierre-Joseph, 10–11; and the family, 19–20, 166; and Karl Marx, 17

Radical Liberal League (Philadelphia), 92
Radical Library (Philadelphia), 136
Red Ruin (anonymous novel), 108
Red Scare, 121
Re-generation, 75
Religion, 60–61, Voltairine de Cleyre on, 138
Replogle, Georgia, 55, 95–96
Replogle, Henry, 96
Revolution: and anarchism, 7–15, 17, 106, 139–45, 150
Robinson, John Beverly, 55, 60, 87–88
Rockefeller, John D., 30–31, 109, 114
Rodman, Henrietta, 163–64

Sanger, Margaret, 18, 93, 120
Schools. *See* Education
Schwab, Michael, 7
Sennett, Richard, 63, 68
Sexual abuse, 76–77
Sexuality, 94; anarchist views of, 65–70, 72–91; and women, 22, 40–41, 46, 74–75, 78–91
Sklar, Kathryn Kish, 47
Slosson, E.A., 117–18
Sochen, June, 165
Social feminists, 57–58
Socialism, 15, 17, 151–52; and the family, 63; and social class, 21; and women, 56, 153–66, 168–70, 176–81
Socialist-feminism, 153, 158–60, 164–65, 168–70
Socialist Labor Party, 162–63, 166
Socialist Party of America, 17, 160–62, 164, 166
Socialist Woman, 161–62
Social Purity, 48, 68–69, 93
Societies, communal: anarchist, 117–21; and feminism, 118, 121–22. *See also* Communitarianism
Soviet Union, anarchists in, 38
Spanish Civil War, 38
Spies, August, 7
Spiritualism, 70–71, 73–75
Stanton, Elizabeth Cady, 16, 46–47, 62, 70
Steimer, Mollie, 29, 32, 38–39, 114
Stelton, New Jersey (anarchist colony), 117, 118–21
Stone, Lucy, 24, 67
Suffrage. *See* Woman suffrage
Suffragists, 49–50
Supreme Court, 32, 39

Teachers: anarchists as, 11, 43, 118–19, 124; socialists as, 163. *See also* Education
Technology: anarchists and, 15–17; socialists and, 152
Temperance, 58, 67–68
Terrorism, 8–9, 107–10
Thayer, Adelaide de Claire, 125, 127
"They Who Marry Do Ill" (de Cleyre), 92
Thoreau, Henry David, 16, 107
Tilton, Theodore, 70
Tucker, Benjamin F., 10–11; on children, 95–96; on marriage, 86–87, 89; on women, 24, 55
Tufts, Helen, 27
Turner, John, 137

Urbanization, 8–9, 171

Varietism, 46, 70, 172. *See also* Sexuality; Free love
Veysey, Laurence, 119

Index

Violence, 21–22, 62; and women, 107–14, 181
Voluntary Motherhood, 68–69, 95. *See also* Birth control

Waisbrooker, Lois, 53, 118, 125; on free love, 73–75; and Home, Washington, 117–18; on woman suffrage, 59–60
Walker, E.C., 76–77, 86–87
Warren, Josiah, 10–11, 70, 115
Weinberg, Chaim, 113
White, Lillie D., 60, 118
Wollstonecraft, Mary, 50
Woman Question, 46, 67–68; and anarchists, 50–51, 62–63, 121–22, 166–67; Voltairine de Cleyre and, 131–35; socialists and, 153–66, 168–70. *See also* Feminism; Woman suffrage

Woman Rebel, 93
Woman suffrage, 47–49, 66–69; and anarchism, 58–60; and socialism, 158–60, 163–64, 168
Woman Under Socialism (Bebel), 155–57
Woman's Christian Temperance Union, 48
Women's National Liberal Union, 60–61
Woodcock, George, 3, 17
Woodhull, Victoria, 70–71
World War I, 14, 32, 121

Yarros, Victor: on the family, 84–86; on woman suffrage, 59; on women, 24, 54–55

Zelm. *See* Holmes, Sarah Elizabeth